After the Revolution

D1509185

13

Editor: William Buford
Assistant Editor: Diane Speakman
Managing Editor: Tracy Shaw
Associate Editor: Graham Coster
Executive Editor: Pete de Bolla
Design: Chris Hyde
Editorial and Office Assistant: Emily Dening
Editorial Assistants: William Campbell-Taylor, Michael Comeau,
Margaret Costa, Michael Hofmann, Alicja Kobiernicka
Editorial Board: Malcolm Bradbury, Elaine Feinstein, Ian
Hamilton, Leonard Michaels
US Editor: Jonathan Levi, 325 Riverside Drive, Apartment 81,
New York, New York 10025

Editorial and Subscription Correspondence: Granta, 44a Hobson
Street, Cambridge CB1 1NL. (0223) 315290.
All manuscripts are welcome but must be accompanied by a
stamped, self-addressed envelope or they cannot be returned.

Subscriptions: £12.00 for four issues.

Back Issues: £2.50 for *Granta* 3; £3.50 for *Granta* 5 to 12. *Granta*
1, 2, and 4 are no longer available. All prices include postage.

Granta is photoset by Lindonprint Typesetters, Cambridge, and is
printed by Bell and Bain Ltd., Glasgow.

Cover by Chris Hyde

Granta 13, Autumn 1984

ISSN 0017-3231
ISBN 014-00-75669

Published with the assistance
of the Eastern Arts Association

CONTENTS

ANDRÉ BRINK
LOOKING ON DARKNESS

The powerful and controversial novel about a South African coloured actor awaiting execution for the murder of his white lover. £2.95

Caroline Blackwood
ON THE PERIMETER

A remarkable depiction of life in the women's peace camp at Greenham Common – the conditions, the fears and the prejudices.
£1.95

A Journey in Ladakh
ANDREW HARVEY

Andrew Harvey's astonishing account of his travels through a strange and magical land located on the very edge of civilisation. 'A remarkable evocation of another life.'
Sunday Times
£2.50

Editorial

In June, Conor Cruise O'Brien devoted his column in the *Observer* to a discussion of the issue of *Granta* that featured the work of Milan Kundera and Salman Rushdie. Dr O'Brien's column was a curious achievement. And a mystifying one. It somehow succeeded in making *Granta* an accomplice in its own kidnapping: it managed to praise *Granta* while using the writings that were published in it to support an argument that, to me at least, sounded pretty wrong-headed.

Dr O'Brien's column continued an argument that he had begun four weeks earlier. Dr O'Brien has, of course, many passions, and the one to which he seems especially dedicated is disabusing wimpy liberals of their soft notions. In this particular exercise, he addressed the wimpy liberal's notion of black Africa: that it was once a pretty good place, but, since the whites arrived, it's become a real mess—so much of a mess that black leaders are still unable to clean it up. It's a fairly prevalent idea, and Dr O'Brien offers a number of strong antidotes to fortify intellectual softies against it. So, for instance, we learn that pre-colonial Africa was 'more oppressive than European rule' and, to particularize the point, that the 'Matabele rule over the Shona' was as bad as the white domination that followed it in the shape of a country that came to be known, for a while anyway, as Rhodesia. Even the practice of selling Blacks around the world was not really a European thing: 'Liverpool did well out of the slave trade, but so did Kumasi.' Dr O'Brien's argument presupposes real intellectual muscle, and if you're feeling strong—ready to take off your weedy spectacles, throw out your chest and resolve never to be a wimp again—you will not be made uneasy by all the different senses that tend to crowd into his use of the word imperialism: tribal rule, for instance, seems to mean the same thing as Western colonialism—the same thing, that is, as economic domination based on racism and the exploitation of labour and natural resources. And if you're feeling *really* strong, you'll read Dr O'Brien's conclusion with glee: 'The racism *previously* inculcated and practised by European countries was obviously *demoralizing* to Africans *in its day*. But the form of demoralization which Africa is currently importing from the West is something more insidious: flattery.' (My italics.) By 'flattery', Dr O'Brien means, I believe, the gooey liberal blandishments we offer tyrannical black leaders to excuse their tyranny ('Don't worry, Idi,' I remember reading so often in the press, 'we made you do it').

There are, predictably, a lot of wimps in the world, and invariably not all of them are strong enough to throw off their spectacles. And so they protested. And this is where *Granta* gets involved. *Granta* appears to have supported Dr O'Brien's argument by publishing two writers: Salman Rushdie, one of the wimpy liberals, it seems, and Milan Kundera, one of the tough guys.

Salman Rushdie suffers from a malady—its symptoms are evident in his polemic on the vogue in Raj films, 'Outside the Whale'—to which so many writers and intellectuals in or from former colonial territories are susceptible: 'The Collective Self-Pity of Former Subject Peoples' or what Dr O'Brien, in his inimitable way, calls COSEPIOFOSUPE. And the antidote, again revealing a strong grounding in history, is simple: Rushdie should just stop wailing so much in public—O'Brien cites John O' Leary's 'No man should cry in public, even to save his country'—because the complaint is no longer justified. There is no point insulting the old masters—'most of whom are, in any case, dead.'

In contrast, there are the likes of Milan Kundera. And while Dr O'Brien acknowledges that Kundera insists that his work not be read as a denunciation of a regime, the temptation is obviously too great. 'Kundera has more to wail about,' Dr O'Brien observes, 'than just televised versions of a vanished Raj. His own country, Czechoslovakia—from which he is an exile—is ruled today by a form of Raj which is very much alive, not to say kicking.'

There are some good reasons why Kundera resents his work being read as a political denunciation. The popularity in the United States, especially among the 'Neo-Conservatives', of writing by dissident émigrés seldom derives from an appreciation of its literary merit. Analogously, Ronald Reagan (whose first act as President was to fire the entire nation's air-traffic controllers because they went on strike) and Margaret Thatcher (whose first legislation was to curb the powers of the trade unions) did not lament the fate of Solidarity so loudly because of their love of workers' militancy. Their lament expressed not sympathy but vindication: the fight for freedom does not occur in the West; the fight for freedom means we hate communism.

Elsewhere Conor Cruise O'Brien is hardly an uncritical apologist for the West, but what he writes here is a typical example of the strange spasm that occurs somewhere in the mind when it is exposed to evidence of a totalitarian—and especially a communist—regime. An otherwise healthy facility of perception collapses into a kind of tunnel vision that reduces the world to simple, comprehensive terms. Dictatorships, totalitarianism, censorship, communism—you find the words in Eastern and Central Europe, China and Africa—mean *unfree*. And it's the sense of this *unfree* that defines and validates what we have come to understand

7

in the West by *free*: what we have come to understand by the words free society, free press and free trade. Over there you have something to wail about. Here wailing is indulgent and shameless public display.

But it's not impossible that the real sense of this word *free* is a little more complicated. Some of the complication is evident in the very newspaper in which Dr O'Brien's column appeared.

Since 1981, the *Observer*, or at least eighty percent of it, has been owned by the Lonrho Group. The Lonrho Group's chief executive, whose unacceptable face was duly celebrated by Edward Heath eleven years ago, is Tiny Rowland. Unlike Conor Cruise O'Brien—who regards black Africa as a continent of dictators—Tiny has said that he loves black Africa, believes in the independent countries, and promises, moreover, to help them 'achieve their full economic potential.' This isn't quite as generous as it may initially seem as, ultimately, a great deal of this economic potential goes straight back to Tiny Rowland. A list of the African businesses owned by Tiny includes those that grow tea, sugar and wattle; those that sell records, Mercedes cars, Pepsi *and* Coca-Cola; those that make lipstick, sleeping pills and African beer; and those that retrieve from the earth great chunks of platinum, coal, copper and gold. He also, like so many of the wealthy in Britain, tends to own newspapers. And while Tiny's African businesses account for only thirty percent of his company's turnover, they make up for it by being seventy percent of its profits.

Tiny's love for black Africa is of the forgiving sort, able to overlook differences, even ideological ones. So, for instance, at a time when the British Parliament was investigating him for breaking sanctions against Rhodesia, the Rhodesian government was investigating him for relations with the guerrilla movements. And while Ian Smith was praising Tiny's talent, it was said that Tiny was offering money to an ostracized man named Mugabe (immediately refused). Because Tiny basically just wants everyone to be happy: why, when there is so much suffering in the world, would anyone want to irritate friends?

Some idea of the strength of these friendships was perhaps evident in a recent tiff Tiny had with his editor at the *Observer*, Donald Trelford, who, after interviews with Mugabe and his government ministers in Zimbabwe (some arranged by Tiny himself), returned to London with a story that wasn't about the Prime Minister at all but about the brutalities performed by the Fourth Brigade. This obviously upset Tiny, as is evident in Donald Trelford's recollection of their chat just before his story went to the printer's. 'I hear you're trying to destroy my business in Zimbabwe,' Tiny is said to have inquired. 'If you damage my Zimbabwe interest, I may sell my newspapers because I won't be able to afford to keep them. You should think about the consequences.' Some people might conclude that friendship, in Tiny's world, comes before freedom.

Inevitably, however, Tiny's love for black Africa, like so many affairs of the heart, is complicated by the occasional infidelity. And one of them is in South Africa, where Tiny owns a number of mines. One such mine is called Western Platinum, and it's located in one of the Black 'home countries', in Bophuthatswana.

What do you think it would be like if you were a black man, loved by Tiny, and had to work in his mine? For a start, you wouldn't come from Bophuthatswana, even though unemployment there is high, but from one of the central labour organizations scattered throughout Africa, because this way Tiny, despite his love, can pay you less money. You wouldn't be able to come with your family either, because Western Platinum allows only three percent of its workers to live with their wives. Instead you would sleep in one room with twenty new friends, with whom you would share one stove to cook your food. It's reasonable that you would expect to be paid the national average for a black miner—lower of course than the average for a coloured one, lower still than the average for an Indian, and about a tenth of what the white miner would get (but there aren't many of them anyway)—because this would allow you to earn 'the lowest possible amount' on which a person 'can live under humanely decent conditions in the short run.' You probably wouldn't know the quote, which comes from a British publication, *Wages and Conditions of African Workers Employed by British Firms in South Africa*, or what it refers to, which is the Poverty Datum Level. But you would know that there's not a lot you could buy with the money (a few things like two pairs of cotton underpants and a jumper every year, or a pound and a half of meat and six ounces of beans every month). But, unfortunately, Tiny's love won't extend quite this far. In fact, over the last ten years, Tiny's companies have had an embarrassing tendency to pay below the Poverty Datum Line. If, for instance, you had been working in one of Tiny's mines three years ago, you might have been represented in the figures published in the 1982 edition of *Wages and the Conditions of African Workers*, when 'the lowest possible amount' on which a human being could 'live under humanely decent conditions in the short run' was established to be about forty pounds a month. You would then have been one of Tiny's 2,479 black miners who earned only twenty-six pounds a month—and fourteen pounds of this you would have given back to Tiny to pay for your food and lodging.

'Fair makes your blood boil,' Conor Cruise O'Brien said of Salman Rushdie. So it does. And he also said a number of other things, like 'The racism *previously* inculcated and practised by European countries was obviously *demoralising* to Africans *in its day*,' And all this, and so much more, was said in a newspaper owned by a man who only six weeks before was unanimously censured by its independent Board of Directors for trying to influence the paper's coverage of Africa: the same man whose exploitation of labour reinforces the practices of apartheid and whose businesses, in effect, support the regime of South Africa. In the West, there are many different senses to the word *freedom*—and one is unpardonable licence.

One hundred years ago, Britain was sustained by an economy that was easy to name: colonial imperialism. What name describes it today? And how much does our definition of it derive from what it is not—communism? 'The fact is,' Nadine Gordimer has said,

> black South Africans and whites like myself no longer
> believe in the ability of Western capitalism to bring about
> social justice where we live. . . . Whatever Western
> democracies have done for themselves, they have failed and
> are failing, in their great power and influence to do for us.

Gordimer's comments are from a lecture entitled 'Living in the Interregnum'. By 'Interregnum', she refers to the period between the end of South Africa's regime and what will replace it. But the interregnum has a larger context, beyond the particulars of South Africa. It sets the idealism and dreams of socialism against the barbarities of El Salvador and the curbing of Solidarity, the Russian tanks in Prague and the prisons of South Africa and Latin America. The ways of Western capitilism are not humane; but if Western capitalism cannot bring about social justice, what will? 'Communism,' Gordimer says, 'has turned out not to be just or humane either; has failed, even more cruelly than capitalism. Does this mean we have to tell the poor and the dispossessed of the world there is nothing to be done . . .?' What will follow the interregnum?

In August, Conor Cruise O'Brien's regular column in the *Observer* was discontinued, not, according to the Editor, because of 'outside pressure'. Dr O'Brien's view is different; his last column was devoted to the idea of ESP: 'editor subordinate to proprietor'. He was not, of course, crying in public.

MILAN KUNDERA
PARIS OR PRAGUE?

W hen I arrived to spend a few days in the West in September 1968—my eyes still seeing Russian tanks parked on Prague's streets—an otherwise quite likeable young man asked me with unconcealed hostility: 'So what is it you Czechs want exactly? Are you already weary of socialism? Would you have preferred our consumer society?'

Today, sixteen years on, the Western Left almost unanimously approves of the Prague Spring. But I'm not sure the misunderstanding has been clarified entirely.

Western intellectuals, with their proverbial self-centredness, often take an interest in events not in order to know them but so as to incorporate them into their own theoretical speculations, as if they were adding another pebble to their personal mosaic. In that way Alexander Dubček may in some circumstances merge with Allende or Trotsky, in others with Lumumba or Che Guevara. The Prague Spring has been accepted, labelled—but remains unknown.

I want to stress above all else this obvious fact: the Prague Spring was not a sudden revolutionary explosion ending the dark years of Stalinism. Its way had been paved by a long and intense process of liberalization developing throughout the 1960s. It's possible it all began even earlier, perhaps as early as 1956 or even 1948—from the birth of the Stalinist regime in Czechoslovakia, out of the critical spirit which deconstructed the regime's dogma little by little, pitting Marx against Marxism, common sense against ideological intoxication, humanist sophism against inhuman sophistry, and which, by dint of laughing at the system, brought the system to be ashamed of itself: a critical spirit supported by a crushing majority of the people, slowly and irremediably making power aware of its guilt, less and less able to believe in itself or in its legitimacy.

In Prague we used to say cynically that the ideal political regime was a decomposing dictatorship, where the machine of oppression functions more and more imperfectly, but by its mere existence maintains the nation's spirit in maximum creative tension. That's what the 1960s were, a decomposing dictatorship.[1] When I look back,

---

[1]Despite official ideology, there was an extraordinary flowering of Czech culture in these years. The films of Miloš Forman, Jiri Menzel, Vera Chytilova, the theatrical productions of Otomar Krajča and of the brilliant Alfred Radok, the plays of the young Václav Havel, the

I can see us permanently dissatisfied and in protest, but at the same time full of optimism. We were sure that the nation's cultural traditions (its scepticism, its sense of reality, its deeply-rooted incredulity) were stronger than the eastern political system imported from abroad, and that they would in the end overcome it. We were the optimists of scepticism: we believed in its subversive force and eventual victory.

In the summer of 1967, after the explosive Writers' Congress, the State bosses reckoned that the decomposition of the dictatorship had gone too far and tried to impose a hard-line policy. But they could not succeed. The process of decomposition had already reached a guilt-ridden central committee: it rejected the proposed hardening of the line and decided to be chaired by an unknown newcomer, Dubček. What's called the Prague Spring had begun. The critical spirit which up to then had only corroded, now exploded: Czechoslovakia rejected the style of living imported from Russia, censorship vanished, the frontiers opened and all social organizations (trade unions and other associations) intended to transmit meekly the Party's will to the people, became independent and turned into the unexpected instruments of an unexpected democracy. Thus was born (without any guiding plan) a truly unprecedented system—an economy one hundred percent nationalized, an agriculture run through cooperatives, a relatively egalitarian, classless society without rich or poor and without the idiocies of mercantilism, but possessing also freedom of expression, a pluralism of attitudes and a very dynamic cultural life which powered all this movement. (This exceptional influence of culture—of literature, theatre and the periodical press—gives the sixties as a whole its own special, and irresistably attractive, character.) I do not know how viable the system was or what prospects it had; but I do know that in the brief moment of its existence it was a joy to be alive.

---

novels of Josef Škvorecký and Bohumil Hrabal, the poetry of Jan Skacel and the philosophical works of Jan Patocka and Karel Kosik all date from the 1960s. European culture has known in our country few better or more dynamic decades than the Czech sixties and their importance is the yardstick by which the tragedy of 21 August 1968, which killed them brutally, must be measured.

Since the Western Left of today defines its goal as *socialism in freedom*, it is logical that the Prague Spring should henceforth figure in its political discourse. I note more and more often, for example, comparisons between the Prague Spring and the events of May 1968 in Paris, as if the two had been similar or moving in the same direction.

However, the truth is not so simple. I won't speak of the almost too obvious difference in scope between the two (in Prague we had eight months of an entirely original political system, and its destruction in August was a tragic turn in our nation's history), nor will I descend into 'politological' speculations which bore me and, worse still, are repugnant to me, for I spent twenty years of my life in a country whose official doctrine was able only to reduce any and every human problem to a mere reflection of politics. (This doctrinaire passion for reducing man is the evil which anyone who comes from 'over there' has learned to hate the most.) All I want to do is to put my finger on a few reasons (without masking their hypothetical nature) which show that despite the common non-conformism and the common desire for change, there was a substantial difference in the climate of the two Springs.

May '68 was a revolt of youth. The initiative in the Prague Spring lay in the hands of adults who based their action on historical experience and disillusionment. Of course youth played an important rôle in the Prague Spring, but it was not a predominant rôle. To claim the opposite is to subscribe to a myth fabricated *a posteriori* in order to annex the Prague Spring to the epidemic of student revolts around the world.

May in Paris was an explosion of revolutionary lyricism. The Prague Spring was the explosion of post-revolutionary scepticism. That's why the Parisian students looked towards Prague with mistrust (or rather, with indifference), and the man in Prague could only smile at Parisian illusions which (rightly or wrongly) he thought discredited, comic or dangerous. (There is a paradox worth meditating upon: the only successful—if ephemeral—implementation of socialism in freedom was not achieved in revolutionary enthusiasm but in sceptical lucidity.)

Paris in May was radical. What had paved the way over many years for the Prague Spring was a *popular revolt of the moderate.* Just as Ivana the Terrible, in Škvorecký's *Miracle in Bohemia,* replaces 'bad quotations from Marx with less bad ones', so everyone in 1968 sought to blunt, soften, and lighten the weight of the existing political system. The term *thaw,* sometimes used to refer to this process, is very significant: it was a matter of making the ice melt, of softening what was hard. If I speak of moderation, it's not in any precise political sense, but in the sense of a deeply-rooted human reflex. There was a national allergy to radicalism as such, and of whatever kind, for it was connected in most Czechs' subconscious minds to their worst memories.

Paris in May '68 challenged what is called European culture and its traditional values. The Prague Spring was a passionate defence of the European cultural tradition in the widest and most broad-minded sense—as much a defence of Christianity as of modern art, both equally denied by the authorities. We all struggled for our right to this tradition, threatened by the anti-Western messianism of Russian totalitarianism.

May in Paris was a revolt of the Left. As for the Prague Spring, the traditional concepts of right and left are not able to account for it. (The left/right division still has a very real meaning in the life of Western peoples. On the stage of world politics, however, it no longer has much significance. Is totalitarianism left-wing or right-wing? Progressive or reactionary? These questions are meaningless. Russian totalitarianism is above all else a different culture—and therefore also a different political culture—in which the European distinction between those of the left and those of the right loses all sense. Was Khrushchev more left or more right than Stalin? The Czech citizen is confronted today neither by left-wing terror nor by right-wing terror but by a new totalitarian culture which is foreign to him. If some of us think of ourselves as more right-wing or more left-wing, it is only in the context of the West's problems that we can conceive the distinction, and not at all with reference to the problems of our country, which are already of a different order.)

All this created a spiritual atmosphere rather different from the one familiar to opponents west of the Elbe, and Josef Škvorecký represents this atmosphere better than anyone else.

He entered literature with *The Cowards,* an exceptionally mature novel written just after the war, when he was a mere boy of twenty-four. The book stayed in a bottom drawer for many years and was not published until the brief thaw which followed the year of 1956—unleashing an immediate and violent ideological campaign against the author. In the press and in many meetings, Škvorecký had the very worst epithets flung at him (the most famous was 'mangy kitten') and his book was banned from sale. He had to wait until the sixties and another thaw to be republished in an edition of a hundred thousand copies and to become not only the first big bestseller of the postwar literary generation in Czechoslovakia but also the very symbol of a free and anti-official literature.

But why in fact was there a scandal? *The Cowards* does not denounce Stalinism or the Gulag and does not fit what the West calls dissident writing. It tells a very simple story of a young schoolboy who plays in an amateur jazz band and tries his not always lucky hand with classmates of the opposite sex. The story is set in the last days of the war and the young hero watches the spectacle of Liberation in all its derisory unworthiness. It's exactly that aspect which was so unseemly: a non-ideological discourse dealing with sacred subjects (the Liberation is now enshrined in the gilded showcases of all European museums) without the seriousness and respectfulness which is obligatory.

I have dwelt at some length on Škvorecký's first book because the author is already fully present in it, some twenty-five years before this *Miracle* was written in Canada: in both we find his special way of viewing history from underneath. It's a naïvely plebeian view. The humour is coarse, in the tradition of Jaroslav Hašek. There's an extraordinary gift for anecdote, and a mistrust of ideology and the myths of history. Little inclination for the preciousness of modernist prose, a simplicity verging on the provocative, in spite of a very refined literary culture. And finally—if I may say so—an anti-revolutionary spirit.

I hasten to gloss this term: Škvorecký is not a reactionary and he would no doubt not have wished for the return of nationalized factories to their owners or for the dissolution of farm co-operatives. If I mention an anti-revolutionary spirit in connection with him, it is to say that his work represents a critique of the *spirit* of revolution with its myths, its eschatology and its 'all or nothing' attitude. This critique does not touch on any concrete revolutionary demands or policies, but concerns the revolutionary *attitude* in general as one of the basic attitudes which man can adopt towards the world.

The Western reader can only be surprised. What can one expect from a Czech writer who emigrated after the 1968 invasion except that he should write a defence of the Prague Spring? But no, he hasn't done that. It's precisely because Škvorecký is a child of his country, faithful to the spirit whence issued the Prague Spring, that he writes with unwavering irony. What strikes the eye first is his critique (through anecdote more than through argument) of all those revolutionary illusions and gesticulations which tended as time went by to take the stage of the Prague Spring.

In its originating milieu, Škvorecký's view of the Prague Spring has already provoked violent polemics. In Bohemia, his novel is not just banned (as are all the writer's other works) but it is also criticized by many who hold the current regime in contempt, for whom (understandably enough) ironic distance is not possible when they look at themselves in the tragic and difficult circumstances in which they live. Each of us is free to enter into a polemic with this novel, but on one condition: without forgetting that Škvorecký's book is the fruit of a rich experience, in the best realist tradition.

All that is to be read here carries the stamp of truth and contains many accurate renderings of real people and events; this applies also to the main plot—a 'miracle' set up by the police who manage thereby to convict a priest of fraud and to invent a pretext for a violent anti-religious campaign; only the real name of the village, Čihošt, has been changed to Písečnice. Ivana the Terrible, the headmistress who picked out the least bad quotations from Marx, is a real *heroine of moderation*: I knew dozens of her sort. She struggles patiently, silently, against one kind of radicalism, only to fall prey in the end to an opposite kind. (Incidentally, I doubt whether any communist writer has ever managed to create a more moving communist than Škvorecký—a convinced non-communist—gives us here.) The poet Vrchcoláb, the playwright Hejl, the chessmaster Bukavec are portraits of real, known, living persons. I don't know whether that's also the case for the Russian writer Arachidov, but whether or not he has a model in reality he seems more real to me than reality itself. And if you suspect Škvorecký of exaggeration, I can assure you that reality exaggerated much more than Škvorecký. Though all these portraits are marvellously malicious, the novel's hero Smiřický (a kind of stylized self-portrait of the author), who calmly writes an official speech for Lenin's birthday without believing a single word of what he sets down, by no means represents the Truth nor does he constitute a 'positive' hero, even if he is presented in a sympathetic light. Škvorecký spares him little of the tide of irony which inundates the entire novel. This book is until further notice the only work to give an overview of the whole implausible story of the Prague Spring, while at the same time being impregnated with that sceptical resistance—in its most authentic form—which is the best card in the Czech hand.

T he fire which Jan Palach lit with his own body in January 1969 to protest against the fate which had befallen his land (his desperate act, it seems to me, is as foreign to Czech history as the ghostly sight of Russian tanks)—that fire brought a period of history to a close. Is what I said earlier on the spirit of the Prague Spring even very true? Can one still speak today of a revolt of the moderates? The Russian invasion was too terrible by far. Even the authorities, moreover, are not what they used to be in Bohemia. They are no longer fanatical (as in the 1950s) nor guilt-ridden (as in the 1960s) but openly cynical. Can plebian cynicism fight authority more cynical than itself? The time has come when the cynic Škvorecký no longer has a place in his own land.

THE EAGLE AND THE SMALL BIRDS

Crisis in the Soviet Empire: from Yalta to Solidarity

Michael Charlton's survey of a particularly turbulent part of Europe in the four decades since the Soviet takeover. It offers evidence of the collapse of ideology within the Communist fold, and shows the Polish Crisis to have been the latest in a chain that includes the Hungarian Uprising of 1956 and the Prague Spring of 1968. The significance of Solidarity still reverberates in the countries of the Communist bloc and in the West.

£8.75

"The Eagle should permit the small bird to sing, and care not wherefore they sang"
Winston Churchill to Josef Stalin, Yalta 1945

BBC
PUBLICATIONS

The new series for the 1980s and beyond

PALADIN MOVEMENTS AND IDEAS

Series editor:
Justin Wintle

This important new series aims to provide clear and stimulating surveys of the ideas and cultural movements that have dominated history. It has been planned to furnish a broad approach for students, teachers, and general readers. **Paladin Movements and Ideas** takes the whole sweep of human history as its provenance. It will build into a complete library of authoritative, readable books dealing with every aspect of culture.

The first three titles are **Rationalism** by John Cottingham: **Expressionism** by Roger Cardinal; and **Darwinian Evolution** by Antony Flew, just published at £2.50 each. Coming in 1985 are **The Psychoanalytic Movement** by Ernest Gellner; **Structuralism** by José G. Merquior; **Western Transcendentalism** by A. Robert Lee; and **The Women's Movement** by Helen McNeill.

GRANADA

JOSEF ŠKVORECKÝ
MIRACLES

H ere we were, the three Czechs: Mr Kohn, the Jew who fled the Nazis in '39. Mr Pohorsky, the recent exile, now tending the lawns of the Connington Golf Club. And me: not an immigrant, nor an émigré, but a visiting 'scholar', courtesy of the Ford Foundation.

'You see,' Mr Kohn was explaining to us, surveying the Connington snack bar with sad, unseeing eyes, 'I'm now an American. I pay taxes. I make a lot of money. But America is not my home. I've lived in the States for thirty years, but I still long for Prague. I still miss the shop that belonged to my father—a bell over the door rang whenever anyone entered it. That was home. But this,' and in waving his plump hand he took in not only Connington but all of New England, 'this, gentlemen, is Babylon.'

'But surely,' Mr Pohorsky asked, 'surely, Mr Kohn, you aren't sorry you left?'

'Sorry? I'm sorry I *had* to leave. That's the difference. It's one thing to want. It's another to have to.'

A bell was ringing, but I didn't know where. Consciousness came slowly: it was night and I was half-trapped in a vague dream—from which, nonetheless, I was happy to escape. Gradually, the darkness in my room thinned out. A yellow street lamp was shining outside the window. It was the telephone that was ringing—an ominous sign at this time of the night. The illuminated clock showed a quarter to three. I reached for the phone: 'Smiricky here.'

'The experiment has failed,' answered a voice.

'Who's that?'

'Ocenas.'

I was relieved. Night calls from Ocenas—the sci-fi writer and well-known soak—were not unusual.

'Are you in heaven?' I asked. 'How did you get there? On Johnny Walker or Châteauneuf du Pape?'

'I'm in the shit, and so are you.'

'I'm not. I'm asleep. And if you want someone to talk you out of your fug, ring Sarka. Goodbye.'

I hung up. The room was quiet, except for the distant growling of an airplane engine. Pilots approached the airport by flying directly over my flat and the noise was terrible. But you get used to it. It no longer disturbed my sleep.

I lay there listening to the noise of the traffic on the Brevnov road—also familiar. But it was also unusually busy for this time of night. I opened my eyes. The yellow street lamp, in a cloud of nocturnal fog, continued shining calmly outside my window.

The telephone exploded again. 'Smiricky here.'

'The experiment has failed.'

'Go to hell!' I said with an impressive show of feeling, while continuing to half-listen to the growling somewhere up above. Slowly coming out of my sleep, I was beginning to understand that this wasn't an ordinary growl: it wasn't someone circling above the airport unable to land because of the fog. And suddenly the sleeping half of my brain woke up. I hadn't been half-trapped in a vague dream: I had merged the nightmare of sleep with the nightmare of reality. 'Go to hell,' I repeated, in a voice that involuntarily had less conviction than before.

'I'm there already. And so are you. The brothers have arrived.'

'Those airplanes? Is that them?'

'Those as well as the armoured column coming up from Melnik. They may have reached your part of town. Have a look out the window.'

'I would have heard them. Tanks rattle like a load of old iron.'

'Of course, I forgot: you were in the tank division.' Suddenly Ocenas gave a horrified yell: 'Oh, my God! Your manuscript is sitting in Foglar's drawer. That was high treason even under Novotny!'

Then I was the one feeling scared—more scared than Ocenas. Against my better judgement, I had moved my novel, *The Tank Division,* from the attic of my aunt's house in Popovice—where it had lain undisturbed for fifteen years—and submitted it to a publishing house that, rapidly joining the liberalization, had thrown out the dreaded Vohnout, replacing him with Foglar, the man who had earlier already been thrown out by the dreaded Vohnout. In the context of the current developments—which were not unrelated to the growling of alien airplanes—my venomous satire of the people's army did not leave me feeling particularly secure. 'So what?' I said valiantly, trying to hide that I was trembling.

'My dear colleague,' Ocenas replied, 'if I'm in the shit up to my neck, you're in it at least up to your waist. If I were you I'd find that manuscript right away and get it back to Popovice. Vohnout is sure to be on the first Soviet tank, and once he's here you'll never see your manuscript again. Except perhaps in court.'

'Go to...' But then I heard it—a noise I know very well. In the early days of my army service it terrified me. Then I got used to it. Eighteen years later I was unused to it, and my heart sank. 'They're here.'

'The tanks?'

'Yes.'

'See you in Siberia. Goodbye.'

And he put down the phone.

I leapt out of bed and, on legs that kept giving way underneath me, went to the window. Outside was a scene from Ocenas's science fiction, but with sound-effects: a rattle that suggested the mass-mobilization of endless pots and pans. From the morning mist, they emerged, one after another: flattened monsters, the envoys of truth. Adolescents, clustered on top, gazed down the barrels of their guns and into our windows. Youths from the land where tomorrow is yesterday.

And today the day before yesterday.

I felt relieved: my sarcasm hadn't deserted me yet. And my knees slowly began to obey me.

M r Kohn continued: 'I did not want to leave. I was still in Prague in May 1939, and couldn't make up my mind. There were terrible rumours that the Germans would put us into camps, that they treated people like cattle, that we would all die there. But no one knew anything for sure. That was the worst thing. And on the other hand, I was forty-five. I didn't speak anything but Czech and a bit of German. I had a little factory, no capital abroad, and it was impossible to take money out. You see, Doctor Smiricky, it was a difficult decision. I was pushing fifty: nothing was certain, and everything looked terrible.'

I understood Mr Kohn well. I was forty-five and had no capital. But Mr Kohn was now an American citizen. All this was behind him, and the worst he could expect was death. And probably a luxury death in a good sanatorium. I looked at his sorrowful eyes, at the pink face of a well-preserved seventy-five-year-old man. I suddenly envied him. I still had to make up my mind.

I walked quickly through the morning streets. I didn't bother to take my car: the stream of tanks was endless and steel jammed the crossroads. The boys outside the house were throwing bottles and stones at the panzers.

It was four in the morning but already the streets were full. Women were weeping. Unshaven men shouted insults and younger men in colourful shirts raised clenched fists. Schoolgirls were running alongside the jolting tanks, calling out in Russian: 'Why? Why did you come here?'

I just walked on. Nervous Russian adolescents, embracing deadly weapons, gazed out at an alien world from the same sort of tanks I had described in my imprudent novel: they tried to take in the girls jogging along beside them, the unexpectedly defenceless crowd that met them instead of the Zionist bands armed with the latest American weapons they'd been promised in their briefings. They looked out on a strange, un-Russian, medieval town. Their officers, in newly-issued tunics, stood above the gun turrets, glowering. Every now and then a soldier glanced up, as if asking for instructions, but the officers, sphinx-like, did not respond. My city, which had survived the plunderings of Swedish mercenaries and the undisguised power-hunger of the National Socialists, was now being covered by a flat darkness led by computers.

On the corner by St Anthony's Church the road turned sharply right and the tanks, one after the other, had to execute elephantine manoeuvres before they could proceed awkwardly towards the embankment. I overtook one that, with its left track, was tearing up the paving stones and tramlines. On its hull sat the perfect officer. Small, puffy, padded in a body warmer, pointing his revolver. He had a potato face and a nose borrowed from Maxim Gorky. And above the nose, a beautiful, symbolic red star. The shaggy brows under the star expressed irritation, assurance and righteousness, but also the faintest suspicion that he might be in the wrong country. A gaggle of girls in miniskirts gathered around his tank, shouting, with thick Czech accents, the question that was becoming increasingly familiar: 'Why? Why? There is no counter-revolution here.'

The soldiers bunched around the perfect officer were staring, hypnotized, at the girls' thighs. It seemed that they had never seen so much so publicly exposed.

'*Pachemu? Pachemu?* Why? Why?' the girls cried, and real tears poured from their eyes.

The perfect officer, furious, looked at them. Many emotions appeared on his potato face: but righteousness won. Miniskirts, he had probably been taught, were among the telling signs of the return of capitalism.

'Why? Why?' wailed the girls in their school Russian. Suddenly their shouts, the metal rattle of the armoured vehicles and the roars of their engines were broken by the siren shriek of one woman. The shriek was also in Russian, but a classical Russian, perfectly enunciated: '*Idite domoy, russkiye fashisty!* Go home, Russian fascists!'

The perfect officer raised his pistol. The young Russian at his feet burst into tears, sobbing like the girls in miniskirts. The officer's shaggy brows furrowed as he looked to see who was shrieking: there, high above the crowd, was the grey head of Bozena Pokorna, the six-foot translator of Russian classics. She was in pink curlers and a shabby dressing-gown: 'Russian fascists, go home!'

For a moment, they stared at each other, the perfect officer and the translator of Russian classics, in mutually-felt antipathy. He waved his pistol, paused, and then, not like the perfect officer but the perfect drill sergeant, bellowed: 'Death to fascism! Death to the counter-revolution!'

The crowd swelled and roared. The young men whistled and mocking shouts rose from the multitude. A little boy chalked a swastika on the front plate of the tank, under the feet of the sobbing crewman. The high voice of Bozena Pokorna shrieked again, once more in the purest Russian: 'Death to Soviet fascism! Death to Soviet counter-revolution! Go home!'

The girls in miniskirts, momentarily silenced by the exchange, quickly took up the slogan: '*Idite domoy, russkiye fashisty! Idite domoy, russkiye fashisty!* Go home, Russian fascists! Go home, Russian fascists!'

It was charming. And it was hopeless. I turned the corner without waiting for the frightened Russian adolescents to resolve the exchange with gunfire.

'And all the time, I kept thinking,' said Mr Kohn. 'Will they do something to us? Or will they leave us alone? Will they put us in a ghetto and let us live, or will they load us into the trains and kill us? That was the question everyone asked, morning till night, night till morning. A living nightmare, Doctor Smiricky. The streets were filled with people who were in no danger at all, and there was me: would I be a man without a country or a man condemned? No one cared. But why should they, anyway?'

Mr Kohn fell silent. Some blacks with their sexy girlfriends pushed past us to the bar.

'I know the feeling, Mr Kohn,' said Mr Pohorsky. 'Like the time in 1951 when they took me down through Wenceslas Square in a prison van, and I saw the sign on a cinema we were passing: 'TOMORROW THERE'LL BE DANCING EVERYWHERE'. And they were taking me to the uranium mines in Jachymov.'

'Well, fancy that,' said Mr Kohn. 'So you know what it's like, Mr Pohorsky. That terrible feeling: not quite free, but not quite dead. Well, to cut a long story short, I hung about Prague until May 1939. And then it was too late. The cage had closed. Jews weren't allowed out. *Then* anything seemed better than sitting in a cage. Anything. Begging in the streets. Slaving from morning till night in Patagonia. Dying in a paupers' hospital. The important thing was to die in a bed. Anything but the cage, the feeling of being caught like an animal. Men aren't animals, Doctor Smiricky: there is nothing worse than dying like an animal. And those poor things—well, you know, gentlemen—those poor things died like cattle.'

I recalled a photograph taken by an SS man who then caught a bullet. The photograph got into the hands of an allied soldier, who sold it to a picture magazine, probably for a good sum. It showed naked old women and fat, naked middle-aged women running up the side of a mucky trench. A few of them sat, resigned: naked, shameless before the camera, stomachs hanging over the triangle of human fur, drooping breasts. Naked, not sexy, not desirable. Undressed by an order. Terribly naked, gripping—senselessly, absurdly—equally naked children. Pale, white women's bodies, swollen with age and a lack of exercise. Once, when dressed, they had been dignified Jewish mammas with perfect hairdos, with earrings in their old ears. Yes. There is nothing worse than dying like animals.

'And if it hadn't been for Bondy,' Mr Kohn added, 'I would never have got out. Today I would have been soap—well, used up long ago actually—just like the poor things who stayed behind.'

I was pushing my way through the crowd in front of the Museum. One of the tanks had knocked down a telephone box. I remembered a terrifying phone call many years ago. It was from Ludmila, whom I called Lizetta.

'*Howdy,*' she said. It was eleven o'clock at night, and I immediately recognized her. No one else I knew said 'howdy'.

'Hello, Lizetta.'

'Get your things together and come here.'

'Now? Why should I?'

'There was a time when you wouldn't have asked.'

'But it's almost midnight.'

'There was a time when you would have come at three in the morning, darling.'

'But that was before.'

'Don't you love me any more, Danny darling?' she insisted.

'I do. It's just a bit late.'

'It's never too late for love.'

'For mine it is.' She was silent. I imagined her as she lay on her bed—tattered by a succession of dissatisfied lovers—and felt her anger.

'I'll tell you something, darling. It's never too late. So get your things and be here. *Now!*'

'Oh, get stuffed, Lizetta!'

'It's in your own interests,' she said.

In my own interests? I was seized by an uncomfortable feeling, a particularly socialist feeling: of being, once again, in some kind of trouble. 'What do you mean?' I asked.

'I'll explain when you get here.'

'But I'm not curious.'

'You will be. I have an interesting novel here. *The Tank Division.* Do you understand, Danny darling?'

Ten minutes later I was in a taxi, my heart beating furiously. It wasn't love: it was the thought that the aforementioned novel, of which I was the author, contained a venomous account of Lizetta's numerous infidelities, neatly embellished with technical but accurate descriptions of her various amorous skills. Oh my God, how did she get hold of the thing?

I soon found out. Lizetta, her naked body loosely draped with a thin nightgown, was full of threats: 'Look, darling, I couldn't care less that you lend your rubbish to your friends without first checking to see if they are *my* friends as well'—thus implicating Ocenas who, when I gave him the manuscript telling him not to show it to anyone, had certainly not been Lizetta's friend—'nor do I care that you describe me as a tart, nor even do I care that you describe me as a completely dumb tart, nor that you say I have an arse like a horse. What really offends me is your cynicism. I am not one of those stupid communists, but this is too much. This, Danny, in spite of my tolerance and my sense of humour, offends me as a socialist'.

I was petrified. The connection between this woman—more possessed by vaginal desire than any other I had known—and socialism was surreal: like a roast leg of mutton lying on a communion plate.

'Moreover,' she said, 'I believe that your book betrays military secrets.'

'Not that,' I exclaimed.

'I don't know!' she said. 'The powers-that-be will have to decide. I think I will have to take the book to the Ministry of Interior.'

She fixed me with her evil, beautiful eyes, her tits stiff under the thin nightgown. My heart once again beat madly, this time with the certain knowledge that there was nothing of which Lizetta was incapable. That night she played with me, in the way that a very cruel cat plays with a very frightened mouse. It was only much later that she finally allowed me to take off that nightgown and rape her from behind—so as to prove, no doubt, that she did not have an arse like a horse. But, actually, she did have an arse like a horse. In this, as in everything else, my description was accurate.

Bondy?' Mr Pohorsky asked, 'Was that one of your American relatives?'

'No,' Mr Kohn replied. 'A friend. I met him at the end of May on the embankment. Bondy was, as usual, dressed perfectly—he even wore a carnation in his buttonhole. By then Jews kept to the side streets, but Bondy behaved as if nothing had changed. No cage, no restrictions. He saw me looking worried and asked,

"What's up?" And so I told him how, unable to make up my mind, I had got stuck in Prague. I could have run away, I said, I could be in South America or living in poverty somewhere, but at least out of danger. And Bondy said, "Kohn, old friend, come with me!" And so we went. You'll never guess where.'

'Where, Mr Kohn?' Mr Pohorsky asked.

'To the Wehrmacht Headquarters, gentlemen,' said Mr Kohn. 'There was a guard at the gate, but Bondy just showed him a pass, and he let us in. And you can see, Doctor Smiricky, what I look like. And Bondy was worse. There couldn't have been any mistake.'

And Mr Kohn pointed, sadly, to his massive conk.

She lay beside me in her favourite position—on her stomach—her magnificent posterior shining white in the moonlight.

'Lizetta,' I said, 'Where is the manuscript?'

'In the safe. Over there.' She pointed with her foot to a small strong-box on the bookshelf, in which she locked all the letters of her lovers from her jealous but impotent husband.

'Give it to me.'

'I'll think about it.'

'Do you want to blackmail me?'

She raised herself on her elbows. In the white light, her breasts formed two beautiful white hills, divided by a narrow path. 'Do you find this blackmail so unpleasant?'

'No. But it would be pleasanter if you returned my manuscript.' I was, I realized, in a predicament of classic proportions: I was helpless. But I had an idea. I got up. There were cigarettes on the writing table. There was also her handbag—in which were her keys.

'What are you doing?' she asked, as I set to rummaging. Then, with a thump, she was out of bed. 'Give it back.' She grabbed the handbag. I grabbed her waist. We struggled and I threw her on the bed. We rolled over each other—under the soft surface of her smooth body she had muscles—and she shoved the handbag under her back, holding it there with both hands. I sat astride her and grabbed her by the throat.

'Do you want to kill me?' she taunted.

'I will kill you,' I said, but her prostitute's instinct told her that the fight was going out of me.

'But not like this, surely. You'd get caught immediately.'

I let go of her neck. The moon lit her green eyes, and, protecting her handbag, she leapt out of bed—once again the gleam of her bum—and ran out of the room. I couldn't run after her. Her parents, strict Catholics, slept in the room across the hall: they had added an inexplicable tolerance of their daughter's fornications to the many mysteries of their faith, but it was not a tolerance I wished to test. I turned on my back and lay on the bed, angry, tense, full of hate, scared and destroyed. As she returned, the moonlight gave her skin a seductive opalescence. She leaped on the bed, where I lay with my hands behind my head, and sat astride me as if on a horse. Her hands rested on my shoulders, her full white breasts waved their dark tips before my face.

'Now you're mine, Danny dear, and you'd better remember it. You'll come when I call, and if you don't, you'll have to answer your door to the police.'

And this thought excited her so much that her beautiful bottom started to work assiduously between my legs.

'And another soldier,' Mr Kohn continued, 'opened the doors for us. Inside, behind a table that could seat twenty people, sat a general with a monocle, all alone. As soon as he saw Bondy, he said in German, "Hello, Bondy! What can I do for you?" You won't believe it, gentlemen—I didn't believe it—but that's what he said. A Nazi general. And do you know who it was?'

'No,' said Mr Pohorsky.

'It was General Blaskowitz. Does that name mean anything to you?'

It did. General Blaskowitz was inscribed in my generation's memory. It was his signature at the bottom of the first of many public announcements that ended in the beautifully unsentimental warning: 'Anyone resisting the armies of the Reich will be shot.' Yes, we knew General Blaskowitz.

The steel porridge continued to pour down the centre of Wenceslas Square. Near the pavement a heavily-loaded tank, like a stegosaurus, was trying to avoid a munitions carrier. The carrier angrily tore out a piece of the pavement along with the roots of a tree. It rubbed screechingly against the tank's iron flank. Then something cracked, and the enormous, fiery body of the stegosaurus ran onto the pavement scattering us, and stopped. On top of the tank sat a little soldier looking as frightened as I was: his boots pointed at the breasts of a crying girl in a miniskirt. The sight was another significant symbol. A shot rang out, and an ancient lorry with a load of old newspapers emerged from a gateway. Another shot exploded from its exhaust. I looked at the little soldier. His eyes darted nervously from window to window, and, as he raised his gun, a cluster of gunbarrels emerged just above his head. A clapping sound rose from the arch of the Museum and the lorry backfired again. A flock of pigeons flew up from the ramp. The soldier, only a moment before aiming his boots at the breasts of his Prague coeval, raised his gun quickly and discharged a whole load of bullets somewhere in the direction of the pigeons. The barrels just above his head also turned in the direction of the clapping and the tank crew fired a cannonade. I fell to the ground and watched the gun turret turn towards the Museum and shoot arrows of light in a beautiful curved trajectory at the neo-Renaissance façade. Sparkling glass poured down, like a waterfall. Panic: people on all fours were trying to squeeze into doorways. A fat lady was next to me, lying on her stomach like an enormous beetle, groaning and powerlessly wriggling her hands and feet in the air. I crawled behind a lamppost. Artillery men with automatics were kneeling on the front of the stegosaurus. An officer, identical to the perfect officer I'd seen by St Anthony's, instructed, bellowing, the soldiers to take aim—the target, it turned out, being the pigeons.

High above, at the top of a tree, something trembled. I raised my head. A gentle white dove fell to the pavement, shuddered and died. Everything in my life is often so embarrassingly symbolic.

'And,' Mr Kohn said, 'Bondy then said: "Just a little thing. My old friend Kohn here needs exit papers." "Just for himself?" asked General Blaskowitz, "or for his family too?" Bondy looked at me. It was like a dream. "Also, for my wife Gerta," I said, plucking up courage. "And for my daughter Hana and my son Jacob, my mother-in-law Berta, and also, if possible, for my brother Arnost. He's a bachelor." And I kept thinking, General Blaskowitz is making fun of me—people like him always made fun of the Jews—but he said, "Easy," and called a secretary. Half an hour later, I was running for home, with exit visas for the whole family.'

33

'That's incredible,' said Mr Pohorsky. 'What do you think was the reason?'

'Don't ask me, Mr Pohorsky. I didn't ask Bondy. It was a miracle.'

'A miracle?' asked Mr Pohorsky.

'How else can you explain it?'

When I finally reached the publishing house, I saw that everything was lost. By the gate stood yet another product of fertile Soviet mothers: he had an automatic rifle and his dusty boots were firmly planted. Behind him a little officer with a cigarette in his mouth leaned against the sign saying WRITERS' CLUB, observing the events in the street with a mixture of curiosity and inculcated hate.

I felt a chill. My first, fifteen-year-old counter-revolutionary novel was up there—together with the illustrations by the homosexual painter Brabenec. In them, the officers look like animated potatoes. Brabenec was also famous for his painting *Alice in Prickland.* And all that will now fall into their hands.

I imagined the nightmare that awaited me, one far worse than the one I experienced under Lizetta—even though her perversions would have astounded Ancient Rome and her sexual needs were virtually insatiable.

'Perhaps,' asked Mr Pohorsky, 'Bondy and Blaskowitz were old comrades from the First World War?'

'Bondy? Don't make me laugh! He got out of the First World War by faking idiocy. It was a miracle! But I've paid for it by being a man without a home country. And without a mother. Because my dear mother didn't come with us. She said she was too old to cross oceans. She was sixty-three. And anyway after my father's death she married a Christian, which saved her. Can you imagine—she survived it all. The war, Stalin, everything. She's alive to this day! She's ninety-two! But she hasn't seen me since 1939. In fact I understood it all only last year: I was saved so that I could be punished.'

'But what for, Mr Kohn?' I asked.

'For cowardice. For unforgiveable cowardice. And selfishness.

When one thinks what they had to go through before they were killed.'

Mr Kohn pulled out a monogrammed handkerchief and blew into it. It sounded like a sad, hopeless trumpet call.

'You see, gentlemen, I wanted to return the moment the war ended. But that was just when my business in America started to prosper. So I put it off, and I kept putting it off until 1948. By then I was, as they say, a made man. And by then the communists had taken over. Well, tell me: could I, an American capitalist, return to Czechoslovakia then? I couldn't. And anyway, my dear mother sent a message that I shouldn't come back yet, times were difficult: they seemed to be cooking up something against the Jews again. So I said to myself: I'll wait a little longer.'

Mr Kohn once again played a lament on his tragic conk.

'But all the time, gentlemen, I kept dreaming of home. But do you know what always woke me from my dreams? That cage. That feeling of the cage closing. That terrible, inhuman feeling, because men were not made for cages.'

Mr Kohn took, against doctor's orders, a careful sip of his gin.

'And my instinct was right,' said Mr Kohn. 'They closed the borders, like the Nazis before them, and no one could get out. People tried to get out through the Sumava forests, and they were shot. And once again they sent innocent people to the camps: just four years after the war. And once again men died there like animals. Even though there weren't so many of them, murder is always terrible: it does not matter whether you're talking about one man or a hundred.'

'It was more than that, Mr Kohn,' said Mr Pohorsky. 'Some 200 were executed even if you don't count those shot while escaping, or those who died in hospital. Only those who were hanged. And some of them were hanged more than once.'

Mr Kohn was horrified: 'More than once, Mr Pohorsky?'

'Yes, more than once,' the habit of a lifetime made Mr Pohorsky look round him. 'There was the case of Franta Vohanka, who was in the same cell as me. A police informer got him for CIA links, so they gave him the noose, but first they wanted names. They gave him a list and said they won't hang him if he names his accomplices. But Franta was strong. So they led him out into the courtyard, put him under the noose, tied his hands neatly by his side, and the executioner was about

Josef Škvorecký

to pull the rope when Judge Ryba, that filthy swine who spent the war licking the arse of the Nazis, said: "Stop!" And Franta was untied and they marched him off to the cell and back to interrogation. And again: if he'd just tick the names on the list he'd get prison instead of death, and would be free to go home when there's an amnesty. Franta, however, did not know any of the people on the list. He could easily have pointed to any name which came to mind, but he was as solid as a rock. So two days later it was back to the noose, hands tied to the body, and the executioner about to pull the rope—'

'But that's terrible!' said Mr Kohn, reaching for the forbidden gin with a trembling hand.

'To cut a long story short,' said Mr Pohorsky, 'they played this game with him for half a year. Franta even stopped counting: he got so accustomed to it he used to say that he felt something was missing if they didn't tie him up like a salami twice a week and shove him under the noose. At least it provided a bit of excitement because otherwise prison was as boring as hell. Well, one day, Mr Kohn, they tied him up again, put him back in the noose, the executioner reached for the rope again, but Judge Ryba didn't say anything and *crack*! Franta was swinging on the rope like the discarded pupa of a butterfly.'

Mr Kohn had to have another gin.

It was afternoon. By now the Soviet military machine had probably reached both the Austrian and the German borders. I packed two suitcases and loaded them into my car. I was expecting the classic ring at the door. On my way home I'd heard the first broadcasts of the underground stations and the first manifestos of the heroes—or suicidal maniacs—who, under their own names, cursed the arrival of the fraternal armies. A woman announcer, her voice terribly familiar, warned people to look out for an ambulance with the number AC 3215. It belonged, she said, to the KGB, and its crew was collecting the people on their list in alphabetical order. There was a chance that my name was on it.

As I packed my second case the bell rang. For a second I felt faint, but the ringing was repeated at regular intervals. It was the telephone.

'Danny? This is Sylva.'

I felt a flood of relief.

36

'Danny, listen, I don't know what to do. Milan is in Paris, I tried to telephone him, but I can't get through.'

That's what you'd call bad luck. Sylva had returned from Paris with both their kids only the day before.

'I'm just packing. We can go to Paris if you like.'

'That's perfect. Thanks,' Sylva answered, as if I'd just promised her a trip into the country.

Half an hour later I was loading Sylva, her two little children Martin and Martina, and their three enormous suitcases into my small convertible. One case wouldn't fit.

'Can't we leave it here?'

'Oh. No, please!' Sylva begged. She looked out of this world. She'd dressed for the long and dangerous journey in a postage stamp snake-skin miniskirt which she'd brought from Paris. The awkward trunk was probably full of similar treasures. The sight of this perfect specimen of Czech womanhood awoke my patriotic pride and I decided that I'd somehow get all her minis and maxis to Paris, even if it was going to cost me my life.

I put down the roof of the car and placed the trunk on the back seat.

Little blonde Martina was very pleased. 'Uncle, are we going in an open car? What fun!'

'What fun,' added Martin. 'We'll catch cold!'

'That's enough,' said Sylva. 'Get in!'

She lifted Martina and put her in the back next to the trunk. Then, as she bent down for Martina's little brother, the miniskirt revealed Sylva's wonderful legs, and once again, in place of the more traditional male responses, I felt a wave of impersonal pride. The two Czech children sitting next to the trunk also looked irresistibly beautiful. I realized that it was my mission to get this load of Central-European beauty through the cordon of oriental steel, and, in the grip of my wild chauvinism, I forgot all fears for myself.

We left the peaceful Prague suburbs by the main Dejvice road. The pavements were framed by tanks, and each tank was surrounded by debaters practising their Russian. The soldiers were getting hoarse with ideology.

We turned the corner past a wooden hoarding surrounding a building site. It was covered in graffiti. 'BASTARDS GO HOME' was emblazoned in enormous, almost man-size white letters. The six-foot figure of Bozena Pokorna, no longer in curlers, now wearing a flower-printed dress instead of a dressing-gown, was passing from slogan to slogan. In her left hand she held a bucket of white paint, in her right a brush. She was carefully correcting the imperfect Russian spelling of the graffiti left by her less literate predecessors.

'And so the years passed, as they say,' Mr Kohn continued. 'Things in Czechoslovakia began to improve. Around 1956, my dear mother wrote saying she'd been promised a passport. You can't imagine my joy. I hadn't seen her for seventeen years! But then another blow. Hungary! And my dear mother didn't get her passport after all. She was eighty by then, so I said I had to go and see her myself. By then, of course, I was an American citizen. And whenever I thought of going back, I felt the same old fear. My head kept saying: What are you afraid of? But my fear wouldn't listen. After all, even my head couldn't be one hundred per cent sure.'

The tanks on the road ahead of us were crawling at a snail's pace, enveloped in clouds of dust. I glanced at Sylva and met her honey eyes. They were magnificent, but in spite of my patriotic determination the situation looked anything but rosy.

'Shall I try to overtake?'

'If we stay behind them we'll never make it to the border.'

I put my foot on the accelerator and a moment later we were behind the back of the last tank. Eight pairs of booted legs hung from the sides. We swam slowly past them in clouds of dust as the amazed eyes above the boots fixed on Sylva's proud face. She looked a little like Queen Nefertiti and she was fully aware of it. She kept her lower lip contemptuously puckered until we'd got past the side of the tank and back into the middle of the road. The horrified eyes of yet another mass-produced perfect officer, sitting on the barrel of the tank ahead, rolled at the sight of Sylva's thighs as we passed. We were overtaking another tank drowning in dust, and both the quiet little Czech children were gazing with equally horrified eyes at the hot iron monsters.

'I kept having the same dream.' Mr Kohn went on with his tale. 'That I'd crossed the border, panicked, but the barrier was down. The cage. That's an émigré's dream, gentlemen, and you'll have it too, if you haven't had it yet.'

'We have, Mr Kohn,' Mr Pohorsky nodded. 'The same dream.'

'And it wouldn't take much to kill me. One kick, perhaps, I've got a weak heart and my liver is bad. It wouldn't take much.'

'That's what you think, Mr Kohn,' said Mr Pohorsky, trying to console him. 'But you wouldn't believe what a man can endure. Do you know how often they put me in solitary during those years? At least fifty times. And I'm here.'

'Solitary?' Mr Kohn was horrified again.

'It was kind of a concrete balcony.' Mr Pohorsky spoke with the passion of an inventor. 'Or, if you like, a concrete hole in the ground. You could get either. It was designed so you couldn't lie down—it was that narrow—and you couldn't sit down: the guards wouldn't let you. And in some, the floor was at an angle, so standing wasn't easy, either. It all depended on the imagination of the commanding officer. And when they put you in there, you had to strip naked, winter or summer, and if you felt sleepy the guards doused you with cold water.'

'In the winter? Good God! What if there was a frost?'

'That's just what I mean. A lot of people got pneumonia and died. But most survived. A camp makes a man of you. I've even survived the uranium mine, Mr Kohn. Want to know how? Only thanks to—'

And he acquainted Mr Kohn with his theory about the curative properties of tea.

'You won't believe this,' Mr Kohn then replied. 'But I've never been afraid of death. I'm only afraid of dying like an animal. It's a modern fear. The world is a terrible place, gentlemen! And I see a sort of meaning in it all that makes it even harder to get rid of my fear. That they'd find something to get me on. That I'll die like those poor creatures. Like an animal.'

'I'll tell you something,' said Mr Pohorsky, 'they're the animals actually. There was a man called Valchar in Rovnost prison, who specialized in something he called 'tomato ketchup'. Can you imagine what it was?'

Mr Kohn's eyes were wide. 'Please, perhaps it would be better—if I didn't know—'

'Crushing men's balls,' said Mr Pohorsky. 'And you know, they survived even that. Some did, anyway.'

The vehicle in front of us braked sharply, and I nearly crashed into its back. The tanks, evidently on command, turned off their engines. A terrifying silence reigned. From the back seat came Martina's clear voice: 'Mummy, I'm thirsty!'

'I'm thirsty too!' echoed Martin.

'We're in trouble,' said I. 'It looks as if the brothers have lost their way.'

Excited voices were arguing in the commander's tank and I noticed an old woman with a goat observing the unusual visitors.

Sylva gave Martina a bottle of Cola.

'They've lost their way,' I said.

'What a joke,' said Sylva.

A Russian voice somewhere near us said: 'Give us a drink, little girl!'

Behind us Martina burst into tears. And Martin joined her.

'Mummy, mummy, he's taking it fwom me!' bellowed Martina.

Sylva turned fiercely round. In my mirror I could see a dusty soldier snatching his hand back with the guilty face of a kid caught stealing apples.

'Who's taking what, Martina?' Sylva asked with threat in her voice.

'That Wussian! He's taking my Cola!'

What terrible things you tell us, Mr Pohorsky,' said Mr Kohn. 'Did they really crucify him?'

'For a joke, naturally,' said Mr Pohorsky. 'They wanted to take him down again. But they didn't actually nail him in. No, they just tied him up by his legs and and feet, saying they'd give him vinegar from a sponge, just like Jesus. But he had a bad heart, so he died on them.'

A nd she pointed an accusing finger at the shaven culprit. 'How dare you!' Sylva shouted at him.

'How dare you, bastards!' added Martin.

'Mawtin!' said Martina.

'It's OK,' said the soldier with an embarrassed smile. 'I just wanted a drink. Why won't you let me have a little of your drink, little girl?'

'Drink your own stuff!' Sylva's lower lip was delightfully contemptuous.

'We haven't had a thing to eat or drink since the morning. They forgot to bring our rations.'

'You'll just have to tighten your belt, you Siberian plague,' said Sylva. 'Martina, don't let some stupid Russian make you cry!'

'She's not cwying because of the Wussian,' volunteered Martin. 'She's spilt Cola all over herself.'

That made Sylva really mad: 'Bloody hell! See what you've done? That's a new frock, and now it's covered in Cola!'

'Is that Coca Cola?' The soldier pointed at the bottle with an expressive curiosity.

'Hands off!' shrieked Martin.

'What's happened?' said a Russian bass from behind us.

I turned round. One of the mass-produced perfect officers was glowering suspiciously at my elegant little red car from the side of the road.

'What are you doing in our column?'

'A nd then that Dubcek business,' said Mr Kohn. 'You know, for a long time I didn't believe it. One communist is much like another. They're like those policemen in detective stories. Some act good, some bad, but when it comes down to it they're all the same. But with Dubcek we heard all these strange things. Former prisoners had formed clubs. Political parties were to be allowed again. Rehabilitation. And the people who visited there returned full of enthusiasm. Finally even Lewith, you know, the one who makes Venus chocolates, plucked up the courage. He was a big man in industry back home before the war. They confiscated his factories in 1945. I asked him to visit Mother. And he came back and said: "Kohn, you've got to go! Either there's a miracle occurring there, or we've all gone mad. It's probably the latter, so you'd better go while you can. And your mother," he said, "says the same, and she doesn't expect to live much longer. Anyway," he said, "you'd better go as soon as possible. You can't imagine how beautiful it is. It's like a fairytale. Kohn," he said, "get a move on, it won't last beyond Christmas."'

I shrugged: 'I don't understand Russian.'

'Tell him to get knotted!' said Sylva.

'Give me your passport!' the officer ordered.

I looked at Sylva: 'It looks as if we're in the shit.'

'Don't be wude, uncle!' Martina commented from the back, still snuffling.

'Shut up, Martina!' said Sylva.

'Give me your passport!' the officer repeated. 'Are you foreigners?'

'*Da,*' said Sylva.

The officer was taken aback. He went off and returned with another. They looked at our number plate.

'Now you've done it, Sylva,' I said. 'Car numbers must be one thing they understand.'

One of the officers pulled out a little book, leafed through it, and then they gazed at our number plate again. My fears were justified. The first officer said, very unpleasantly: 'You are Czechs. Why did you say you are foreigners?'

'*Da,*' said Sylva stupidly. Or not so stupidly, it turned out. The second officer leaned towards the first one and whispered loudly: 'They don't understand Russian!'

The first officer gave us another dirty look. Then his glance was drawn by Sylva's enormous trunk next to the two tiny children. He pointed: 'What have you got in your luggage?'

'What business is that of yours?' asked Sylva aggressively. The threat to her property had a remarkable effect on her linguistic abilities. Luckily the officer, gripped by an interesting suspicion, failed to notice this.

'We have come to destroy the counter-revolution!' he instructed the bristling young woman before him. 'This case may contain weapons.'

Sylva misunderstood the Russian: 'Why's he talking about roses?'

'*Oruzhiye* doesn't mean roses,' I replied quietly.

'What does it mean?'

I did not answer. Even though I didn't expect Sylva to be carrying any kind of weapon to Paris, I felt a chill.

The officer stepped up to the back of the car and looked around proudly. Then he summoned two soldiers from the tank next to us and pointed at the trunk.

Mr Kohn's Cadillac had been in the hold and his black driver had travelled in Tourist Class. They had reached Le Havre, got into their Cadillac and by the evening they were on the Franco-German border. The journey through West Germany had taken them two days. They slept in clean motels and as they neared the Czechoslovak border Mr Kohn's fear had turned to panic.

'At the last moment,' Mr Kohn said, describing the journey he finally decided to make, 'I told John to turn round, mother or no mother. That's how frightened I was when we got to the barrier. A man in uniform came out of the customs building. I know that customs officials the world over wear uniform, but this one terrified me. There was nothing unusual about it, he wasn't even wearing high boots, and when he got near he was just a man like any other. But he had that star on his hat and his uniform was so untidy and crumpled, so *eastern,* that I said to myself: My God, if I get on the wrong side of someone like him—'

A hairy youth with both a Phi Beta Kappa sign and a red star on his sweatshirt looked round and headed towards us. Mr Kohn fell silent, like a man in a trance.

'*Guerrilla Newspaper,* gentlemen?' asked the hairy youth in the tone of a paper boy and placed before us a tabloid with a traditional portrait of Lenin. 'Only twenty-five cents!'

Mr Kohn, still like a man in a trance, pulled out a silver half dollar with a portrait of John Fitzgerald and bought two copies of the paper from the hands of the young man.

'I know it's persecution mania,' said Mr Kohn, waking slowly. 'Why should they go for me, some Kohn from Providence? But that didn't help. Anyway, if it hadn't been for my wife Gerta I would have told John to turn back. But Gerta took my hand, gave it a squeeze and we drove through the barrier.'

'Leave it, won't you?' exclaimed Sylva and turned to me. 'Tell them to leave it!'

'Have you got authorization to search private citizens?' I said rather stupidly given the situation, which was aptly symbolized by my tiny car squeezed between tons of steel. I too had forgotten that I don't speak Russian.

The perfect officer took a deep breath: 'We have come to destroy the counter-revolution!'

Then he looked round the countryside, illuminated by an attractive sunset. For a while he rested his glance on the meadow, where a diminishing old woman was dragging a protesting goat out of view, and then he silently nodded at the two soldiers. They grabbed the trunk and lifted a pick. Sylva shrieked and threw herself at them.

'Halt!' bellowed the officer and pulled out a pistol.

'Leave it, won't you? It's not yours!' Sylva was shrieking and fighting like a cat. She had no idea that a pistol was pointing at her back. 'How dare you?'

'Mummy! Mummy! He wants to give you one!' shouted Martina.

'In the bum!' said Martin knowingly and got a slap from his pure-minded sister.

'Or he'd put you in a bath full of shit and piss,' said Mr Pohorsky. 'Believe me, Mr Kohn, that wasn't much better than his tomato ketchup. I was sick into that bath. And you should have seen how that pleased him!'

Sylva turned like a flash, straight into the black mouth of the gun. Her lip curled in a familiar expression. 'Listen, put it away, won't you? It might go off!'

'*Ruky vverkh*!' said the officer.

'What's that he's saying?'

'He's telling you to put your hands up.'

'But why, for God's sake?'

Offended, she turned to the officer.

'Come on, put it away! You're making me nervous.'

But the officer didn't lower the pistol. It was still pointing at Sylva's breast and once again he gestured to his subordinates. Hesitantly they applied the pick to the lid of the trunk.

'Leave it, damn it! It's a new trunk!' Paying no attention to the weapon, Sylva was again about to throw herself into battle, but the officer dramatically leapt between her and the trunk and put the barrel of the gun against her stomach.

'Come on, stop that, I'm ticklish!'

'Sylva, you'd better leave them to it,' I said.

'Well, at least let me unlock the trunk, damn it! It's a brand new trunk! It cost me nearly a thousand crowns on the black market, and they're attacking it with that—'

I explained the proposal to the officer. He removed his pistol reluctantly from Sylva's belly and she, with her lip curling as contemptuously as possible, unlocked the trunk and threw back the lid with a dramatic gesture. 'Get on with it, stupid idiots!' she said.

A rich treasure of the finest ladies' underwear in colours that ranged from delicate pastels to diabolical blacks, reds and stripes—all, absolutely all, completely transparent—greeted our eyes. The soldiers were startled. The officer slowly straightened up and said with threatening suspicion in his voice: '*U vas eto dlya blata?*'

'Now what's bugging him?' asked Sylva.

'He suspects you of speculating in knickers.'

'Tell him to keep such thoughts to himself, OK?'

'It's all hers,' I said.

'You're lying—'the officer was about to say, but something stopped him mid-sentence.

His angry glance took in the car and the two perfectly-dressed children, and then the landscape with the disappearing old woman, and he gave a strange sigh. He plunged his arm into the trunk and grabbed the first thing which came to hand. It looked like a bra with the top half cut off. The officer held the thing between both hands, with amazed distaste in his face, then he shook his head and gave out the sound expressive of the state of mind of a man who'd just been reassured of some great truth.

'Damn it, tell him not to wave it about in front of all these milksops, man!' said Sylva with undisguised fury. 'The next thing you know they'll rape me.'

'That's Mummy's!' cried Martina joyfully.

'Naughty man!' added Martin, pointing at the perfect officer.

The officer shook his head again and replaced the bra among the shameless objects in the overflowing trunk. At his order, and with considerable difficulty, the soldiers closed the lid then jumped back on their iron vehicle, and the officer climbed up on the gun. The engines roared, a cloud of orange dust rose, and the flat monsters headed in the supposed direction of Putim.

Later, in Paris, Sylva told me that they'd stolen a box of contraceptive pills from the trunk. For a while we hopefully meditated on the effect of a massive dose of the Pill on a tank squadron. But probably they had no effect at all. They've always had a strong stomach.

'I t was ten by the time we got to the Hotel Hubertus,' Mr Kohn sighed. 'I remember it all clearly. And it was half-past eleven when we lay down in a fragrant, enormously wide bed. The forest was rustling outside the window, and above the trees you could see stars. I was completely calm by then. Like the forest, like the night. And I began to make plans. We'll buy a little villa somewhere, because Lewith said there were lots for sale, and we'll move in with dear mother, and everything will be fine at last, after those thirty years. I'll be home. I fell asleep and I dreamed of the bell above the door of my father's shop, and I saw mother, smiling at the customers, looking just the same as she had thirty years ago. Ah, yes!'

We reached the main road, I put my foot on the accelerator and got out of the grip of the column, which had stopped in indecision: an enormous officer was once again studying the map and his perfect officer was pointing to the setting sun, perhaps to show him where the West was.

It was already dusk, a conspicuously symbolic black cloud was rising in the east, lit from the opposite direction by the orange and gold rays of the sun wreathed in a Technicolor sunset. The officer made a decision and the rattling column headed for the black cloud, and we for the ruby sun. We were quickly driving along the road, which was suddenly empty and quiet, and in a moment we found ourselves in a forest. Martin and Martina in the back seat had long been silenced by sleep, and Sylva said: 'Please stop, before I have an accident!'

I stopped at the side of the road and Sylva reached for the handle.

'Why didn't you tell me before?' I said.

'Come off it. And what about them? They'd have had to stop the whole armoured division, or whatever it was.'

I'd just gone to sleep when I could feel someone shaking me,' said Mr Kohn. 'I came to a little, and saw the chambermaid. "Mr Kohn," she said, and I could see she was crying. "Get up, Mr Kohn! The Russians are here!" And do you know, gentlemen, what I felt when I got over the first fright?'

I shook my head. Mr Pohorsky did too.

'That the cage had closed! That it had finally closed! But this time there would be no Bondy and no General Blaskowitz!'

Something crackled and a relieved Sylva emerged from the thicket of ferns. 'Danny! Just a little bit further there's a side road, and someone is talking English there!'

'Don't be stupid!'

'Do you think it could be a relief force? Let's have a look!'

I thought it absurd that American armies might cross our borders over such a local matter.

'You stay here with the children,' I reminded Sylva of the duties of motherhood and plunged into the ferns.

The forest soon thinned out and a white side road, for some reason running parallel with the main road, emerged ahead. An enormous American limousine shone in the light of the stars. Voices could be heard inside:

'We won't get out of here! We won't! We won't! I know it!' one of them was lamenting hysterically while another, deeper voice was saying soothingly:

'Oh calm down, boss! Let's just wait here for dawn.'

'They're goin' to find us! They'll kill us!'

'Oh, c'mon!'

For a while there was silence. And then: 'How could you've got lost? Don't we have the map?'

'No fucking roadsigns anywhere. You know that, boss.'

'Oh God! Oh, my God! This will be the end of me!'

The conversation was far too nervous for this to be an invading force. I jumped across a ditch and into the road and walked up to the limousine.

'Good evening. Can I help you?'

A Black in a chauffeur's cap stuck his head out of the window. 'Good evening, sir. We've just run out of gas.'

'Sir, please be so good, are you a Czech?' said an anxious voice from inside.

'Yes. At your service.' I said.

'I am someone called Kohn,' said the voice.

Translated from the Czech by J.R. Dorrell

SOMETH MAY
THE FIELD BEHIND
THE VILLAGE

S hortly before Christmas 1979, at a time when the stations and underpasses of London were full of carol-singers collecting for the Cambodian famine appeal, I received a letter forwarded from the Red Cross Tracing Agency in Bangkok to 'The News Stastesment, London WC1'. 'Dear Mr. James Martin Fenton!' the letter began, 'I hardly say to you that I could be alive up to now.'

The author, Someth May, went on to inquire politely about the health of my family before telling me about the misfortunes of his own. His father, his sister, three of his brothers and his brother-in-law had died during the Khmer Rouge regime. Now he was living in a refugee camp on the Thai-Cambodian border and wondering whether I could find him an office job. 'I'm free right now,' he wrote, 'and especially I'm very very poor.'

The fact that this letter had got through to me gave me profound satisfaction and relief. Anyone from the West who worked in Cambodia before the Khmer Rouge victory in 1975 and formed friendships there, followed the news reports from that area with a particular horror and helplessness. When the Vietnamese invaded and swiftly defeated (or appeared to defeat) the Khmer Rouge, a large number of those who had suffered most during the previous four and a half years decided to escape into exile.

However, it seemed to me highly unlikely that I would meet any of my Cambodian friends again. I heard that Dith Pran (the hero of Roland Joffé's forthcoming film, *The Killing Fields*) had escaped and contacted his former employer, Sydney Schanberg of the *New York Times*. That was great news, but it was not entirely surprising. Pran, a most respected figure, was known to be the best operator in the Cambodian press corps. If anybody could survive the Khmer Rouge, it would be him.

The pressmen who did not survive the new regime included one who, in the early days after victory, voluntarily confessed to having taken photographs for a Western agency. After he apologized, he was congratulated for his honesty and shot.

While the foreign press were in Cambodia, the men we employed as drivers, interpreters, photographers and assistants were, despite the dangers of their jobs, privileged people. They earned enough to maintain their large families. They were protected from service at the front line. And some of our special status rubbed off on them. But when Phnom Penh fell, the press card became a death certificate. Only by luck, secrecy and the avoidance of informers could our old friends and colleagues win through.

There are many people who, given a clearer understanding of what was going to happen, could have saved the lives of their employees by organizing their evacuation. But in contrast to Saigon there was, in Phnom Penh, no developed sense of panic at the prospect of Khmer Rouge victory. Very few people had an idea of the scale of the impending revenge, although when Phnom Penh and all the cities were forcibly evacuated I think that many of us recognized that our worst, half-suppressed fears were being realized. By then it was too late to do anything for our friends.

The Cambodian press corps was an exceedingly friendly and eccentric operation during this period: the 'Decent interval' between 1973 and 1975 when direct American military involvement in Southeast Asia was meant to have ended. We met every morning and evening at the Groaning Table Restaurant and Cocktail Lounge for what was called the Briefing. The Briefing was not like the famous Five-o'clock Follies in Saigon. Indeed, if you didn't know where to look for it, you might miss it altogether. It was a piece of paper which emanated from the offices of General Am Rong and was pinned to a noticeboard, detailing the views of the Etat-Major as to what had happened in the previous twelve hours. One of Am Rong's favourite phrases was *Aucun incident significatif.*

The sign for the Groaning Table Restaurant and Cocktail Lounge was nailed to a small kitchen hut in the shady grounds of Am Rong's office. We sat under awnings at a group of tables, calling out for *croques monsieur, oeufs au plat au jambon* and iced coffee with evaporated milk. The central table was favoured by the westerners, who spent an hour or so chatting and cleaning their cameras before setting out for the Front. There was a quieter and more exclusive table for the Japanese, and a riotous table for Cambodian journalists and Am Rong's officers.

In the evenings before dinner we returned to swap notes on the day's events. It was then that Someth, the author of the ensuing article, served me the most extraordinary gin and tonic in the world. It came in a pint-size straight-sided glass into which a brick of ice was inserted: the gin (the local brand from a bottle labelled simply GIN) filled up all the remaining space. The tonic water was electric blue and came in a separate bottle. So the first task of the drinker was to try and find some way of balancing just a little tonic on the meniscus and drinking that off before it dissipated in the clear threatening spirit. The first thirsty minutes of this operation, if rushed, knocked you out for the rest of the evening. And yet I remember that I sometimes managed two of these gins. The Western pressmen were divided between the dope-and-opium set and the drinkers. We all had to relax, after all.

When he was not serving the press corps, Someth was studying sciences, and in the last year of the Lon Nol regime he began a medical course at the by then chaotic university. We struck up a deal whereby he would try to teach me Cambodian, in return for which I would correct his English essays. I could never, as a stringer living hand to mouth, afford a full-time interpreter, so this informal arrangement was extremely useful. Someth used to try to explain to me how Cambodian poetry worked. I remember, in return, taking him through a Wordsworth sonnet. Among the books that he read with pleasure at that time were Eric Williams's *The Wooden Horse* and Orwell's *Animal Farm*. This last book was in his luggage when, in April 1975, Phnom Penh fell to the Khmer Rouge and its entire population was forced to go and work in the fields. All books were confiscated.

After Someth's first letter in 1979, we lost contact for a while, until he turned up on the Thai side of the border, in Khao-i-Dang camp. It was there that I went to visit him in order to arrange for his transfer to the West. It goes without saying that the always smiling and obliging schoolboy I had known had changed greatly in the intervening years. His front teeth had been smashed in and the lines of his face showed continual tension, worry and fear. The shelter that he was living in with his three remaining sisters was open and it was impossible to have a private conversation without being watched on all sides. So when we wanted to talk we went for a stroll around the huge camp, and he showed me the place where the smugglers were shot, and confessed to the fears besetting all the refugees—that they were at the mercy of the Thai soldiers every night

53

when the UN officials left the camp. The place was in effect a prison. The Thai authorities made sure that it never became attractive enough to lure yet more illegal immigrants (as they were classed). The learning of English, for instance, was officially disallowed because that would give the impression that every one of these illegal immigrants to Thailand was bound for the United States. The aid officials and the US embassy were operating with extreme caution. On the say-so of the Thais all the refugees could be forced back into Cambodia against the guns of the Vietnamese. This was a real threat. The Thais and the Vietnamese are the traditional enemies of the Cambodians. So nobody in the camp could feel in the slightest bit secure. They were desperate to get out as quickly as possible.

Because he had worked for me as an interpreter when I was stringing for the *Washington Post,* I was able, with the help of the American Embassy and the *Post* itself, to get Someth and his family accepted for the States. But between acceptance and actual exit there was a long delay, and at any time the camp might have become embroiled in the war again. Someth had joined a group of classical dancers and spent much of his time organizing and performing with the group. But there remained the incredible tedium of camp life and the dreadful delay in processing. I remember pointing out that several of the refugees had planted small vegetable gardens by their huts, and suggested that this might prove a distraction. Someth replied tactfully but firmly that having spent the last few years slaving in the fields the last thing he wanted to do was to grow vegetables. So I suggested that he should begin to write his memoirs.

It is likely that in every family that escaped from Cambodia someone has written, or is in the process of writing, his memoirs. But although there have been books about the Khmer Rouge written by westerners, very little of the story has been told by the Cambodians themselves. Someth believes that the best Cambodian writers must have been killed. There are other reasons. Autobiography itself, a long established tradition in the West, is not a particularly familiar mode in Cambodia. Sihanouk's memoirs were written as a political tract by Wilfred Burchett. *L'Utopie Meurtrière* by Pin Yathay describes the experiences of one who escaped in 1977; published in France in 1979 it is again a work of collaboration. Useful as it may be for historians and political analysts, it is written too close to the events it describes.

There is another reason why satisfactory accounts of the period are thin on the ground. That is, the traumatic nature of the experience itself. In order to describe, in the kind of detail which might begin to satisfy the wonder and horror of our curiosities, the nature of life under the Khmer Rouge, it is necessary for *somebody* to be prepared actually to relive that experience in his imagination. During the last years as I have watched Someth at work on the successive drafts of his book, there have been times when I have wondered whether the pain of this effort was not too great. Yet now that the book is on what we hope will be its last draft, now that the whole outline has been recorded and the worst details set down, it does begin to appear that the ghost may have been exorcised. What has been set down on paper will horrify the reader, but it no longer gives the author quite such sleepless nights.

When I first saw the draft of the piece which follows, I realized that the book he was writing had reached an essential stage of articulacy. The narrative is classic. We are at the height of the crisis in the Cambodian revolution. The Old People (those who lived on the Khmer Rouge side from 1970–75) have already killed off many of the adult males from the New People (those who, at the end of the war, were in the capital and other cities). In the name of the Angkar Loeu (the High Organization, the mysterious state itself, a cross between the traditional conception of the Party and the Tontons Macoute) they are now in the process of working the younger men to death. Authority among the Old People is vested in teenage boys, peasants who have learned to hate the New People for all they have suffered. And now this authority is challenged by two young men—the thief and the boy who asks the wrong question. In their respective fates we learn a great deal about how that authority was maintained. There is an awesome simplicity in the fact that, despite interminable meetings for political education, the New People only asked two questions. The first, 'What is the Angkar?', received some kind of answer. But the second question was fatal.

James Fenton

T his was the way with the Khmer Rouge: we would work for months on one project, like this rice field where I guess that two out of ten of us died or were killed in the course of three months. Then one evening, well before the ploughing was finished, the new field leader (the old one seemed to have been liquidated) appeared at the commune meeting and told us we were to go back to our co-operative. What that meant, quite simply, was that all our work had been pointless. There was nobody else in this isolated region to continue it, and anyway the land we had been preparing was so dry and infertile that it would never have been much use. Now we were told that the rice growing on our co-operatives was in urgent need of protection from birds. We had to pack our things, return communal property such as ploughs and oxen and bullocks to the labour field headquarters, and go back the next day.

At about five o'clock in the morning our unit leader, Comrade Khann, told us what our duties would be. The next work would not be difficult. We would have to stay in the fields waiting for flocks of birds, and as soon as we saw them we had to shout and make as much noise as possible in order to scare them away. We had all our belongings with us at the meeting. Mine were: one torn mosquito-net, one broken spoon, one ragged cloth called a *kramar*, one yoke, one torn tarpaulin.

'And now,' said the unit leader, 'we can leave,' and he got on to his rusty Chinese bicycle and pedalled away ahead of us.

At this moment there was a great movement in the meeting. Everybody who still had relatives back at the co-operative went off in a state of excitement, hungry and exhausted though they were. But I was not excited. None of my family was at the co-operative, and I envied those who had parents or relatives waiting for them. When they arrived, they would be fed in secret. But when I arrived, who was going to give me any food? Who would welcome me? I thought of Comrade Ran's mother, who was the only person I knew there. But would she recognize me? I was skin and bone. I had no idea what my face looked like.

I was near the end of the group, walking along the track. From time to time, Comrade Khann cycled back to order the stragglers to hurry. His bicycle—that is, the communal bicycle, the unit's only bicycle—was black and very old and without brakes. Digging his feet into the dust track, he would bring the bike to a halt and tell us to get a move on. He was in a childish good humour and to look at him you might think he had nothing to do with the revolution. But I knew it was dangerous even to joke with Comrade Khann. Whatever you said he might distort and relay to the Angkar Loeu. And there was another thing: without my wishing it, I had been his rival in love. That is, Comrade Khann had fallen in love with Comrade Ran, but she had rejected him before turning her attention to me.

Comrade Khann was small and slim—a teenager, between sixteen and eighteen years old. Like all the unit leaders, he had a little servant, an eight-year-old orphan whose job was to guard his master's possessions while we were at work in the field. The servant walked along with us, with a shoulder bag on both shoulders. His own bag probably did not contain much more than mine, except he would also have two sets of clothes—two neat black uniforms in good condition. His master's bag would have more in it: tobacco (I think this is why he needed a guard), western medicines, clothes, US camouflage blankets, a mosquito-net, pens and paper. You could tell it was the unit leader's bag for several reasons: its colour—bright blue or yellow; the red flash sewn on to it; the green nylon American hammock that, tied to a strap, was trussed up with string, like a joint of meat; and, finally, the US spoon of bright, stainless steel that stuck out of the bag, or was slipped into the hammock string (so that it could be seen).

These little boys, working as batmen to the unit leaders, were always orphans, but they might be drawn from the Old People or the New People. When I saw one of them carrying such a bag, I always knew at once what his job was.

We had set out around six o'clock in the morning, with no food in our stomachs. When I needed water, I took off my palmleaf hat (which also served as a rice bowl) and scooped a drink from the ditch beside the track. My group consisted entirely of male teenagers. Behind us came the female group, which included my sister Bopha. Although I had seen her working in the field, I hadn't been able to talk to her for the last three months. We walked through the heat of the day, about twenty miles, arriving at the co-operative in the mid-afternoon.

The unit leader got off his bike. 'All right,' he said, 'we're going to stay here. Leave your things. You can go to see your relatives if you want—but be back within an hour.' Then he went off to visit his mother. I prepared a place to rest on the ground and tried to forget my hunger. But the more I tried, the more hungry I felt. Our unit was near the commune's potato field. Along the edge of the field was a row of sugar palms which produced the sugar for the co-operative.

I ought to explain something about the sugar palm. During the harvest season the trees produced flowers, each about the size of a small, floppy rolling-pin. Every day, in the early morning and late evening, someone had to climb the palm and cut the end of the flower, which was then squeezed into a bamboo flask tied to its stalk. Twice a day the flasks were replaced, and the juice inside was boiled down to produce the sugar. This job, which took eight to ten hours, was the favourite occupation of the Old People. It was an easy job and there were plenty of opportunities to drink the juice on the side. More than that: the Old People were able to filch some of the thick brown discs of sugar and use them as currency, to trade with the New People for clothes, jewellery and especially for watches. Sugar and salt were the things that the New People wanted most.

I lay down, resting the back of my right hand against the bone of my forehead. One of the Old People, with a knife like a short sword and a set of flasks tied to his waist, was climbing up a palm. As I watched him, an idea occurred to me. If he can climb palm trees, why can't I? If I get the chance, I'll have a go tonight.

But that evening, after a meal consisting of two boiled green bananas, I was chosen as part of a ten-man detail to work in the fields at the back of the village, rebuilding broken dikes. I gathered my belongings again and promised myself that at the next opportunity I would climb one of the sugar palms.

We set off at about ten. When we reached our destination, a couple of hours later, it was too late to build a temporary shelter and we had to sleep in the open, on the dike. The next three days passed slowly. The nights especially were cold and windy. It drizzled and, worse, our rations had not been sent on. We had to live on apple-snails and paddy-crabs, which were roasted in the fire. On the fourth day, when we were called back to the village, I thought: This, at last, is my chance.

That night I waited till everyone was asleep, and crept out from my mosquito-net, making my way towards the sugar palms. They were about sixty feet high. I looked up, wondering whether I had enough energy to reach the top. I was weak from hunger. I had never climbed such a tall tree before, and this was the first time that I had rebelled against the discipline of the Angkar. I was scared, but I was more hungry than scared. What I was doing could cost me my life.

I began to climb the tree, slowly and carefully. It took me the best part of half an hour to get to the top. Once there, I drank as much of the palm-juice as I could. I drank and drank, and then I had to pause, since my stomach was like a balloon. As long as I was at the top of the tree I felt safe. The village ahead of me was quiet and dark. To my left lay the potato field. To my right, I could see the cattle-pen, where a bonfire burned all night to keep off the mosquitoes. A few of the cows were standing near the fire and I could see them swishing their tails. I felt happy at the heaviness of my stomach. I suppose I waited ten minutes or a quarter of an hour and then I climbed back down and returned to my sleeping-quarters, which were in the open barn. Nobody moved or said anything. I had succeeded.

The next night, and for the next few days, I repeated my routine. I used to look forward to the moment when everyone was asleep, and I became quicker and more practised at climbing the trees. I chose the flasks carefully, first taking a sip to see whether the juice was really sweet, and I never drank to the bottom in case of sediment. I discovered that, despite the Angkar's ban on alcohol, some of the Old People were secretly preparing toddy (or palm wine) in these flasks. One person was in charge of a dozen trees, and he might allow himself three flasks for toddy. I always avoided these.

At the co-operative meeting, a couple of weeks later, the leader announced that somebody was stealing palm-juice from the flasks. The single-male unit was near the sugar palms, and the leader suspected one of us. After this I stopped my nightly visits.

It was late 1978 and the rice was due for harvesting. Our job was to scare the birds away from the crop. The day began at five o'clock with the leader's whistle calling us to the regular morning check-up, where the able-bodied men received their rations immediately and were sent out to the fields. For lunch the healthy got a boiled potato or half a tin of boiled sweetcorn. The sick received about a third of the rations of the healthy. The cold windy weather continued and as soon as we went out into the fields we looked for anything edible to supplement our diets.

We went out, five or six to the field, and sat on the paddy dike waiting for birds, which generally arrived at about ten o'clock in the morning and three or four o'clock in the afternoon. There were flocks of pigeons, parrots, robins and sparrows, and cuckoos as well. The worst were the pigeons and sparrows. When anyone saw them coming he would shout to his neighbours, and the message would pass from field to field. As the flock came over us we stood and yelled; the birds wheeled away to the next field, where you could hear the process repeated. When we were not scaring the birds, we of the New People were keeping our eyes open for anything to eat. We went for any suitable green vegetation; or for snails, tadpoles about the size of your thumb, baby frogs, grass-snakes, mice, paddy-crabs and millipedes. Anything you could eat raw, you ate immediately. The rest you concealed by turning over the waistband of your trousers, so after a good day's work you might return to the village with what felt like a cartridge-belt of food—a rat, a couple of apple-snails, a few live paddy-crabs—and as you walked home you continued looking for millipedes. We were always longing for rain, because then the birds wouldn't come, and the wild life of the paddy would crawl out from the centre of the field towards the dike. But it seldom rained during the day.

At night all the creatures we caught were roasted on sticks over the remains of the cooking-fires, but this had to be done in secret (we would say 'with my eyes on my forehead') so that the leader wouldn't know. Within a few weeks, all these animals became scarce, and the New People began eating ants' larvae (raw) and catching red ants from the trees, putting them in water and making a kind of vinegar. They took a bucket of water on a long pole and held it under the ants' nest, shaking it so that the larvae fell to the bottom of the water and the red ants floated on top. These buckets were stolen from the camp kitchen, and hidden out in the fields.

For myself, I confined my eating to baby frogs, paddy rats and crabs. If you want to know what they tasted like, all I can say is that frog was like frog, and rat exactly like rat.

The unit meetings were held once every three days, normally at seven in the evening, after we had eaten. A meeting was usually a series of speeches made by the unit leader, the company leader and the group leader, in which we were told to 'attack' our work, to lose our feelings of possessiveness and to give everything to the Angkar. The speeches were endlessly repetitive, meandering, wandering backwards and forwards as the leaders tried to think of another way of saying the same thing. They were punctuated by long pauses, and it was not unusual for members of the audience to keel over into sleep: they would be woken up and warned. At the end, the leaders opened the meeting to the people, but nobody dared ask any questions. A year before, one man had asked for the meaning of the word *Angkar* to be explained—but although he had survived, nobody else had thought of copying him.

Then one day, Comrade Chhith, a boy of about seventeen—a quiet character who seldom chatted to anybody and always sat by himself—suddenly put his hand up and asked whether the unit leader would answer some questions about the revolution and explain a few points which Chhith had not understood so far. His request was granted and he rose to speak.

'Friends and Comrades, it is a great opportunity for me,' said Comrade Chhith, 'that the meeting has allowed me to ask some questions about the revolution. In every meeting, thousands of them so far, I have been told that the people in the revolutionary territory are equal and that equality has been achieved everywhere. Could you please tell me, Comrade,' said the boy, looking straight into the eyes of the unit leader, 'what is the meaning of the word equality?'

The unit leader, Comrade Khann, stood up to reply.

'Equality,' he said, 'means the *same*. In other words, it means that the people in the revolution are the same....' And he paused as if stumped by the boy's question. 'That is, there is no supervision in the revolution. Everyone is the same.'

The boy stood up again. 'You've just said that everybody is the same and that there is no supervision in the revolution,' he said, and I noticed that he was becoming excited and that his voice was trembling. 'Then why am I always told or ordered to *do this* or *do that*?' And he sat down again.

'Well, that is a very good question indeed,' said the unit leader sarcastically. He was beginning to get annoyed. 'If you are not told what you're supposed to do, none of the work that our Angkar wants will get done.'

Now Comrade Chhith sprang to his feet and came straight back into the argument. 'I see. Now let me return to the word equality. From what you have said, the people in the revolution are equal. But why doesn't equality exist in every unit of the co-operative?' he asked. You could see anger and excitement mounting in him.

'How do you mean—equality does not exist in the units?' asked the unit leader, his tone hardening.

The unit leader was not a Khmer Rouge soldier. He was a peasant who, until 1975, had been working under the Khmer Rouge. It was only with the arrival of the New People that he would have been put in charge of a unit. He was not a well-educated man. He had the handwriting of a child.

Comrade Chhith, who now returned to his feet, was (I later gathered) the son of an officer in Lon Nol's army. He was obviously well-educated, and he had thought out his argument a long time before beginning it. Now he reached the crux.

'Well, let me explain. Take, for instance, our own unit. Why do you all, who call yourselves the Old People, have enough food to eat, when we don't? This is the main question I want you to answer.'

Heads shot up when this question was put, but Comrade Chhith had not finished. Indeed he had lost his self-control: 'As far I can tell, from listening to the songs that were broadcast every evening at Wat Chass labour field, I can't see any *equality* in our unit. We have two meals a day—quite often none. *You* and your *Old People* always eat more than three times. Please, Comrade. Tell me more about the word *equality*.'

'Comrade,' the unit leader's voice was more menacing, 'you should think very, very carefully before you open your mouth again to ask more questions. We Old People have been fighting very hard over the last few years to achieve equality and freedom for all of you here. We suffered all kinds of miseries while you were in luxury villas in the capital, doing nothing but enjoying yourselves in the decadent culture of the East and West. Do you think what *you* did was fair to *us*? What right do *you* have to complain about the food you have eaten? Come on, tell me more about the way we Old People have behaved.'

The boy was really brave and seemed to have recovered his control a little. He stood up again and said: 'What I want to know from you Old People is—is there any *equality* in our unit, and, if so, what sort of equality is it?'

The unit leader was calmer in turn: 'I admit that there doesn't seem to be equality in our unit. But if we Old People didn't have enough to eat, we would be starving like you. Leaders have to eat more in order to have enough energy to lead you the way our Angkar wants. As I told you a few minutes ago—you have to be told, otherwise none of the work would get done. Any more questions?'

'No, I think the answers are very good,' said Comrade Chhith, stressing each word. 'Thank you. They are very understandable.'

The meeting broke up at one in the morning. We went off to our sleeping-quarters with much to think about. I was pleased by the boy's questions, and worried for his safety.

About once a week, the unit and company leaders had a fourth meal around midnight. On one such night, they sat by the fire cooking the rice, and the New People watched, as usual, from their sleeping-places. As they began to eat, Comrade Chhith got up from his mosquito-net and went straight to the fire, sat down and without a word began eating with them. Conversation around the fire stopped immediately, but nobody prevented Chhith from eating. Then, one by one, the leaders got up and left him alone with his meal. When they had gone, several boys from the unit came over and started to join in. During the whole incident nobody said a word.

Some time during the next week, the unit's rations were stopped without explanation. After working a day without food, I could think only of finding some way of filling my stomach. I thought of the potato-field next to the village. If I was careful, I might go there in the night. Most of the people in the unit were asleep by midnight, except for three groups huddled around camp-fires, roasting the small creatures which they had caught during the day. The clouds were thick. It would rain soon, and I thought that this was a good opportunity.

As the rain began to fall, I wandered over to one of the fires and chatted a little with one of the men. When it seemed a good moment, I slipped away in the direction of the potato-field. It took about twenty minutes to cross the open ground, and I stopped and hid for ten minutes, listening for voices. Then I tried to pull up a potato stem, but I was too weak for the task.

I should explain that this form of potato grows like a small tree, about the height of a sunflower but with a strong woody stem. The part you eat is the tuber, which can grow to the size of your forearm. Most flour used in Southeast Asia is made from this potato. It is also boiled as a vegetable.

Normally I could have pulled up the plant without any difficulty, but now I had to dig out the tubers with my hands. I ate as much as I could, raw, and then dug up some more to take with me. When I got back to the camp-fire everyone had gone to sleep. The rain had just stopped and the fire was nearly out. I put the potatoes among the coals—covering them with wet dead leaves—and blew gently.

I heard a voice calling my name. The voice came nearer and nearer and I recognized it as Comrade Khann's, the unit leader. I called out: 'I'm over here, Comrade.'

'Hey, Comrade Meth, what are you doing here?' asked Comrade Khann, joining me at the fireside, squatting and warming his hands.

'I couldn't sleep,' I replied. 'I want to warm myself. It's too cold over there.'

'Come on, go back to sleep. You have to get up early to work.'

'Okay, Comrade, I'll go in a minute after I've warmed myself,' I replied, glancing at the potatoes in the fire to see if they were well covered.

'Come along, now. It's not right to sit out in the middle of the night like this. Come on!' He slapped me on the shoulder, but in a friendly way he was ordering me to leave. I was sorry to lose the potatoes. It was months since I had eaten a properly cooked potato.

'Please, Comrade,' I said, 'I can't sleep over there. It's too cold.'

'No problem,' said the unit leader, 'I'll lend you my blanket. Come on, let's go now.'

Lend me his blanket! I'd never had that kind of generous offer before. He must be 'chasing a footprint,' as we say in Cambodian. I got up and followed him reluctantly to the sleeping-quarters, where he gave me his blanket and saw me to my mosquito-net.

That night the raw potato I had eaten attacked my stomach and I couldn't sleep at all.

The next night I went off to the potato-field again. Nothing happened. By the third night, I'd got into the swing of it. I went off again, and while digging for the potatoes—this time with a piece of dead wood instead of my bare hands—I heard a group of people coming towards me.

As they approached I wondered whether to run or stay still. If I ran, and if they happened to have a gun among them, I might get shot. I hesitated. They moved closer. I lay stock still on the ground and tried to stop breathing. They paused about sixty feet from me, and I could see by the moonlight that there were four men. Each wore a black uniform and carried a long parang. I knew from this that they were the reconnaissance team, drawn from the most senior of the Old People. We called them *Kang Chhlob*. When we had first come to this place they patrolled the sleeping-quarters at night, and if they heard anyone say something wrong, that person would be called away by the Angkar the next day, and would not reappear. Once they called you, you were never seen again.

They were speaking among themselves. One of them said, 'It's my turn. If I catch someone, I want to show what I can do.'

His friend was irritated. 'Enough. Do whatever you want. But don't do it here. It's not allowed.'

I closed my eyes and tried to stop shivering. Hunger disappeared. I could think only of what I would do if I was caught.

They stopped and stood still for about five minutes, watching the field and trying to catch the slightest noise. I held my breath. Eventually they moved on. I thought: I'm alive again! I swore never to come back here at night, however hungry I was.

As soon as they had gone, I got up and tried to work out how to get back to my quarters. I had been lying on a nest of red ants and was bitten all over. I was nervous and did not know which way to go. Very slowly I edged in what I thought was the right direction, but ten minutes later I found myself at the wrong end of the potato-field. I retraced my steps towards the village. As soon as I was out of the field there was a noise behind me.

'You there, stop and put your hands up. You're the one we're looking for.'

I stopped and turned around. It was the four men I had just seen, the members of the reconnaissance team. Although I had seen them often around the village, I never knew their names and I had never even looked into their faces. Whenever they passed, we simply stared at the ground and continued our work.

'What are you doing?' said another of them. 'We've been watching you and we know that you were in the potato-field.'

'No, Comrade...' I stuttered, 'I'm going for a walk because I couldn't sleep.'

'Going for a walk? Come here. Walk slowly and keep your hands up.'

I did as I was told and as I came closer I noticed their wristwatches in the moonlight. One of them stepped towards me, grabbed my hands, twisting them behind my back. I looked at the ground.

'You're a liar. Tell us the truth. How many times have you done this?'

'What have I done, Comrade? I don't understand what you're talking about.'

'You've been stealing potatoes from the commune field.'

'No, I'm going for a walk.' By now I was trembling violently and my voice was out of control.

The man in front rolled up his sleeves and placed his hands on his hips. I noticed a great scar on his forearm.

'Scum, I said tell us the truth before you get hurt.'

I couldn't answer. I could only, with great difficulty, raise my eyes from the ground and look in his face, which I then saw for the first time. It was the face and weirdly cruel expression of a man who had spent a long time on the battlefield. His eyes were bloodshot and bulging and the lines in his brow were deep with anger. His hair was greying and his skin was dark.

My mind seemed to drift. I do not know what I was thinking when I felt a terrible blow to my mouth. His fist had knocked out one of my teeth, and my mouth and tongue started to bleed. My eyes were filled with tears and the pain spread immediately through my skull. The man on my right pulled a piece of parachute cord from his pocket and went behind me. As he tied my arms together at the elbows he kicked me in the back several times.

The man tying me up asked: 'What are we going to do? The field behind the village?'

'I don't know,' said another, after a short pause, 'I've no idea.'

'Let's take him to the field behind the village,' said another.

That phrase 'the field behind the village' meant the killing ground. I'd never been to it, but I'd heard about it when I was company leader. There were in fact, for our village, two main killing grounds. The bigger one was near the re-education centre, the former pagoda. When people were taken to the re-education centre, and afterwards killed, their deaths were reported to the regional Angkar Loeu. But if for some reason they wanted to kill one of us without reporting it, they took the victim to the field behind the village.

The field was about two miles away, a patch of open ground with a small wood at one end. When we went to work, we passed it and could see from a distance three large open pits from which came the most horrific smell. We could have gone there if we'd wanted to, since they were intended to keep us in terror. But nobody I knew ever went. There was always a flock of crows around.

(There was a separate graveyard nearby for victims of famine and disease, and for those who didn't survive the hospital. Formerly in Cambodia we always cremated our dead, but the Khmer Rouge believed that corpses fertilized the ground. Only once during their regime did I witness a cremation. That was in the bamboo jungle, and the ashes were used afterwards for growing vegetables, which we then ate.)

As I listened to the conversation of my captors, all sense seemed to drain from me. I couldn't understand anything. Blood flowed from my gum where my tooth was broken. I tried to swallow as much of it as I could, thinking that this would conserve my energy. I spat out the broken tooth.

One of them said 'We've no right. We can't take him there. We need permission from his unit leader. Otherwise we'll be in trouble.'

'Nobody will know about it, except the four of us, unless someone talks,' said the one behind me.

'But the Angkar is smart. Sooner or later someone will talk.'

'Stop arguing. Take him to his leader,' said the one holding my arms. He was irritated and he pushed me forward.

They continued hitting me with their fists on the way back to the village. A few people were awake in the sleeping-quarters. They were shocked at the state I was in and roused their neighbours, pointing at me and wondering what it was I had done. One of the reconnaissance team went to the unit leader and spoke to him. Then he and his companions left.

It was about two in the morning. I was thrown on the ground with my arms still tied, and Comrade Khann began to ask me what I had done. I told him that I was caught while walking near the potato-field, but he did not believe me and began searching my pockets. He found a small piece of potato.

He kicked me in the ribs. Instinctively I rolled with the blow, but I was too weak to avoid the impact altogether. He came at me again and aimed another kick in the same place. This time I took the full force and fell, immediately unconscious.

I was woken by a cold breeze. My mouth and ribs were still hurting, and I tried to move my hands and feet in order to curl up and keep warm. My right foot felt heavy. Opening my eyes with great pain, I discovered that my foot had been chained to a tree.

The sky was clear, showing all the stars and a half moon. From its position I reckoned it was around four in the morning. I was outside the unit camp. I was shivering. My shirt had been removed, I didn't know when. I was wearing only a pair of shorts. I closed my eyes and tried to sleep, but I was too cold. The pain in my mouth and ribs was excruciating. I began to recall the conversation of the four men. I assumed they were waiting till daylight to take me to the field behind the village. I tried to resist the pain. I was scared.

The sky began to glow in the east. I began thinking about my sisters. Did they know what had happened to me? And, if I was killed, what would happen to them? One of my sisters had already been executed for criticizing the revolution. Now that I was found out, perhaps they would decide to destroy my whole family. And then I thought of Comrade Khann, and how he had been turned down by Comrade Ran, and how she had subsequently asked to marry me. Comrade Khann had every reason for taking his revenge. I was at his mercy.

As it started to grow light, Comrade Khann came towards me with three other men. He was armed with a parang, and another man was carrying a spade. I was going to be killed.

It was still not yet light when we set out across the fields. At this time of day, everyone would be getting ready for the regular morning check-up, and so we did not meet anyone on our way. I was limping in front, dragging my chain. There was no conversation, just a series of orders barked out in my direction: hurry up, left, right, get a move on. The sun had not yet dispersed the mist, and I could only just make out the small patch of woodland which marked the mass graves.

We walked about a mile.

I knew something of the pleasure they took in killing people. When we were working on the Ream Kun dam, the men from the reconnaissance team used to come and sit near us, and we could not help overhearing their conversation. They would boast about how somebody screamed and cried for mercy before he died. They said that after people had had their livers cut out they could do nothing—they couldn't talk, only blink their eyes. They said that fat people had small livers and thin people had big livers. They would sit there laughing together as they exchanged these details. I once heard one of them say that when you put human liver in the frying pan it jumps.

When we were within a mile of the open pits, they suddenly told me to stop, and walked away to talk. I couldn't hear their conversation, which lasted about five minutes. When they returned, they told me to start walking again, to the right. We were not going to the open pits after all.

A quarter of an hour later we came to a field I did not know. There were several grave mounds, some of them new, some old. Comrade Khann tied my chain to a small tree, took the spade from one of his companions and threw it down in front of me.

'Here is your pen!' he said. 'Go ahead and dig the ground.'

I understood and I began digging my own grave—began immediately to avoid being hurt. Two of the men left, and Comrade Khann and the fourth man sat on the low dike at the edge of the field, chatting and laughing together just out of earshot. At around noon, when I had finished digging a grave about a foot and a half deep, Comrade Khann came up to me and told me to lie in it. He asked me whether I felt comfortable or not. I made no reply. It was slightly small for me. He told me to make it a bit wider. When I had done that, by about three o'clock, I was told to rest. I sat on the edge of the grave, looking into it. A piece of cooked potato was given to me. I was not hungry.

'Why don't you eat?' asked the leader. 'Is it because you've had too many potatoes in the last few days?' He was smiling and he slapped my back.

'No, Comrade... I'm very hungry indeed.' I started eating the potato and continued staring into the grave. I used to like potatoes. This one tasted like rotten wood.

In the distance I saw the two other men returning, with three others. They were carrying something which looked like a log, wrapped in a piece of old matting. I thought it must be a corpse. They dropped it on the ground near the grave, and one of them said with a smile: 'You won't be lonely here. We've found a friend for you.'

He unwrapped the matting. There lay the body of Comrade Chhith, the boy who had asked the meaning of the word equality. I closed my eyes.

'Come on,' they said, 'look at your friend.' They weren't smiling now.

They rolled the body into the grave with their feet.

The unit leader walked towards me with his parang in his hand and ordered me to fill in the grave. I started shovelling, but the whole time I had an intense feeling that something was about to hit the back of my neck, and that I would fall into the grave. Dusk was falling as I finished. I was taken back to the unit camp, my right foot still chained. I was tethered to the support of the barn and given a small bowl of rice soup.

That night the unit meeting took place as usual, and after the regular, long speech, the leader, Comrade Khann, came to my case. A fourteen-year-old boy from the reconnaissance team was sent to fetch me. He told me to crawl to the meeting. I went before the comrades on all fours. Comrade Khann said: 'This person is a thief of the Angkar. He has broken the rules of the commune by stealing potatoes from the field. However, I am very glad to say that the co-operative leader told us not to put him away. He will have to work very hard in the next few days.' He paused a moment and then turned to me: 'Now, Comrade Meth, come and address the meeting and tell us what you want us to do if you are caught again, or if you do something else to destroy the discipline of the Angkar.'

I stood: 'Friends and Comrades, this is a very great opportunity for me to re-educate myself in the way our Angkar requires. If I do anything wrong again, please banish me from the Angkar's territory. Friends and Comrades, do not emulate my behaviour.'

At the end of the meeting I was allowed back to the sleeping-quarters. As I lay down and closed my eyes, the body of Comrade Chhith reappeared before me with a horrible vividness. I realized that he had been beaten to death. The back of his neck was bruised and his skull was smashed in. I lay there for about an hour thinking about him.

Suddenly two boys crept in under the mosquito-net.

'We're hungry,' one said. 'Take us to the potato-field.' I was irritated and told them to leave. But they were insistent.

'Nobody will know. You need not be involved. You can watch. We'll dig.' I threatened to tell the leader. They left.

The next day the company leader spoke to me. 'You are lucky. If you had followed the two boys last night, you wouldn't be here today.'

The immediate effect of my experiences was to make me ashamed in front of my friends and to withdraw from all company. I don't know why I should have felt so ashamed. Before I was exposed as a thief, I used to be held up as an example of hard work and revolutionary potential by my company and unit leaders. Now I worked hard to recover my lost position. Try as they might, the Khmer Rouge could spot no fault in my labour. I worked in continual terror, and as I toiled away I often wondered why I had not been killed. Was it because I had previously been a good worker? Or had Comrade Ran's mother intervened with the co-operative leader on my behalf? And if she had done so, why had she not also intervened to save my sister Mealea's life? These are questions I still ask myself.

Now the harvest season had come, and all the New People were happy at the size of the rice crop. However, as far as I could see, it wouldn't last more than a couple of months.

At the co-operative meeting we were told of a new project: another labour field, another dam! The place was called Tram Kang; it was very near a re-education centre, and the water it would hold would be for the use of the inmates. We were advised to be well-behaved because the re-education centre would be under our noses.

THE BIG FIVE FROM VERSO

Ronald Fraser
IN SEARCH OF A PAST

Using the techniques of oral history and psychoanalysis, Ronald Fraser has created a remarkable childhood autobiography.

"A remarkably honest and revealing study – like a fiction, it recreates a past world; yet this one is unmistakably real." **John Fowles**
Cloth: £15.00 Paper: £3.95

Tariq Ali & Ken Livingstone
WHO'S AFRAID OF MARGARET THATCHER?

Britain's most controversial politician, leader of the GLC and of Labour's socialist left, here talks about the political strategy and the prospects for the left with the most charismatic figure to have emerged from the generation of 1968. *Cloth: £14.00 Paper: £2.95*

Jean-Paul Sartre
THE WAR DIARIES
Notebooks from a Phoney War 1939-40

Found among his papers after his death, the *War Diaries* are among Sartre's most brilliant writings. Stationed in his native Alsace as a radio operator during the phoney war that preceded the invasion of France in 1940, he employed his time – often during the night shift – making an extraordinary series of notes on philosophy, art, politics and literature. In terms of sheer literary verve and readability, they anticipate and often surpass his later work. *Cloth Edition Only: £14.95*

Terry Eagleton
THE FUNCTION OF CRITICISM

The Function of Criticism argues that criticism emerged in early bourgeois society as a central feature of that 'public sphere' in which political, ethical and literary judgements could mingle under the benign rule of reason. The disintegration of this fragile culture brought on a crisis in criticism, whose history since the 18th century has been one fraught with ambivalence and anxiety. Eagleton's account embraces Addison and Steele, Johnson and the 19th century reviewers, such critics as Arnold and Stephen, the heyday of *Scrutiny* and New Criticism, and finally the recent proliferation of literary theories, especially deconstructionism. *Cloth: £15.00 Paper: £3.95*

Isaac Deutscher
WHAT'S PAST IS PROLOGUE
Marxism, Wars and Revolutions

Isaac Deutscher, the world-famous author of the Trotsky trilogy, was also a highly prolific and versatile essayist. His work in this field represents one of the most consistent attempts to apply the method of Marxism to the original political realities of the modern world. This new collection, comprising material hitherto unpublished or long out of print, spans four decades of his life and provides an accessible introduction to his thought.
Cloth: £18.50 Paper: £5.95

V

To the Memory of
Yevgeniya Semyonouńa Ginzburg

JOHN BERGER AND

NELLA BIELSKI

A QUESTION OF

GEOGRAPHY

Of the seven principal characters in our play, four are former 'Zeks', political prisoners, condemned under one of the various sections of Clause 58 of the Soviet Penal Code, which deals with 'political offences'. After serving sentences of between five and fifteen years in various Siberian labour camps, they have now received their White Passes and are obliged to live in 'liberated' but forced residence in the town of Magadan. They find work—for example, Dacha works in an infants' school—but they live under constant surveillance, in bleak material conditions, and with the continual threat of being rearrested. They have the habit of referring to the rest of the Soviet Union as the Continent because it is as if they live in a world, on an island, apart.

The other three principal characters are, first, Ernst who is still a Zek, with five more years to serve in a camp near the town. Because he is a doctor who, besides working in the camp hospital, treats the families of the 'Bruise', the military guards in town, Ernst has been given the privilege of a free pass between camp and town, provided he returns to the camp each night. It is within the few free, problematic hours of this 'Free Pass' that he lives his 'domestic' life with Dacha. The second is Sacha, Dacha's son whom she hasn't seen for fifteen years. Since his mother's arrest he has lived with his aunt in Leningrad on the Continent. The third is Micha who has served a sentence as a common criminal. In the camps, common criminals enjoyed many more privileges than the political prisoners. Micha is not in forced residence and could leave for the Continent tomorrow. If he stays it is because (sentimental reasons apart) he earns good money as a lorry-driver.

The guards and camp administrators are commonly referred to as the Bruise for obvious reasons, and also because their uniforms were blue.

1952 was the year before Stalin died. In the camps his death was awaited as a possible promise of better times.

Our play, edited here for publication, is not about the Gulag as such. The Gulag is the darkness against which the scenes take place, and what we want to show is the light emanating from those scenes. How can people, deprived of everything which we understand by security, continue to survive, and not only survive, but make meaning of their lives? The horror of the Gulag continues to be ideologically exploited by all sides. In this play we have tried to address a more intimate—and perhaps a more universal—question.

John Berger and Nella Bielski

1

It is a June evening in 1952. A room in an apartment house in the port of Magadan, the principal town of Kolyma in Eastern Siberia. The room, on the ground floor, is large and very simply furnished. A woman, wearing an apron and glasses, is reading a book. Her name is Dacha. There is food ready on a table—potatoes, herring, black bread. Above the table a lamp, shaded with an orange scarf. On a massive primus stove, a fifty-litre saucepan of water is simmering. On the floor a zinc bath. A tall, thin man in his late forties, with white hair, enters the room. His name is Ernst. He limps slightly. He places on the table a string bag with two newspaper packages inside it. Then he opens his suitcase and takes out a stethoscope and an old instrument for taking blood pressure. Dacha rolls up her sleeve. The man takes her blood pressure. Meticulously.

ERNST: Sixteen. It was seventeen yesterday, no?

DACHA: On Monday I had nineteen.

ERNST: I want to keep it at sixteen. For a 58/11, aged thirty-eight, that's not bad. [*He goes to wash his hands.*] Five terminal cases today. Three scurvies. Two TBs. It's a good omen. The Bruise may be getting more human.... A 58/10 will probably die during the night. If I can do without some sleep...

DACHA: You need sleep. Who is he?

ERNST: A poet.

DACHA: You saw his file?

ERNST: Yes, I remember his name—Sérébriakov.

DACHA: Pavel Sérébriakov?

ERNST: [*He unwraps the newspaper packages from the string bag.*] Look, some greengroceries.

DACHA: Not a present from the poet!

ERNST: They're from the Agrobase. The Colonel called me out this afternoon. His daughter has measles. Mother and father were beside themselves: they thought their little daughter had scarlet fever. I reassured them. [*Ernst begins to eat.*] There are two conflicting points of view about the Colonel, since his arrival. Some say he is scrupulous but sadistic; others say he is sadistic but scrupulous! I don't take sides. Either way he is sadistic, and at his little daughter's bedside he fusses like a hen. My diagnosis of measles earned me the lettuce and radishes.

DACHA: The Colonel is generous!

ERNST: [*Ernst finishes eating and is more relaxed. He gets up to look out of the window.*] I'd like to measure how many centimetres a beanstalk grows in a day. Everything is accelerated here, the season is so short.

DACHA: In five years, when you have a White Pass you can measure your beanstalks.... You've probably forgotten that Lydia works as a maid in the Colonel's house.

ERNST: So you said. Has she been working there long?

DACHA: A week. She found out by accident that the Colonel's wife wears a crucifix.

ERNST: It can happen even among them.

DACHA: Lydia says the Colonel's wife is not a bad woman. She saw her crying once.

ERNST: A good omen. [*Ernst stands behind Dacha, his hands on her shoulders. She leans her head back against his chest.*] Twelve visits in the town this evening. Eleven of them for nothing. The twelfth had cirrhosis of the liver. A sergeant of twenty-five drinking himself to death. I warned the Colonel that in the Zone operating-theatre we have no gauze left. We have to sterilize rags. I told him even twenty kilograms of gauze would be something to go on with.

DACHA: And do you know what I want to go on with?

ERNST: What?

DACHA: Twelve square metres of hardboard.

ERNST: What?

DACHA: And if that's not possible, twelve square metres of thick cardboard.

ERNST: Nobody, my love, could say you lack imagination. [*He starts to undress. His white body is badly scarred.*]

DACHA: You have teeth like Gary Cooper.

ERNST: That's because of the stone pines! *Convit,* by the way, is no longer obligatory, a new order from Moscow.

DACHA: You'll always be the most beautiful man in my life, and the stone pines have nothing to do with it.

ERNST: [*Naked, he walks over towards the window.*] What's the hardboard for?

DACHA: [*Pouring water into the bath.*] Patience, Doctor, patience. Everything in good time. [*He sits in the bath. She soaps and washes him.*] The last time I saw Sacha I was bathing him. There was a knock at the door. There were four of them. What's it for? I asked. I knew what it was for. My one worry was who was going to finish giving Sacha his bath. They're thoughtful, the Bruise; they had already warned the neighbour's wife.

ERNST: And now your Sacha knows how to bath himself and he doesn't need you for that. But me, I do!

She pours water over his head. Both are laughing. There is a knock on the door. A Bruise pushes it wide open.

BRUISE: Citizen Oizermann!

ERNST: [*Ernst remains seated in the zinc bath.*] Citizen Oizermann present! [*To Dacha*] Give me my glasses. [*He puts them on. To the Bruise*] What can I do for you?

BRUISE: You are required to report immediately to the Commandant. [*The Bruise approaches the bath, stiffly. Ernst stands up, dripping, naked.*]

ERNST: You want me to come like this?

BRUISE: You have five minutes. The Colonel's daughter has vomited up her supper. I'll be waiting outside. [*The Bruise leaves. Ernst steps out of the bath and starts dressing.*]

ERNST: I told the Colonel's wife not to give her too much to eat.

DACHA: Too much to eat!

ERNST: Calm, Dachenka. Don't fret. Why do you want the hardboard?

DACHA: A telegram came today.

ERNST: From whom?

DACHA: Leningrad.

ERNST: Bad news?

DACHA: From Sacha.

ERNST: Sacha! Your son!

DACHA: That's why I want the hardboard.

ERNST: Dacha, I have to go, don't talk in riddles.

DACHA: Sacha has taken the decision to come to Magadan.

ERNST: Taken the decision!

DACHA: When the school year is over.

ERNST: This year?

DACHA: Ernst, he's coming, he's coming here!

ERNST: And the hardboard?

DACHA: To make a room for him in the corner there.

ERNST: It won't happen.

DACHA: I believe he will come.

ERNST: May God protect him and may he never come here! [*Ernst goes towards the door. Pauses. Takes a wrapped sweet out of his pocket.*] The Colonel's other child gave me a sweet.... Keep it for Sacha.

Ernst leaves. Dacha, alone in the room, folds the towel, empties the bath. She moves slowly as if her own gestures were now company.

DACHA: This autumn it'll be exactly fifteen and a half years since I saw you. [*She takes the telegram out of her pocket.*] DECISION TAKEN BY SACHA TO SPEND VACATION IN MAGADAN STOP LETTER FOLLOWS STOP KATYA. You were bigger than me, Katya, and more serious and more beautiful, yet you were jealous. You couldn't be jealous of me now, Katinka, could you? It wouldn't be reasonable. [*She hangs the zinc bath on the wall.*] Every time Maman said it was bath time you howled so loud, Katinka. Papa would come out of his study and say: 'Be quiet, Miss. The Great Blanqui is just about to make his speech to the massed crowd at Bourges on 15 May 1848. How can I follow such an historical moment with you making this din?' How could we know then, Katinka, that Papa's following of historical moments would earn him a bullet in the neck? [*In the street outside, in the dusk of the arctic night, some drunks are singing a song. Dacha shuts the window peremptorily, and notices the sweet that Ernst left on the table.*] DECISION TAKEN BY SACHA. Ernst is frightened. He thinks you shouldn't get to know this world. Perhaps it's your mother you need to get to know. Katya has been a mother to you. But Katya can't be Dacha. Perhaps it's Dacha you want to get to know now.... [*She lies on the bed in the corner.*] Do we, of the same flesh, need to get to know each other? Your father used to come and fetch me after class. He'd wait by the bridge and we'd cross it together, and he always carried my books. He had very blue eyes, like yours, full of light. He had tiny feet and wore pointed shoes—as if he wanted the least contact possible with the ground. He saw us all and the whole history of our planet from way, way above, from where everything fitted together perfectly into circles and the circles into spirals going higher and

79

higher. The great hymn of history! When I told Papa I was going to marry Serge, Papa joked: 'So your children will be young Hegelians!' How could we know studying Hegel would lead to six millimetres of pointed steel in the back of the neck.

Dacha jumps up from the bed because of a knock on the door. A sixty-year-old man enters, holding a herring wrapped in paper, as if it were a bouquet of flowers. His name is Gricha. They embrace.

GRICHA: Hedgehogs are the only animals who make love looking at each other face to face. Don't argue. I've just seen them doing it. My compliments! The only woman of Magadan who stays the same. [*He displays the herring.*] Fished off Vladivostok! It's not Swedish, it's not Norwegian, it's not Icelandic—this fish was caught in the waters of Holy Russia! Fat, juicy, and the spices, oh, the spices that go with it—cinnamon, bay leaves, cloves, nutmeg, peppercorns—all, like perfumes on the breath of our motherland! Ten barrels full. Do you have a cigarette? I unloaded a ton of tomatoes today. Don't look so surprised. If the cases drip, we say they're loaded with tomatoes. Take it, sweetheart, it's not a stinging nettle. Grasp it firmly from underneath, move the hand up—never down—and it won't sting.

DACHA: You've been drinking.

GRICHA: We'll never know when the ball is over. [*He pretends to dance with the herring clutched to his chest.*]

DACHA: Better to dance with me! [*They dance a few steps. Abruptly the man steps back.*]

GRICHA: Fuck it! I've never seen you dance before, not even when you got your White Pass.

DACHA: My son's coming.

GRICHA: Children are the flowers of life! And who is the Best Friend of All Children, Everywhere?

DACHA: Be quiet!

GRICHA: You've given yourself away! No wonder they picked you up and did you with Article 58. You are incorrigible, you refuse his edification—he who is the Best Friend of All Children Everywhere, The Best Trainer of all Athletes, the Great Linguist.

DACHA: Sacha's coming here.

GRICHA: [*Gricha takes out of his pocket a small bunch of daisies and places them beside the fish on the table. Suddenly he can think of no more jokes and looks tired.*] You haven't got a cigarette?

DACHA: [*Dacha finds him one on a make-shift shelf above her bed.*]
Gricha, dear, can you lay your hands on some hardboard and a little
door?

GRICHA: You should catch the rabbit before you build the hutch!

DACHA: The rabbit is now sixteen.

GRICHA: And what the fuck is he coming to do here?

DACHA: You're all the same. Even Ernst. What's the matter with you all?

GRICHA: A hard day, a hard day....

DACHA: How's the pain in your chest, Gricha?

GRICHA: You must be wondering how your son will feel about you and
Ernst.

DACHA: I suppose—

GRICHA: Forget it. More to the point: how will he feel about the white
frozen fog. One should never underestimate the importance of
geography.

DACHA: 'Decision taken'—that's what it said—read it! [*She offers
him the telegram.*]

GRICHA: IMPRUDENT DECISION TAKEN BY CITIZEN DACHA TO IGNORE
GEOGRAPHY. STOP.

DACHA: He never knew his father.

GRICHA: Think of Ernst as Father Elect.

DACHA: Ernst is frightened, Gricha.

GRICHA: Ernst was born to be a father.

DACHA: Were you?

GRICHA: If you want to have a large family you must know how to count.
Counting comes naturally to our Ernst.

DACHA: I saw him once in the Zone, counting the number of leaves on
the one and only tree in the station yard.

GRICHA: It must have been a snow-ball tree.

DACHA: What?

GRICHA: 'Where there's a snow-ball tree, there's always an uncle.' A
variety of viburnum.... And your Sacha, he lives with his uncle?

DACHA: Yes, the husband of my sister, Katya. He's an architect who has
built two universities.

Gricha is lying on the bed under the bookshelf, Dacha is sitting and
sewing on a second bed in the corner. Both are suddenly listless.

GRICHA: Do you remember when you came back to the logging camp after working at Agrobase 5? You were a picture of health. At least you were a picture of health compared to the rest of us. The ration had been cut to 500 grams.

DACHA: Why did he let me go?

GRICHA: I told him you had syphilis. And I ought to know! I told him. I made out I was one of your victims.

DACHA: You were my guardian angel.

GRICHA: He didn't want to believe me. He said that on the list of Zeks there was no mention of your having the clap. It's just happened, I said, since the last examination. And cunt that he was, he believed me!

DACHA: You should have been a diplomat, Gricha, not a porter at the Special Provisions Depot.

GRICHA: You're right and what's more I speak French like an actor! *'Dans l'orient désert quel devint mon ennui'* —Racine.

DACHA: At Logging Camp 28, I never thought I'd live to see my son.

GRICHA: Miracles only happen in this world, Dachinka, not in the next.... [*He slumps into fatigue and then comes to life again.*] Take the miracle of the Holy Trinity. For two millennia it had them all foxed, and only now at the beginning of the fifties in this century, which is so full of promise, has your Gricha discovered the secret. Do you know what it is? I've discovered I'm my own Father, my own Son and my own Holy Ghost.

DACHA: I think the Holy Ghost has had enough. Suppose he sleeps here tonight?

GRICHA: He is tired, it's true. Do you know what he saw today with his own eyes? Two cases of oranges!

DACHA: Can you get some for Sacha?

GRICHA: There's always a grass about.

DACHA: Don't run any risks.

GRICHA: I never run risks. I'm an untouchable.

DACHA: [*Dacha goes to the mirror and undoes her hair before lying down on the bed in the corner.*] Good night, Gricha. Sleep well.

GRICHA: [*Gricha is sitting on his bed, his head between his hands.*] Good night... Good night... Those must be the words they still repeat on the Continent before they are arrested. Good night! Sweet dreams! The shits of this mother-fucking motherland... Sssshhh,

Gricha. Ssshhh, my little boy. Sshh, Papa. Good night, my boy. Good night, Maman, Good night, motherfuckers. [*He takes off his shoes and bringing one of his maimed feet to his mouth, kisses it.*] There's the cleverest...ah!...the brains of the foot...

2

An evening one week later. In the far corner of the room a cardboard partition with a door has been put up to make a bedroom for Sacha. In the doorway, reluctant to enter, a thirty-year-old lorry-driver, whose name is Micha. Behind him, Sacha, sixteen, dressed in clothes from another world.

MICHA: I'll be leaving you here. This is where she lives.

SACHA: There's no one here, come in. Look!

MICHA: You're feeling a bit lost?

SACHA: A bit.

MICHA: Don't worry. They've seen everything here. You'll find a place for yourself.

SACHA: I was meant to arrive tomorrow, you see, that's why there's no one. I came today because tomorrow's flight was cancelled....So she lives here. I've seen a photo of her, a marriage photo, but nothing since.

MICHA: In the Zone here, there aren't any picture-framers.

SACHA: She has dark eyes and she's not very tall. She'd come up to my chest, I'd say.

MICHA: I've never seen your mother. I've just heard about her. She works at the Infant School.

SACHA: [*Sacha walks around the room, examining the few objects.*] What have you heard?

MICHA: You'll have so much to tell each other, the summer won't be long enough.

SACHA: [*Sacha opens a small wooden-framed triptych on the bookshelf and reads the title of one of the reproductions framed inside.*] *Flight into Egypt* by Nicolas Poussin. [*He looks at Micha.*] What brought you here?

MICHA: The legal system.

SACHA: You're free now?

MICHA: I could leave for the Continent tomorrow, if I chose.

SACHA: Why don't you?

MICHA: Sometimes I ask myself that. The pay's good here.

SACHA: It isn't the same for my mother. She can't leave.

MICHA: Your mother is an Enemy of the People.

Ernst suddenly appears in the doorway.

ERNST: You've come! Dacha was expecting you tomorrow. Was the door open?

MICHA: Yes, Doctor, the door was open.

ERNST: Wait! She'll be here. [*Ernst runs into the street.*]

SACHA: Who's he?

MICHA: He's your step-father.

SACHA: How?

MICHA: Your mother's been with him for years.

SACHA: They aren't married?

MICHA: I wouldn't know, but they met in the Zone, and there aren't any wedding dresses there.

SACHA: You called him 'Doctor'?

MICHA: One of the rare good ones. Uncle Permanganate we used to call him. Poor sod, he's still got five years to do.

SACHA: How's that? You say he lives here, with my mother.

MICHA: In the afternoons he treats the Bruise....

SACHA: The Bruise?

MICHA: The Bruise are law here. He treats some of them and their families. That way he gets a free pass out of the Zone into the town until eleven o'clock each night. He's gone to fetch your mother, so I'll be off.

SACHA: How did they meet here—in the Zone?

MICHA: Don't ask me. I don't know how they got away with it. Love is listed as a crime for 58s.

Enter a large forty-five-year-old woman, wearing the once smart, now hand-me-down clothes given her by her employers. She works as a cleaner for the wives of camp officers. She is carrying a saucepan; her name is Lydia. She pointedly ignores Micha and goes straight to Sacha.

LYDIA: One didn't hope to see you here so soon.

SACHA: Nor did I.

LYDIA: So, your mother's great day has dawned even sooner than she was expecting! You must know that for years, my boy, she never dared to hope to set eyes on you again. All she could take with her, when she was transferred under escort, was your name... Sacha. Nobody could steal that from her.

SACHA: She could imagine me more easily than I could imagine her.

LYDIA: She didn't imagine, she *saw* you.

Ernst comes back, smiling, and limps across to Sacha still carrying his suitcase. He taps Sacha on the chest, a caricature of a chest examination.

ERNST: Fit. Congratulations! How on earth did you get here?

MICHA: I picked him up at the airport.

ERNST: You have a vehicle? [*He examines Micha more closely.*] Haven't I seen you before?

MICHA: From time to time I deliver medical supplies.

ERNST: Yes, yes, a free worker. What article were you convicted under?

MICHA: Nothing special. Pick-pocketing.

ERNST: Ah! An artist!

Lydia is preparing food in the kitchen corner. Gricha, an orange in his hand, rushes in.

GRICHA: Our prodigal son has returned! Get out those trumpets, you stomping archangels! The horses are coming, the angels are marching in! Everybody outside! Line up! The prodigal son has returned. Down on your knees. Everybody down on your knees. The sweetness of the mother's breast, the authority of the father's hand on the son's head! The family home with all modern conveniences, gas, electricity, running water. Oh the miracle of running water, hot and cold!

Dacha appears, taking off her scarf. Gricha does not see her; his back is to the door. But Sacha, looking over Gricha's shoulder, sees her immediately and cannot take his eyes off her. Dacha, as if mesmerized in turn, leans against the doorpost, staring back at her son.

GRICHA: Long live all miracles! Never again to limp out of bed into the frozen skimmed milk of the fog. Never again to be knocked over and held down by the dogs! It's finished now. Well and truly over. Long live all fairy tales! Warm yourself, little one, by the radiator. May milk and honey melt in your mouth. [*Abruptly he senses the presence of Dacha and turns towards the door.*] Mother and son, may honey melt in your mouths. Madonna and Child!

DACHA: Dear Gricha, let us be.... Let us look at each other.

The others busy themselves with laying the table and arranging the chairs. Mother and son gaze at each other across the room, as if nothing else, not even the distance between them, existed. A badly dressed, shy, fifty-five-year-old man enters and bows formally to Dacha. He is Igor.

IGOR: I was passing and I saw a light through the window.... What a public occasion it is! Your home is so full of people.

DACHA: Sacha, my son, has come home.

IGOR: May you always return like this, the first time. By airplane or by dream, no matter the means of transport, may you always return like this, Sacha.

Everyone moves and talks at once. Lydia brings in a saucepan of soup. Dacha puts bottles on the table. Gricha takes a few dance steps by himself. Micha protests that he must go, and Gricha insists that he stay. Ernst leads Sacha to a place at the table and everyone sits down. The chair next to Sacha is left vacant for Dacha, who is the last to sit down. She touches Sacha's cheek.

DACHA: You've shaved.

SACHA: Yes, I shave now.

GRICHA: And supposing we drink? Red for the ladies, white for the gentlemen. [*He hesitates before Sacha's glass.*] And what will the Continent drink?

SACHA: The Continent likes vodka. [*Dacha puts her hand over the glass to prevent Gricha serving Sacha vodka.*]

ERNST: Let us drink to Dacha's and Sacha's happiness!

DACHA: And yours, Ernst.

SACHA: And my father's.

GRICHA: To be alive at all is a sin.

IGOR: How fine the soup is.

LYDIA: There's wild sorrel in it.

ERNST: An official order came this morning. *Convit* is no longer compulsory.

GRICHA: Everyone struggles for himself. It's obligatory.

SACHA: What is *Convit*?

ERNST: A concoction made from the needles of stone pines, that everyone in the Zone is obliged to eat before the evening ration.

LYDIA: It makes you want to vomit and it takes away even the appetite of the famished. They invented it to punish us.

ERNST: The Academy of Medicine in Moscow has decided that whatever little good *Convit* does to compensate for a lack of vitamins, it has disastrous effects on the liver. It has probably killed thousands.

DACHA: Eat, Sachinka.

ERNST: And now we are to be spared *Convit.*

GRICHA: Ah! The perspicacity of the Academy of Medicine!

ERNST: The poet Sérébriakov died this morning. His face was relaxed, his eyes were closed and he was reciting a verse; it was addressed to a woman called Maria. I asked him if it was an old poem. A new one, he replied.

SACHA: What did he die of?

ERNST: Alimentary dystrophy, on his papers. Exhaustion from years of hunger, in the sight of God.

LYDIA: 'They taught me the science of good-byes in the wild sobs of the night.'

SACHA: Who?

ERNST: [*To Sacha*] Our Lydia is a specialist in Russian poetry of the so-called Silver Century. [*Gricha meanwhile fingers Sacha's shirt and jacket as if he were a buyer in a shop. He takes his own cap from the back of his chair and puts it on Sacha's head*] And Igor—Igor Issaevitch Gertzman—is a violinist. In 1932 he won the first prize at the *International concours* in Vienna.

IGOR: What Ernst says, young man, is not quite true. I am no longer a violinist.

LYDIA: You will play again, I know it. [*Gricha imitates a violinist playing his instrument.*]

IGOR: Never!

SACHA: You could play if you wanted to, couldn't you? Or don't I understand?

IGOR: Understand? When I was first transferred to the Zone, I had a stroke of luck. I caught typhus. Hospitalized, quarantined, with sheets, food, nurses. After the going-over I'd had in Loubianka, it was like paradise. I could almost imagine a Stradivarius in my hands. And it was there, in hospital, that is how I learned to play concerts to myself. You decide on the programme—Bach Prelude in F Minor,

Schubert sonata, Mozart concerto—and then you start. And with all those bars in your head, you forget the barbed wire, you forget everything else.

LYDIA: How many times have I recited Blok's poem to myself? 'Of Russia's monstrous years we are the offspring...'

DACHA: Eat, Sacha.

ERNST: [*To Sacha*] Our Lydia... Lydia Ivanovna—

LYDIA: —Chief of the Planning Section for the Red October textile factory in Kharkov. Arrested for sabotage of the national economy. Now you know all, Sacha!

SACHA: [*To Igor*] So why don't you still play?

IGOR: In '39 I was transferred to the logging camp at Arkagala. There, I caught an ear infection which led to a tympanosclerosis. Yet what is partial deafness for a musician? Nothing. No, it was the music itself which was slowly leaving my soul. It was too cold, there was nothing inside me, the silence was too heavy. And every day even that 'nothing' grew smaller.

ERNST: At minus forty centigrade and with a ration of 400 grams of bread a day that goes without saying.

IGOR: I had a friend. He slept for a while on the bunk above mine. In his other life he had been a professor of comparative religion, Professor Vassiliev. He talked to me about how he envisaged the Sacred. I listened to him and I watched the fog. And then one day, unexpectedly, I heard the sense of his words. Hearing the sense of his words was like listening to another kind of music. A music that nobody can play.... He had a book in English—Vassiliev—God knows how he got it. It wasn't a whole book, just part of a book, without any cover. Written by an Englishman called Fraser. I inherited it from him, along with a scarf, knitted by a woman whom Professor Vassiliev greatly loved. For the Professor died. He had great endurance and it was he who taught me my endurance. Yet he died. He died from the same disease as the poet Sérébriakov.

GRICHA: No music there and no sense. It's pure geography.

MICHA: That's right. There's no sense in the taiga. There's this friend of mine, he's a lorry-driver too. Picked up for slaughtering his uncle's pigs. He meets a girl here in Magadan, she's a 58 in forced residence, like Dacha here. Liola, that's the girl's name, and she lives in Pioneer Street. Slim, dark, with eyes like almonds, that's Liola. When he meets her, this friend of mine, she's pregnant, with no father around. So he does everything for her. Buys her a bed, buys her a bath-tub, buys clothes for her baby-to-be. He'd drive anywhere in the taiga—if it earned him a bonus to spend on Liola.... So one morning he comes to the depot and he's told to load six great drums of barbed wire. For where? he asks. Beyond Arkagala: they're building a new Zone there. It's 2,000 miles and there's a large bonus. Transport that shit! he shouts. Never! Everyone tries to reason with him. Useless. And, there, on the spot, the Bruise pick him up. He's back inside the Zone now, this time as a 58. Now, where's the sense in what he did? Do you see any?

ERNST: There's always somebody ready to unroll the barbed wire.

MICHA: I don't mind telling you, I delivered it myself. Why not? And the bonus, I gave the bonus to Liola. She was weeping her heart out over her hero. Kept on calling him her 'Decembrist'. What's that? I asked her. She explains to me it means a villain who changes into a hero! I look at her and I think: My poor rabbit, where's the sense?

ERNST: Has she had her baby?

MICHA: Last month, a girl. We decided to call her Alice.

LYDIA: The water's boiling.

ERNST: Your Vassiliev, Igor, in the bunk above you, was he Kostia Vassiliev? It must have been. I was once in the same hut with him. He used to tell stories at night for the criminals, and they paid him with bread and protection....

IGOR: Yes, Vassiliev was one of the most sought-after novelists. He could keep twenty men quiet.

LYDIA: I'll serve the tea.

IGOR: Once he refused to go on with *The Count of Monte Cristo* and, instead, he told a story which haunted me for a long while.

SACHA: Can you tell it to us?

IGOR: I've never told it before?

ERNST: No.

IGOR: There was once a people forgotten by the rest of the world. Perhaps they were not entirely forgotten, but they believed they were. They fell silent. And then one of them, a puny man who had lost most of his teeth, said: Let's go and look for the Beginning, then at least we'll be moving, instead of squatting here like fools. And so they set out. Soon they saw the walls of a city where there were great houses, palaces and temples. They said to themselves: Perhaps this city is the Beginning. As they entered it, they were overcome by its stench and they stumbled over carcasses; they were everywhere, all black and swollen. They left the city and continued on their way. Nothing got better. They crossed rivers red with blood. They crossed battlefields. They saw burned villages smoking. On and on they went, discouraged—more discouraged than when they started. Suddenly the puny man stopped and announced: We have arrived! Behind this hill is the Beginning. Behind the hill they found a small tower, broken-down and useless, and a field of earth, freshly ploughed. Nothing else. Only one thing was strange: the sky directly above didn't join the rest of the sky: it was like a separate miniature sky. The people muttered, So that's all there is to the Beginning! An acre of earth and a bit of sky like an old hat! People need many miracles before they believe in one.

DACHA: And one miracle can make many seem possible.

IGOR: But they'd had enough of travelling, enough of forced marches. They said: We'll stop here anyway. Only the puny man kept wondering who had ploughed the earth before they came. The others set to work. They cut down forests, they quarried, they made roads, they built useful towers. The miniature sky grew and grew, until it was completely absorbed into the large sky. A day-to-day life set in, year in, year out, and the Beginning was forgotten.... [*Silence. Nobody reacts visibly to the story. Dacha gets up, takes the alarm clock from the shelf and holds it up for Ernst to see.*]

ERNST: I must be off. My nightly routine...

IGOR: I talk too much. It is so rare that we have a visitor from the Continent. Shall I walk back home with you, Lydia Ivanovna? [*Everyone makes a move to go and gathers round the door.*]

ERNST: [*To Igor and Lydia*] So you're off to play a little duet!

LYDIA: Me? I've never touched an instrument in my life!

ERNST: Never too late!

MICHA: [*To Sacha*] Miles beyond me his story—maybe Liola will understand it. I'll have to remember to tell her. You know where I am if you need me?

GRICHA: Welcome to Magadan, Sacha. Never forget: the feet are the most intelligent part of the human body.

Everyone leaves. Dacha accompanies Ernst into the street to say good night. Sacha sits at the table alone. He searches in his jacket pocket, and finds an envelope which he puts on the table. Dacha returns to sit beside him.

DACHA: Look at your plate, you've hardly eaten anything. [*She notices the envelope.*] Whose is this?

SACHA: It's for you.

DACHA: From Katya?

SACHA: No. It's from my father—or, if you like, it's from your husband.

DACHA: From Serge! [*She takes the letter and stands by the window, her back to Sacha.*] It must be an old letter.

SACHA: No, Mama, it's dated 8 May 1952.

DACHA: [*She speaks with her back turned to him, in order to hide her face. Her voice is low as if addressed to herself. Nevertheless she is speaking to him.*] The last news I had of him was at the public desk of the Cross Prison on 15 November in '37. 'Transferred with no right of mail.' Those were the words. And they meant: Serge had been executed. I'd heard the same words applied to Father in October.... You must be exhausted after such a full day. *Full day.* [*She catches her breath. Walks towards Sacha.*] You see the little room? When we knew you were coming, we built it for you.

SACHA: It was not necessary.

DACHA: There's a basin and a jug of water to wash your face and hands. [*They are standing close, face to face.*]

SACHA: And my feet?

DACHA: And your feet! Your feet! Hello, my boy. [*They embrace.*]

SACHA: I've come, Mama. [*Sacha goes into his room. Dacha returns to the window.*] Come for a little while, Mama.

DACHA: Yes, darling, I'm coming.

3

Early evening, a fortnight later. Sacha is alone in the room. On the table a bunch of wild flowers and a bottle of milk. He is now wearing clothes more in keeping with life in Magadan. He fetches a vase of water, arranges the flowers in it, glances at himself in the mirror, combs his hair. His mother comes in.

DACHA: So the nightbird is at home for once! We had a surprise today! The local radio station is going to broadcast our play at the Infant School.

SACHA: What's it about?

DACHA: Well, first of all, in our version, the Wolf doesn't eat the Grandmother! The Wolf meets Little Red Riding Hood and goes with her, like an escort, to Grandma's house. He waits for her outside, while she delivers her basket of sweets, and then he walks her back home!

SACHA: Does the Wolf look like the Bruise?

DACHA: Of course not.

SACHA: You surprise me! [*He holds out the vase of flowers.*] Not for the Wolf not for the Grandmother, for you!

DACHA: Is the nightbird staying in tonight? It's days since we've seen you, Ernst and I.

SACHA: I'm nearly seventeen now! And think of the years I've lived through, not just any seventeen years—1936 to 1952. Just think what he has seen, your son!

DACHA: We have to wait nine months, my little one, before you are seventeen.

SACHA: The Great Patriotic War, the Great Victory over Fascism, the Transition from Socialism to Communism... I've seen more than you have.

DACHA: And you are still sixteen! And you come home too late.

SACHA: Last night I was back by quarter to one. I walked with Ernst as far as the Zone. Eight kilometres.

DACHA: Where did you meet Ernst? He didn't come last night, but I wasn't worried, as I would have been once.

SACHA: The worst is over, Mother.

DACHA: How much you remind me of Serge.

SACHA: Do I?

DACHA: There are some men who never lose their innocence. And when their white hairs are stained with blood, it's like the night of St Bartholomew. Tell me, Sachinka, how did you meet Ernst last night?

SACHA: That's a story in itself, a Magadan story. Do you know the Continental?

DACHA: I know it's a kind of hotel.

SACHA: What kind? You see how you need a sixteen year-old to tell you about Magadan!

DACHA: That I need you, yes, Sacha.

SACHA: It's a hotel for Zeks who've just got their release and who are waiting to go back to the Continent. An extraordinary place, a real club for gentlemen, nothing like your crummy Cultural Centre.

DACHA: There's a library at the Centre with books which you can't find anywhere else.

SACHA: I met a man at the Continental who speaks six languages, and has been all round the world.

DACHA: Is it far away?

SACHA: It's not far, it's in a little street that leads down to Nagaiev Bay, close to the sea. It's a basement, well-heated—well it's even suffocating in this weather. Where else can they go, your Zeks? They can't all have super love affairs with great doctors. So they hang out there. Greenhorns who have just been released, others who can't make up their minds whether to go or stay, all of them waiting for their ship to come in—they're not in Forced Residence like you. It's a real museum, the Continental. Kids, babies, women. Washing, cooking, songs. Little groups talking—talking about serious things. Girls too, plenty of them, with nail varnish and permanent waves! And all this just a stone's throw from the sea. It must be strange in the winter when the waves on the bay are frozen.

DACHA: The winter is normal here, it's these two months now, the months you are here, that are abnormal.

SACHA: There's a girl there called Helena who has a great voice. She sings gypsy love songs: you wouldn't believe them. And do you know, she offered, just like that, to teach me the guitar.

DACHA: Really?

SACHA: There are men who committed real crimes against the state, not just a question of words like most of you. Hard cases. They think things out, they plan carefully. To hijack a cargo-ship, for instance. The guards are always pissed, so it would be child's play to disarm them...

DACHA: Stop, Sacha!

SACHA: I never drink anything there, Mother, except tea, and I never go alone. I never go without Micha.

DACHA: And what sort of record does Micha have? There are drug pushers there. There's venereal disease. And worst of all, worse than you can ever imagine, there's the Bruise.

SACHA: I never go without Micha.

DACHA: That doesn't reassure me; he was a criminal.

SACHA: What have all you 58s got against criminals? They're victims like you.

DACHA: The villains and the Bruise, they speak the same language.

SACHA: Yesterday I talked to a 58—a Party Secretary of the district of Saratov. Ten years inside and they've changed absolutely nothing for him. He sits in the hotel with a red pencil, correcting the articles he reads in the *Kolyma Star.* And he's convinced that, since now he has served his sentence for the 'regrettable error' he made in '37, he will be able to continue his career in the Party and make up for lost time.

DACHA: [*in a whisper*] And Serge's lost time?

SACHA: If only you could meet Ignatiev! There's a hero for you—like they teach us at school about Lermontov. Captain of a large freighter. At the beginning of the war he was transferred to a cruiser in the Baltic Fleet. He fought the Germans off Leningrad, fought like a tiger. Only when it was hopeless, did he break the German blockade and get his ship and crew safely to Sweden, where they were interned until '45. After the victory he requested to be sent home. Request accorded. The rest you can imagine. He was lucky—only five years. Now he's out, he won't be had a second time! He has the sea in his blood, Ignatiev.

DACHA: 'Fathers can be found anywhere,' that's what Serge wrote in his letter, do you remember? 'My one wish,' he wrote, 'is that Sacha re-finds you, Dacha.' Be careful Sacha!

SACHA: Don't think he's an idiot, Ignatiev, he has it all worked out. Alaska is no distance from here. You wait, they'll make it to America!

DACHA: When you walked Ernst back to the Zone last night, what did you talk about?

SACHA: About God. Why do you ask? [*He glances at the alarm clock.*] Isn't he late?

DACHA: What?

SACHA: Ernst, Mama! Look at the time.

DACHA: Don't worry. Half an hour, an hour, that's nothing. He's not always his own master. I'll put on the supper.

SACHA: Can you imagine Ernst when he was young? When he was my age?

DACHA: Yes, easily, just as I can imagine you in twenty-five years' time....

Enter Ernst with his newspaper packets. He looks tired. He salutes Sacha and then, without a word, takes Dacha's blood pressure.

ERNST: Twenty. [*He washes his hands in the sink. His discouragement is visible in his back.*]

DACHA: Don't worry, Ernst. [*She serves the soup.*]

SACHA: When you were my age, Ernst Moisseevitch, did you know you wanted to be a doctor?

ERNST: Yes I did. When I was younger still, I dreamed of being a sailor. [*Ernst sees Dacha taking some salt.*] More salt! No, Dashinka, not in your condition.

DACHA: I've been learning things about the sea of Okhotsk this evening.

ERNST: Icebound for seven months of the year.

DACHA: It's child's play, it seems, to cross it and go to America.

ERNST: How's that?

DACHA: By boat, of course!

SACHA: Via Alaska.

ERNST: Ah yes! I see. I never thought of that. [*He stops eating.*]

DACHA: How was your day?

ERNST: Eventful.... Last night I was called to the Continental—a heart case. I gave the man an injection and who should I see but our poet here [*he nods towards Sacha*], drinking tea in company. We left together and he accompanied me back to the Zone. When we came out of the hotel, I noticed one of the lorries of the Bruise and I said to myself: A routine check-up. Better, I thought, for Sacha not to be there when the Bruise arrive: you never know, even though they generally turn a blind eye to what goes on at the Continental. I was far too naive. Do you know what happened after we left? They pulled in your entire tea party—they're inside now—Ignatiev and all his friends.

SACHA: I don't believe it! Ignatiev is too smart to get arrested for nothing!

ERNST: I suppose the idea about the Sea of Okhotsk comes from your tea party?

DACHA: Ernst, how to tell him, how to explain to him? [*Sacha leaves the table and turns his back.*] For a whole hour he's been telling me stories about hi-jackings, heroes, Alaska, escapes. Everything is like an adventure film to him. What can we do? What can we say so they understand?

95

ERNST: Our lives here, Sacha, can never be a film, never. We have lost many things, things that people take for granted elsewhere. And one of the most important things we've lost is the right to be seen. What we live is invisible. Even if, by some miracle, somebody made a film of our lives in Kolyma, all that would be seen on the screen would be a blizzard, with visibility reduced to a few metres. The blizzard of our losses. Nobody would be able to see the little we've managed to protect from the blizzard. The grains on which we live are invisible. You come here. I'm not sure what a boy of your age thinks. It's a very long time since I was sixteen. Probably you find us colourless, a peculiar mixture of passivity and nervousness.

SACHA: That's not true!

ERNST: I'm sure you believe that somehow we can choose. Choose like Ignatiev to put to sea and cross the Bering Straits! You are wrong. Ignatiev has been arrested. Here there are no choices—choices as you imagine them.

SACHA: None of you can choose?

ERNST: Everything outside prevents it. The choices we make are inside. [*He taps his chest. He is still eating his soup, spoon in one hand.*] When you drag yourself back after a day's work in the taiga, when you are marched back, half dead with fatigue and hunger, you are given your ration of soup and bread. About the soup you have no choice—it has to be eaten while it's hot, or while it's at least warm. About the 200 grams of bread you have a choice. For instance, you can cut it into three little bits: one to eat now with the soup, one to suck in the mouth before going to sleep on your bunk, and the third to keep until next morning at ten, when you're working in the taiga and the emptiness in your stomach feels like a stone. [*Sacha moves from his place by the window and goes towards the cooking stove. Ernst slowly gets to his feet. Dacha stops sewing and watches both the men.*] You empty a wheelbarrow full of rocks. About pushing the barrow to the pile you had no choice. Now it's empty you have a choice. You can walk your barrow back just like you came, or—if you're clever, and survival makes you clever—you push it back like this, almost upright. If you choose the second way you give your shoulders a rest. [*Sacha moves towards the bed. Ernst takes the chair on which he was sitting and places it close to Dacha, before sitting down on it.*] If you are a Zek and you become a gang leader, you have the choice of playing at being a screw, or of never forgetting that you are a Zek.... When I receive a new contingent of the dying I have a duty to look after them all, as best I can. In addition, I have the *choice* of trying to do even more, of trying to do the impossible, for one of them whom I feel must be saved at all costs. [*Sacha gets up and moves towards his cardboard room.*]

SACHA: Why not all of them?

ERNST: Because I do not have the means to choose that. Look at us, your mother and me. In '47, when Dacha got her White Pass with Forced Residence, she had no choice about staying here in Magadan. But she could have chosen, she can still choose, to leave me. Me, a Zek, with another five years to do inside.

DACHA: About love there is no choice. And I have only one son. Tell him, Ernst.

ERNST: The Continental and its gang—you understand, Sacha, all that must stop. Once and for all, you understand? You can see how your mother is. Do you want to kill her?

SACHA: What do you want me to do with my time? Who do you want me to see? The kids of your client officers? You want me to arse-lick the Bruise? Or do you want me to kick my heels here all day while both of you are out working? Forced Residence for everyone!

Sacha opens the door to his cardboard room, goes in and slams it behind him. Ernst, equally angry, seizes the doorhandle and pulls it violently. The makeshift door comes off its hinges. Ernst tries to put it back. Fails. Dacha comes to his help. Together they carry the door and lean it against the wall, near the front door. When they turn they see Sacha, framed in his doorway, wearing a sailor's cap.

SACHA: Never mind, I don't need the door. Without a door, we can communicate better, no?

DACHA: Your cap?

SACHA: A present from Captain Ignatiev.

DACHA: It quite suits you.

ERNST: You can't go out in a cap like that.

DACHA: [*Adjusting the cap on her son's head.*] Like this.

SACHA: Look at the time, Ernst Moisseevitch. [*To Dacha*] Let's both go with him tonight.

ERNST: Not in that outfit.

SACHA: No, chief, without it. [*Takes off cap.*]

97

All three leave. The room is empty, the window open. A man's voice reads a letter he has just written.

SERGE'S VOICE: Dacha, my little darling, how to find the words now? Can you imagine, out of the darkness, out of the darkness of so many years, I received a letter from Katya. Like one of those flashes of light in Plato's cave. I learned that you are alive, that Sacha is almost grown up. How can such miracles happen? I have to pinch myself to make sure I'm awake. Yes, I am. Fifteen years! For fifteen years too, I haven't held a pen, so don't be hard on my handwriting. A guard fetched me this morning, brought me here to the office, gave me this pen and paper and said: You have the right of addressing one letter to your wife. And me, idiot that I am, I started to cry. Where are you, my little one? I go back and back to the bridge in front of the Hermitage. Each paving stone, each arch of the bridge which we used to cross together, you in your black dress with a satchel—all, all is engraved. We were always in a hurry—for we had to go and fetch Sacha. I have lost my teeth and I have lost the toes of both feet. For three years I have been on the stoves in the bath house, a merciful job for I'm no longer cold. I don't have much appetite, which is just as well. I suck with my gums and eating takes a long time. I'm not like an old man, I'm more like an old child who has forgotten his age. Hegel used to say that the difference between a dead person and a child is that the child doesn't have a memory. There our philosopher made a mistake, because he couldn't foresee an intermediate category: one who is neither new-born, nor old, nor dead, nor living, yet who has a memory. I always believed that the magic of your hands wasn't in your hands but was in the way your hands obeyed your eyes.

If I'm not transferred to the mines, I'll hold out, and you must go on thinking of me as dead: you will be closer, my heart, to the reality. My soul, my spirit, my memory, have long since joined those of the dead who are, after all, the majority; and, in comparison with whom, the living are rare. Try not to think of me as being here, think of me rather as one who has already joined the Spirit of History which is watching over you from the furthest stars. I know every square millimetre of your body, astonishingly and eternally. My one wish is that Sacha may one day rejoin you. Fathers can be found anywhere. Know all this, my darling. As for me, I know it, and this knowledge is like a guiding star which will show me, until my last breath, where to place my frozen feet. We are already saved! [*A glass jug falls off the table. Silence. Dacha and Sacha return. Sacha notices the broken glass jug and picks up the pieces. Dacha looks round the room, troubled, suddenly anxious.*]

SACHA: It must have been a draught. [*He shuts the window.*] The wind is getting up over the bay.

Dacha wanders vaguely round the room, touching things, a plate, a chair, the glasses. Rubs a finger round the rim of a glass, holds it up to the light. Suddenly decisive, she goes to the bookshelf, chooses a book and from between its pages takes out Serge's letter. Sits down on a chair holding the letter to her breast. Sacha fetches a rag to wipe up the water under the table. After using it, he rolls up the rag, and starts to kick it around like a football.

DACHA: Go and see Gricha tomorrow, will you? He's picked off a tin of corned beef. Lydia is knitting a scarf and mittens. The winter will soon be here. [*She has crumpled the letter and now smoothes it out on her knees.*] The first parcel must get to Serge before November. By a miracle I got a whole salted cod today. He'll soak it in water to get rid of the salt and he'll eat it.

Dacha looks up at her son. He has stopped playing football with the rag and, as if all his energy has gone, has fallen on to his knees. He is sobbing. She stands behind him, her hands on his shoulders.

4

Evening, a few days later. Sacha and Gricha are sitting on two chairs, facing each other, in the middle of the room. Between them is a small table covered with a red cloth. Gricha is wearing an artificial moustache, obviously attached by elastic.

GRICHA: Are you going to confess?
SACHA: I've already said Yes.
GRICHA: In what town?
SACHA: Babylon.
GRICHA: With who?
SACHA: We were two.

GRICHA: Fucking lie. You were three.

SACHA: Not on that spree.

GRICHA: The third came from Prague.

SACHA: I'm just a bit vague.

GRICHA: Pure chicanery.

SACHA: A counter-revolution.

GRICHA: His name please!

SACHA: Diogenes.

GRICHA: Where did you meet?

SACHA: In Gorky Street.

GRICHA: This confirms what has been said.

SACHA: With how many blows to the head?

GRICHA: You scab, you sore, you blight on the People's Body, listen to me. When I pull on this chain, you stand up. When I pull a second time, you sit down. [*He pulls an imaginary chain, in the air by his right-hand shoulder.*] On to your feet! Down! Stand! Sit! Stand! [*While Sacha is standing, Gricha discreetly takes away the chair, resumes his place, pulls the chain. Sacha sits and falls to the floor.*] You scabby shit—nothing, nothing will teach you! If there's no chair there, my sweet little one, you stay like this—just as if there was a chair! If I order you to sit, it means there's something to sit on! Let me see you sit. [*Sacha sits on air, as if there were a chair there. Gricha slightly corrects his posture with his hand.*] All right, my monkey, you stay like that. Twenty-four hours on this chair and ideas will come to you by the hundred. Now—I want the names of your accomplices.

SACHA: Come plis this way, come plis!

GRICHA: [*Pulling the chain continuously.*] Up! Down! Up! Down! Why did Diogenes offer you gum to chew?

SACHA: That's not true.

GRICHA: Shit! Do you think you can reply like that! The only negative reply we permit is: 'Not in my presence.'

SACHA: Not in my presence!

GRICHA: [*Standing up*] Do you want the ice bin?

SACHA: Frederick Chopin.

GRICHA: At last a name!

SACHA: Do you prefer Schumann?

GRICHA: Schumann, Haussemann, Huissman! So you were seven.

SACHA: Yes, seven with Sunday.

GRICHA: That's better, you're learning how to play.

SACHA: We met on Fridays.

GRICHA: Traitors! [*He pretends to think.*] Babylon, Prague, Diogenes, chewing gum, America, Chopin Frederick, the Bering Sea, Alaska: a conspiracy against the Cheka! [*From under the table Gricha picks up a raw herring and begins to slap Sacha's face with it. Sacha, sitting on air, remains immobile.*] Fascist! Archivist! Nationalist! Continental Tourist!

A knock at the door. Sacha stands up. Gricha rips off his moustache, and stuffs it into his pocket. He grabs the red cloth off the table and throws it under the bed.

GRICHA: Come in. [*Enter Micha the lorry-driver. Not as before. Pale, slovenly. He sits down.*]

GRICHA: You look as though you've had a real going-over, my boy. Sacha, do we have anything in the first aid kit? [*Sacha brings over two glasses and a bottle of unlabelled alcohol.*]

GRICHA: Neat or with water?

MICHA: Neat. [*Gricha pours out a drink. Sacha fetches a plate of gherkins. Micha takes a gherkin and knocks back his glass.*] Where's your mother and father?

SACHA: They've gone to the film of the week. With Vivien Leigh and Robert Taylor.

MICHA: You should have heard the abuse your father gave me the other day. For taking you to the Continental. It was like the wrath of God.

SACHA: Do you know, I saw you yesterday on Stalin Avenue? You looked like somebody in a trance. The bronze statues of *The Five Who Don't Drink* looked more cheerful than you did. What's happened?

MICHA: They've picked up Liola.

SACHA: Arrested?

GRICHA: Which Liola? Who is she?

SACHA: Liola—you don't remember? The girl of his friend, the lorry-driver—the girl who was pregnant. A 58 with almond-shaped eyes. She was the one proud of the lorry-driver who got arrested for shouting his mouth off.

GRICHA: When was she arrested, this Liola?

MICHA: They picked her up last night. She was feeding the infant. Alice.

GRICHA: Yes. Yes. I see. So Liola has gone to join her Decembrist—as

the poets used to say. Nobody joins anybody in the Zone. Our Liola
has as much chance of meeting her beloved Decembrist there as the
dead have of breeding.

MICHA: I'm going to wait for her.

GRICHA: Her? Who?

MICHA: Liola. [*Gricha fills up the two glasses. Hands one to Micha and
one to Sacha.*] No, no, not for Sacha. Ernst Moisseevitch would kill
me if I let him drink.

SACHA: [*Winking at Gricha*] Never in my presence! I don't understand,
Micha. This Liola, is she your girl or your friend's?

MICHA: Ten years, twenty years if it has to be, I'll wait for her.

GRICHA: And her Decembrist? What are we going to do about him?

MICHA: That's her business.

GRICHA: Who on earth is this Liola? Under her spell, a simple villain
becomes a knight in shining armour.

SACHA: Who?

GRICHA: I'm talking about her Decembrist. And as for our poor Micha
here: he was an honest thief and now he's transformed into a Don
Quixote! All this for a pair of almond eyes. Ah Kolyma, Kolyma! If I
was in your shoes, Micha, I'd have got the hell out of here long ago.
I'd be in the south sun-bathing.

MICHA: Liola isn't the only one. They are picking up others too. There's
a rumour they're going to arrest all the 58s for the second time.

GRICHA: The third time for me.... Your victim with the almond eyes, tell
me, what's her name?

MICHA: Liola.

GRICHA: Liola *what,* for God's sake? Tell me her surname!

MICHA: Annissimov.

GRICHA: And the others they've arrested, do you know their names?

MICHA: No, I don't think so; let me think. In any case what does it
matter? Hang on, yes, there's this one—he's lost an arm: he lives just
down the street from us. They arrested him this morning, and his
name is Avevtchenko.

SACHA: What's happened to Liola's baby daughter. Alice, you said?

MICHA: She's been bundled into an orphanage—the special one for
children of Enemies of the People.

GRICHA: Annissimov... Avevtchenko... Alice.

Lydia, wearing a smartish dress with a fox-fur round her shoulders enters with Igor. Micha gets up to leave.

IGOR: We were passing and we saw a light in the window....

SACHA: Come and sit down, make yourselves at home.

MICHA: I'm off... I have some friends waiting. [*To Sacha*] I really came to ask you something. Next week I'm making a trip into the taiga delivering supplies for a group of geologists working in the north. I've been there once, and they're mostly from Moscow. Come with me if you can, it'll be company.

SACHA: Is it far?

MICHA: About 200 by road, and then 100 cross-country.

SACHA: I'd like to come but I must ask Ernst first. [*Micha nods and leaves without a word.*]

LYDIA: He looked as if he was in trouble, your criminal friend there; what is it?

GRICHA: Nothing, nothing at all.

LYDIA: Do you know what we did tonight? We went to see a film. A real English melodrama, set in London.

SACHA: With Vivien Leigh and Robert Taylor. My parents are there now.

LYDIA: We went to the earlier programme.

IGOR: Dacha Petrovna and Ernst Moisseevitch will enjoy themselves. It's a love story. The strangest thing of all was that everybody at the Cultural Centre, sitting there in the dark, everybody was wiping their eyes and snivelling. The Bruise with their wives and children, and we who were once Zeks—and will probably be Zeks again—masters and slaves, we all reacted in the same way.... There's a waltz in the film. [*He hums it.*] My mother used to play the same waltz at home when she gave dancing lessons.

GRICHA: Keep it up, Igor, keep it up! The moment has come for you to learn to dance a waltz, Sacha! [*He pulls Sacha to the middle of the room and demonstrates the steps.*] One... two... three—don't walk on my feet—one... two... three... you see, it's simple, simpler than an interrogation: one... two... three.

LYDIA: [*Lydia takes Igor by the hand and leads him to dance.*] You haven't forgotten... you haven't forgotten anything.

IGOR: The waltz was, you know, an invention of the nineteenth century.

Its tempo, according to Spengler, corresponds exactly to the spirit of modern man: the same steps repeated but always at a new level—a kind of diagram in dance of the Hegelian dialectic... If Marx hadn't taken Hegel's dialectic and turned it on its head...

GRICHA: We wouldn't all be here.... [*The four continue dancing. When the music stops, Lydia addresses the others.*]

LYDIA: We are going to give violin lessons.

IGOR: Don't start again, I beg you Lydia Ivanovna. It's out of the question. Music, in every form, is over for me, do you understand? Over, once and for all. And where I am now, in my little caretaker's room, with my notebooks and my little library, I am happy. I earn a living and I have no boots to lick. I sweep the cinema, I pile up chairs, I regulate the radiators.

LYDIA: The lessons would only be for children.

IGOR: *Their* children.

LYDIA: In your basement, there's not even room for a double bed.

IGOR: My bed is still a bed, incomparably preferable to a bunk in the Zone.

GRICHA: This sounds like a family quarrel! Between husband and wife. Ah! How beautiful they were, those family quarrels, which belonged to the time of Little Tom Thumb!

LYDIA: Will you shut up, please?

IGOR: My bed is not a bunk.

LYDIA: We can settle this ourselves.

GRICHA: Perhaps you ought to settle your affairs quickly.

LYDIA: Rumours, rumours. Yes, Yes. There have been a few isolated arrests, I'm fully aware of that. But I have heard, and I have it from the highest authority, that a new wave of arrests is out of the question: there are going to be no mass arrests.

SACHA: How many does that mean? How many Zeks are there on the planet of Kolyma?

LYDIA: Many thousands.

IGOR: A mathematician I knew in the Zone—an expert in statistics in his first life—made his own calculations. He worked as a clerk in the administration, and, according to him, the population was between three and four million.

LYDIA: Igor, please, it's better not to be heard quoting statistics. [*There is a long silence.*]

SACHA: He's going to die. He's not immortal.

LYDIA: What on earth is that child saying? From where did you get such ideas?

SACHA: From here, of course. From you. Everyone has got to die—everyone here knows that. But on the Continent they're scared: they believe he will be the exception. The one who won't die. When he's dead, life will— [*Gricha is pacing round the room in agitation.*]

IGOR: May heaven protect you, Sacha. It has done me a lot of good to see you, Sacha. It's very important for us to have a witness. And you are right: he's not immortal, not immortal, with his arteries thickening with so much blood—not *his* blood needless to say, the blood of others.

SACHA: He's old. He's seventy-two.

GRICHA: Power is an aphrodisiac. Georgians live a long time—with their mountains and their yoghurts and their red peppers.

LYDIA: It's late, late, we really must be going. [*Igor does not stir.*] Igor Issaievitch, there will be all the chairs to stack after the film. [*He still does not move. Lydia takes his hand gently.*] Igorick, come on, dear. [*Igor starts to hum the waltz. The two of them leave. Sacha and Gricha sit down on the two chairs, with the small table between them.*]

GRICHA: Annissimov, Avertchenko, Alice: yes, yes, Alice is a Christian name. Still, you can see the logic. Annissimov, Avertchenko, the cunning bastards.

Gricha takes the moustache out of his pocket. There is a certain resemblance to Stalin's moustache. Sacha fetches a box of matches from the stove, strikes one, and leans across the table to set fire to the moustache. Gricha blows out the match.

GRICHA: You: you understand nothing! You are just a tourist here! A tourist! [*Gricha begins to pull the imaginary chain, but this time it is he himself who stands up and sits down.*] Up! Down! Up! There's no end to it, it goes on and on. Everything starts again; when it is over, it starts again at the beginning: be-gin-ing, be-gin-ing. [*Shouting, but by force of habit, prudently, so that he cannot be heard in the street.*] The in-ex-or-ab-le hell of ge-og-ra-phy....

5

It is nearly September, the days are noticeably shorter. Evening. Ernst, Dacha, Sacha are sitting at the table.

SACHA: When I was there, I understood better what Igor meant about the silence. And I understood something about myself, about my fears. Can you get rid of fears? I don't think so. You have to make a place for them, and then keep them in their place. It's normal to be frightened, isn't it? What's dangerous is when fears break free, then there's panic. It's as if you have to make a room for every one of your fears ... with a window and a door.

DACHA: Yes ... yes.

ERNST: What did they talk about, your geologists?

SACHA: About the Cenozoic era which lasted seventy million years. They were palaeontologists, Ernst. And do you know what they had just discovered? A mammoth—a giant mammoth in perfect condition. He looked as if he were alive yesterday. I brought back a present for you. [*Sacha fetches a little parcel from his room and gives it to Ernst.*] It's for you.

ERNST: Really for me?

DACHA: [*Taking the parcel and unwrapping the paper.*] What on earth is it?

SACHA: A mammoth's tooth!

DACHA: It isn't, I can't believe it! [*She holds it at arm's length, near Ernst's mouth.*] Smile, Ernst. Smile and show us your teeth!

ERNST: Long in the tooth—your Zek mammoth here.

SACHA: Mammoth of my mother's life!

ERNST: Did you know mammoths used their tusks as snow ploughs? They were well adapted to their habitat. By the way, there's no more toothpaste—not even in *their* shop. Deliveries have stopped. [*To Sacha*] Try to send us some from Leningrad. [*He takes out of his pocket a bundle of bank notes tied up with a piece of string.*] This is the money for your ticket. At the latest you should get it for next Friday.

DACHA: Almost a week.

ERNST: That way you'll be there for the beginning of term, and have time to sort out your books. And don't forget to send a telegram to your aunt tomorrow, as soon as you know the time of your plane.... Micha will get you to the airport. The weather forecasts are good. They're not predicting the fog till the end of September this year. The planes won't be grounded. You'll easily get a place, but be good and book it tomorrow.

DACHA: [*Fetching the triptych from the shelf, placing it on the table, opening it.*] Will you do something for me, Sachinka? One day when you have time, walk across the bridge and go and look at these three pictures in the Hermitage. Look at them for yourself—and for us. When I got my White Pass and I found this room for us to live in—in the way you see—well, it was then that I found these three reproductions, and they were the first present, real present, which I ever gave to Ernst.

SACHA: [*Looks carefully at the images, then shuts the triptych.*] I'm not going back to Leningrad. Not for the Hermitage. Not for some toothpaste.

ERNST: You have to be serious now, Sacha, time's running out.

SACHA: I'm staying here.

ERNST: Sacha, arguments are not good for your mother's blood pressure.

DACHA: Please, Sacha.

SACHA: I'm staying.

ERNST: Let us examine the situation carefully. You've spent your holidays here, you've even seen a mammoth! You have found your mother after fifteen years...

DACHA: We'll see each other again soon: we'll spend many, many, many days together.

ERNST: You can come back next year.

SACHA: When?

ERNST: 4 July 1953!

DACHA: You'll have finished school by then, we'll have plenty of time to talk, to talk about your future.

SACHA: What future?

ERNST: We'll be able to discuss what you want to do with your life.

SACHA: What I am—whether I want it or not—has already been decided, once and for all, by my mother and father. [*Silence. Dacha, visibly troubled.*]

ERNST: If what you mean, if what you have just said means that Dacha your mother and Serge your father, both of them Zeks ... if what you mean is that you, as their son, risk being marked for life, you are partly right, and we must admit it, but only partly right. Only partly right, Sacha, because I believe that a man's life is not really determined by the accident of his birth in a particular place during a particular year to two particular parents—all these particulars are what *they* note in their files—and this counts for a lot, but I also believe, from everything I've seen, that the accident of birth is not what finally counts.... Each one of us comes into the world with her or his unique possibility—which is like an aim, or, if you wish, almost like a law. The job of our lives is to become—day by day, year by year, more conscious of this aim so that it can at last be realized. Magadan and Leningrad, geography and history, parents and occupation are accidental. A question of chance. But to beat the accidental, Sacha, is to respect the law and to achieve the aim.

SACHA: And your law, Ernst Moisseevitch, is inscribed under which article of the Constitution?

ERNST: The unfindable one. It's inscribed differently in each one of us—inscribed by God at the same moment as he gave us life.... [*Gricha comes in, sits down. He looks downcast.*]

DACHA: Some tea? What's the matter with you?

GRICHA: Fucked. Can't sleep. Can't sleep a wink. I just lie on my back thinking. I don't want to depress you, last thing I want to do—but I've discovered something which concerns us all.

The door is flung open and a young woman rushes in. Apparently drunk. Dishevelled hair. Unknown to anyone present.

YOUNG WOMAN: Can someone help me? Please, someone. They told me there might be a doctor here. Is there?

ERNST: I'm a doctor.

YOUNG WOMAN: Where have they taken him, tell me, Doctor, where? Can't you, Doctor, can't you give me back my life? He's disappeared, gone, and his shoes are still under the bed. Where have they put his feet, Doctor?.... How many steps? He'll never be late now. And I can't go to the port bar to bring him home. On my two feet, alone, I can't keep going, for how long, Doctor? [*Dacha places a chair behind the young woman and makes her sit.*] It would be easier with one foot, wouldn't it? It would be over sooner. When he came home, we drank a glass each, and we had four feet. He said: Forget it, forget it, Hushaby, I love your freckles, and I said: I want a child.... [*Dacha places her hands on the Young Woman's back.*] He has a habit of scratching his right ear with his left hand. If you see him, Doctor, you'll recognize him. How do they open their own veins? Don't think about it, he told me, have a drink and forget it, Hushaby. Yes, yes. Don't think, no. It is so so hard to say Yes. [*She leans her head back against Dacha's breast.*] Where should I go with a pain like mine to get papers for it? If I find a squirrel, I'll kill it. Two squirrels I'm going to kill, to make him a *chapka.* [*She gets up and walks steadily towards the door.*] He lost his *chapka* last spring. Yes, yes, he must have a *chapka,* yes.

GRICHA: What's his name, please?

YOUNG WOMAN: The same as mine.

She leaves. Dacha, exhausted, grasps the back of the chair on which the Young Woman was sitting. Ernst and Sacha lead her to the bed where she sits down. Ernst puts his arm round her shoulders and sits beside her.

GRICHA: Forget it! Forget it! Not bad advice. Soon it'll be our turn. I know what's happening, I know everything now. Once, the first time, they accused us, they brought a case against us, they forced us to confess, there was a prosecution. This time it's much simpler, as simple as the A B C. They need labour and they're not getting enough from the Continent, and so they're taking us back inside, and it doesn't matter what article we were arrested under. This time it's by alphabetical order. Last week it was the As, this week it's the Bs, it's as simple as A ... B ... C.

DACHA: Poor girl! For her it's the beginning and it's already an eternity.

GRICHA: Next week it will be the Cs, then the Ds. Between their alphabetical order and their geography they have us well and truly fucked.

SACHA: Sshhh....

GRICHA: As for you, Sachinka, listen to your old friend for once. Get the hell out of here, as soon as you can make it. It'll be one worry less for your mother.

SACHA: There are three people living on this earth whom I really care about. They're my world, and they are here.

Gricha leaves almost on tip-toe. Ernst and Dacha are still on the bed. Sacha, very quietly, goes to where the door of his room is leaning against the wall, picks it up, carries it to the doorframe and lowers it on to its hinges.

DACHA: What is it you're doing, Sacha?

SACHA: I'm staying! And if you want to get rid of me, you'll have to carry me out tied to my door!

ERNST: [*He puts his arm round Dacha and speaks to Sacha.*] She had pneumonia when she arrived. She was just one among the other feverish and exhausted bodies. So many arrivals and departures. Some get better, others don't, and the difference between them is so slight. You, you slept all the time. I had four hours sleep a night. Little by little you slept less. And when she could get out of bed, she worked as my nurse. Once I said to her: If all nurses were like you... and she laughed and replied: I was born under the sign of Pisces. In the women's ward of the hospital of Camp 102, you slept in the bed against the wall by the door, and my bed was just on the other side of the wall. One night, you made your way out of the ward, and you came to me, your hands smelling of hay and honey. It was the winter of '44.

DACHA: No, Ernst, it was already the month of April '44. Even with the snow, the air smelt of spring.

6

Two or three days later. Evening. Dacha is ironing. Sacha is lying on his stomach on her bed. While reading, he cracks hazelnuts with his teeth, and eats them.

DACHA: Why don't you read Katya's letter?

SACHA: Later.

DACHA: You shouldn't break the nuts with your teeth.

SACHA: Do you want me to break them with *your* teeth?

DACHA: Find a stone.

SACHA: Takes too long. Why don't you let me read?

DACHA: When you see Katya, please tell her about Ernst.

SACHA: Why do you go on? I've never seen anyone so pig-headed. The two of you, you and Ernst, you make a real pair. Leningrad is finished. Do you understand?

DACHA: [*Arranging what she has ironed on the shelves in the cupboard.*] Look, Sachinka, you have to look now—here on this side are your things. Do you want to make me angry? Listen for once! Here are Ernst's things, here are yours. The household things are on the top shelf.

SACHA: Why do you tell me all that. I know it.

DACHA: Ernst can't tell the difference between a clean shirt and a dirty one.

SACHA: On others, yes, on himself, no.

DACHA: He's like a baby. You must explain to him…. Where in God's name have I hidden my fur boots? Where? This dress could do with an iron. [*Dacha takes out a dress on a coat-hanger and hangs it on top of the open cupboard door. She still hasn't found her boots. Kneeling on the floor, she pulls out a suitcase from under the bed on which Sacha is lying.*] Where, for heaven's sake?

SACHA: What's it you're looking for?

DACHA: My fur boots.

SACHA: We're only at the end of the month of August and she's looking for her fur boots.

DACHA: They need repairing and Ernst has found a man who can do it. If he takes them tonight, they'll be ready in ten days.

Two sharp knocks on the door. Sacha sits up. Dacha still on her knees, buries her head in her son's lap. For an instant.

DACHA: Who is it?

She gets to her feet, opens the door. Enter two Bruise. Sacha stands by the door of his room. The First Bruise hands Dacha a blue paper; she glances at it.

FIRST BRUISE: It's just for a routine check.

DACHA: It was always just for a routine check. No?

The Second Bruise goes to the open cupboard and searches between the clothes, throwing some on the floor. He finds the wad of bank notes tied with string.

SECOND BRUISE: And this—what is it?

DACHA: Some money. In fact, the money for my son's return ticket to Leningrad—I applied for, and received, the authorization for him to spend his school holidays here. He's leaving in a few days.

SECOND BRUISE: We'll see.

The First Bruise examines the wad of money which his colleague has thrown on the table. The Second Bruise, having finished with the cupboard, now goes to the bookshelf and finds the letter from Serge.

SECOND BRUISE: And this document, what is it?

DACHA: A letter from my husband—postmarked Vorkovta.

FIRST BRUISE: It seems then you have two husbands.

DACHA: I don't understand.

FIRST BRUISE: It's clear enough. You have one husband here and another in Vorkovta. [*The Second Bruise picks up the triptych and puts it on the table. The First Bruise opens it, and they both look at it together.*]

SECOND BRUISE: A religious object, used for worship. It's clear. Are you a Baptist?

DACHA: Baptist! Why should I be a Baptist any more than you?

FIRST BRUISE: You believe in God?

DACHA: I don't see the connection.

SECOND BRUISE: It's with this that you say your prayers.

DACHA: Prayers? Why prayers?

FIRST BRUISE: Then explain what you use it for! Explain yourself!

DACHA: On your left, you see a Madonna by Leonardo da Vinci, the so-called *Little Madonna,* fifteenth century; in the middle you can see *The Flight into Egypt* by Nicolas Poussin, seventeenth century, French school; on your right you find David's *Farewell to Jonathan,* painted by Rembrandt, seventeenth century, Dutch. All three pictures are to be found in the Hermitage Museum in Leningrad.

SECOND BRUISE: We're confiscating it.

DACHA: No! You have no right.

FIRST BRUISE: How did you come by these treasures. Were they stolen?

SACHA: It was me. I brought these pictures from Leningrad for my mother.

FIRST BRUISE: Did you buy them? How much did you pay for them?

SACHA: I tore them out of the art magazine *Iskustva.* If you look carefully, you'll see they're cheap reproductions.

SECOND BRUISE: [*Peering close into the triptych.*] They're icons! And disgusting ones! Look. Look at her. Her tits are outside.

DACHA: Even you probably fed at your mother's breast.

FIRST BRUISE: You're all the same, all of you 58s. You think you're clever. I wasn't born yesterday. This object smells of priests. [*He turns round to address Sacha.*] As for you, citizen, you'd better leave without another word.

DACHA: Please give me five minutes. In five minutes I'll be ready, there's no need for anger, nobody is tricking you, nobody is trying to get the better of you. My son is leaving in a few days, and I'll be leaving in five minutes with you. You can be sure, I am ready, everything is ready, there's no need for anything more.

She places her hands very lightly on the shoulders of the First Bruise. He rises to his feet slowly and both Bruise move towards the open door where they wait, leaning against the door frame. Dacha lays out a large scarf on the table, throws her clothes into it, makes a bundle, ties a knot, and approaches Sacha.

DACHA: Beneath so many closed eyes the sleep of no one.... [*She stuffs the wad of money into his pocket.*] Take the plane, my boy, from the airport of Magadan. And never forget: it isn't over. [*She goes to the door, changes into her outdoor shoes and whispers, beside the two Bruise.*] It isn't over. It's not finished. It's not the end. [*She leaves, without turning back to look at Sacha. The two Bruise shut the door behind them. Sacha alone, looks round the room, surveying the disorder.*]

SACHA: [*Picking up his father's letter, re-inserting it into a book.*] And the money, where's it gone? [*He looks on the floor.*] They left it on the table. [*He puts the triptych back into its place.*] Where could it have gone? [*The corner of the suitcase under the bed catches his eye, he pulls it out, looks inside, holds up something wrapped in newspaper.*] The boots she was looking for! [*A boot in each hand, he hesitates, then places them deliberately on the table and goes back to kick the suitcase under the bed. He begins to tidy the wardrobe cupboard.*] Bastards! 'On his side are your things. Here are Ernst's things. The household things are on the top shelf. You must explain to him. He can't tell the difference between a clean shirt and a dirty one. You must explain to him.' [*Suddenly the light is switched on. Ernst stands in the doorway.*]

ERNST: Dacha! Where is Dacha? [*He approaches Sacha by the wardrobe, and puts his suitcase on the table; from his string bag he takes out a loaf of bread and some potatoes.*] Where is Dacha?

SACHA: They came to get her.

ERNST: When?

SACHA: Just now.

ERNST: How many were they?

SACHA: Two.

ERNST: Did they have a warrant?

SACHA: Yes, a bit of blue paper.

ERNST: What did they ask about?

SACHA: The triptych.

ERNST: Nothing else?

SACHA: Father's letter—they found it.

ERNST: Only that?

SACHA: The money. [*He feels in his pockets, finds the wad of notes.*] It was there all the time!

ERNST: Keep the money. What did she take with her?

SACHA: What she had.

ERNST: She didn't take these. [*He takes the boots off the table and places them carefully on the floor beneath the dress. He sits down, pulls up a chair for Sacha.*] Sit down here. You see, now, don't you, you have to leave.

SACHA: I'll wait for her.

ERNST: Yes, in Leningrad.

SACHA: And you?

ERNST: I've a bed at the hospital.

SACHA: If I stay, you'll have a home every night.

ERNST: Home?

SACHA: It's something, isn't it? [*Ernst puts his head between his hands and sobs. Sacha looks at him for a moment, then tip-toes into his room, leaving the door open.*]

ERNST: Sacha... Sacha. [*He looks around the room. Gets up slowly. Puts the chair back under the table. Walks towards Sacha's door.*] I don't want to disturb you...

SACHA: 'I don't want to disturb you.' Sometimes you make me laugh Ernst Moisseevitch!

ERNST: [*Entering Sacha's room.*] Tomorrow you must put your name down for the school. You know where it is?

SACHA: I know.

ERNST: You must send a telegram to your aunt.

SACHA: We must get Mother's boots repaired.

ERNST: I'll deal with them tonight. Take care of the money—it should be enough for three months.

SACHA: Special care....

THE WINNER OF THE FOOKER PRIZE

BY GUY KENNAWAY

In an isolated Maltese bar, a young, neglected
and starving author ekes out a living — by the
consumption, each night, of the most nauseating
and inedible substances…

£7.95   HARDBACK

**Guy Kennaway is a young writer whose first novel, I
CAN FEEL IT MOVING, was published earlier this
year to considerable critical acclaim.**

'a tour de force' THE SUNDAY TELEGRAPH
'consistently funny' BOOKS & BOOKMEN
'quite excellent' PUBLISHING NEWS

QUARTET BOOKS LIMITED   A Member of the Namara Group
27/29 Goodge Street London W1   Tel: 01 636 3992

METHUEN FOR LITERATURE

Contemporary Writers

Iris Murdoch

RICHARD TODD

Iris Murdoch, widely regarded as one of the major British novelists of her generation, is undoubtedly one of the most popular and prolific, having published twenty-one novels since 1954. This study surveys all Iris Murdoch's fiction to date and shows how her fundamental theme, the interplay between the roles of artist and saint, is developed and expressed in her fiction.

112 pages   Paperback   0 416 35420 3   £2.25

Malcolm Lowry

RONALD BINNS

This study considers the significance of the autobiographical elements in Lowry's writing, in the context of his developing concern with fictionality and the romantic sensibility. Special attention is given to *Under the Volcano* together with a survey of Lowry's late experimental novels and stories. Finally, there is an appendix on the recent film of *Under the Volcano*.

96 pages   Paperback   0 416 37750 6   £2.25

Patrick White

JOHN COLMER

Patrick White is a giant among the moderns. His massive novels challenge orthodox notions about fiction and reality. He has created a wholly new kind of prose to embody his prophetic visions of truth and his fierce denunciations of modern society. This study uses fresh autobiographical material, reveals the links between the plays and fiction and stresses White's vision of duality rather than his much praised affirmations of harmony. This is the first study of the Nobel Prize winning Australian to survey all his published works.

96 pages   Paperback   0 416 36790 9   £2.25

New Accents

Metafiction
The theory and practice of self-conscious fiction

PATRICIA WAUGH

Metafiction surveys the state of contemporary fiction in Britain and America and explores the political, social and economic factors which affect critical judgement. Patricia Waugh demonstrates how, in laying bare their own processes of artificial construction, 'self-conscious' texts suggest the ways in which our sense of reality is itself fabricated. The book draws on material from sociology, philosophy and linguistics as well as contemporary literary theory, and suggests the lines along which fiction might develop in future.

192 pages

Hardback   0 416 32630 7   £8.95   Paperback   0 416 32640 4   £3.95

METHUEN
11 New Fetter Lane, London EC4P 4EE

REINALDO ARENAS
COMING DOWN FROM
THE MOUNTAINS

I put on my only nice, dressy dress—I just finished ironing it. I turn on the radio, not too loud, and remain in the dining-room listening to Pedro Infante sing, looking at Hector standing there, in the middle of the garden. What can I do, how can I make him aware that I want to help him?

I write a letter full of foolish things. Read it, and tear it up. I listen to the radio—now Miguel Aceres Mejía is the one singing—and look at you there in the yard while evening falls. I hear my mother rattling around in the kitchen; she's making (*creating*) dinner. Soon I'll turn on the dining-room light, turn off the radio and help set the table. The three of us will sit on our stools. And an unbearable feeling will come with the smell of the food and fill us with fury.

My mother, acting like she doesn't have a conniving bone in her body, *pretending,* will ask Hector again whether there are still no jobs at the factory and when they plan to reopen and whether it wouldn't be a good idea to go look for a job someplace else. Finally she says a friend of hers, an 'acquaintance', told her they needed waiters in who knows what restaurant and tomorrow bright and early he ought to go and start work.

Okay, uh-huh, he says, as he eats.

The next day he goes. They'll try him out for a week. At the end of a week they tell him they don't need him.

And now I hear my mother shouting in the dining-room again. He's a dimwit, she says. The owner of the restaurant told her 'acquaintance' that he was too distracted. He needed a boy who was awake, not a slack-jawed fool people walked out on without paying, who was always breaking glasses and spilling milkshakes and generally being clumsy. It's as if he was living on the moon. And these days, she says even louder, you can't live on the moon. Living right here, even with your feet on the ground, is hard enough now. And she goes on talking, now calling him a moron, a lazy good-for-nothing....

I turn up the radio. Pedro Infante's voice fills the whole house and I start to sing along with Pedro Infante so Hector won't hear the rumpus my mother is making. But it's no use. He's probably heard it all, and he's still standing there in the garden, while the afternoon lengthens, not saying a word, because he never says a word. Why doesn't he ever say anything?... Holy Virgin, tell me, how can I help him if he runs away from me, if he acts like he doesn't even want to see my face? Sometimes I think he doesn't need anyone. But perhaps that isn't true. Perhaps he needs everyone but no one understands him. If only one day he'd come in and beat my mother and smash the radio and set the whole house on fire. If only he'd do *something.* But he doesn't do a thing.... After dinner he goes to his room and starts reading or lies on his back in bed, while Mama takes the fly-sprayer (just like my grandfather did) and fills the house with that awful smell. And I sit on the porch watching the people go by, saying hello, because everyone in this town knows everyone else. I lie in bed too, unsleeping, thinking, trying to think what he's thinking, but I can't...

Dear Mary,

   Don't let my mother find out, but I'm in love with my cousin Hector, and there's nothing I can do to make myself fall out of love with him or make him fall in love with me. And I cry, for him and for myself, but especially for him, because he's a man and it must be terrible to be a man these days. If a woman is insulted she can just break down and cry or ask for help. But what can he do when they insult him? And he's not like the rest. They know how to defend themselves; they have those angry words always cocked and ready, those threatening looks they're always stabbing you with. You have to watch out for that kind, they never let an opportunity slip to fondle you or say something crude....

We are at the annual gala at the Vista Alegre Club. Everyone is dancing. The young men who didn't bring a girl find one immediately, or steal their friends', and go off into the darkest corners. And they do it all in such a natural way (as when they drink beer right out of the bottle) that the world seems made for them, and they understand that, and behave according to those rules, *their* rules. They *fit in,* I think. They're *in their element,* I think. But he is standing in one corner of the room with his hands in his pockets, gazing blankly into space, as though he were in another world. I know (and that is the worst part) that he's not in another world, but in this one, amid the hullabaloo and laughter, and that he's making a real effort to put up with it all. That, at least, I know. When the song is over I excuse myself to my partner (who smiles as though to say, It's all the same to me, I'll find somebody else) and go over to where he's standing.

Let's dance, I say to him. And I take him by the hand. I lead him to the centre of the room. While the organ plays I put a hand on his shoulder and draw him little by little towards me. My other hand clasps his sweating hand; I put my head on his shoulder and let my hair touch his lips. He marks off the steps stiffly, as though he's afraid he'll step on my feet, and he doesn't say a word.

We go back home. I open the door and like always Mama is waiting up for us. Is this any hour to be coming home?

I don't answer her. I go to my room; I undress and lie in bed. I hear her spraying the house and then turning off the lights. In the darkness, it's easier to think. Everything is hidden, blotted out, and although there's no consolation there's nothing noisy or bright or quick either.... I think He is there, next door. Merely by going down the hall I would be in his room. Our Father, I say. Our Father. Our Father, and as I pray I think He is there, just two walls away. Our Father, and he's probably awake, with the lights on.... When at last I say Amen, I am still thinking about him, still seeing him, there, alone. And just about to get out of bed and just, on tiptoe, touching the walls, going down the hall. Our Father, Our Father, if I just went out into the hall and then into his room. Holy Mary, sweet Mary....

Sleep comes over me, but not suddenly—little by little rather, without my realizing it. The noise of my mother in the kitchen wakes me. Her voice vying with the crash of the pots she is furiously throwing on the fire.

Now there's *really* no way out for us, she says, coming into my room, forcing me to listen to her.

Way out, way out, I say to myself aloud, almost laughing, thinking, Has there ever been a way out for us?

Things are going from bad to worse, she goes on, not paying me any heed. The rebels are everywhere, in everything, everything is blockaded. Now we'll *really* starve to death.

So much the better, I say. If they're everywhere that means this can't last much longer then.

She laughs and says, Do you really think it'll topple, just like that? The government has the weapons. What can a rebel mob do without weapons? Eat cows and ruin everything! That's what they're doing, screwing the country up worse every day....

121

Suddenly, hearing her talk like that fills me with fear, not because of what she's saying but because of the way she says it. Anyway, I never pay any mind to what my mother says, only to the way she says it. And what's more there is always some war or other going on here, an attack, some kind of revolution, some monkey business.... At last I reach the conclusion that no war will have any bearing on whether Hector looks at me or not, listens to me or not, guesses how much I think about him. And so I tell myself, *It's all the same to me, it's all the same to me.* But whether I want to or not, I have to hear all about it, have virtually to be part of it all. They are out there, somewhere. They take such and such a town. They now control such and such a province. It topples.... At last I begin to feel a kind of hope, not fully hope because it doesn't make me happy, but at least it shakes me. And it's precisely because, as my mother says, things are getting worse every day. Closed shops, people going off to the mountains. Every second I hear someone say, The canefields are burning, the country is in ruins....

Ruins! Ruins! I close myself up in the bathroom and begin to say the word out loud, laughing at the same time. What on earth do I care whether the country is 'in ruins', what does that mean to me? And I laugh out loud. Although I can see that it's all true. Mama rages more every day. Finally we can eat only once a day, and not much at that. *Ruins! Ruins!* And I laugh and think something, somehow, has to happen. But he is the only thing I worry about.

He speaks less than ever now, although every day my mother is more awful to him and now even says to his face that he has to go find a job, he's the man of the house. And she says the word 'man' so it sounds like an insult. But he, what can he do? What can he say? Where's he going to go?

In bed again. The house totally dark. The reek of insecticide drowning everything. There is the sound of shots, a great roar, the racket of police-car sirens, cries. And he is there, just two walls away from my room, as alone as anyone will ever be, for he has never lost anything because he has never had anyone.... Shots, closer now—it sounds as though the world is coming to an end. And I wonder what he thinks of the world. I sit on the edge of the bed; I sit very still, listening to the uproar. I hear my mother's snoring. I stand up and walk into the hall. I come to the door of Hector's room. The light is on. He is sitting on the edge of the bed with his hands over his face. I stand just a moment at the door and immediately go back to my room. And lie down. Our Father who art in heaven, if only he'd come to my room, if I weren't the one who had to go to him. If only he had come, slowly, barefoot, and pushed open the door. I don't latch it anymore. You don't have to say a word, you don't have to speak—just come in. But you won't come. I will grow old in this house stinking of mosquito-spray, watching the door that he's not ever going to push open.

Finally, the first light of day. I am exhausted. I get up and dress. Before my mother starts yelling at me I'm already polishing furniture, surprised that he still hasn't got up. I finish scrubbing the floor with water and a broom, polishing the tiles; I think—any second now, since he's still in bed, Mama will start fussing and yelling at him to get up, even if it's just to irritate him. And now that I've finished scrubbing down the porch too I begin to feel another worry: Why don't you get up? Perhaps he's sick, really sick perhaps.... I walk down the hall carrying the pail and come to the door of his room.

He isn't there. The bed is empty. The sheets, smoothed over, cover the pillow. Books on the night table. Everything neat, but he isn't there. Where can he have gone so early? I think. When could he have gone without my noticing? I go into the room once more. I open the chest, even look under the bed. Then when I am about to leave, I find a piece of paper on the sheet, next to the pillow. *Dear Aunt, I am going with the rebels, because I'm not doing anything here. Don't let yourselves worry over me.* That's what the piece of paper says. I read it again.

Mama, I say, and I don't know whether I'm happy or sad; happy I think. Mama, come here. She comes in. I show her the note.

He's crazy, she says, throwing the piece of paper down on the bed. I think this war is stupid. That miserable moron, he's as good as dead.

Shut up, I tell her, and I think, That's the first time I ever shouted at her. They're not going to kill him.

How do *you* know? she answers, what do you two know about war? Everybody here has gone absolutely crazy. She goes into the hall, walks all over the house saying, Now we'll really be 'disgraced', they'll come and search the house. That's all we needed, she says, furious and sarcastic at once, a 'rebel' in the family. Now they'll really come down on us.

I follow her around, shushing her, telling her everybody in the neighbourhood will find out. But she goes on yelling, complaining, thinking only about us, about herself. And when she furiously repeats, convinced, certain, that we can give him up for dead, that he'll have no idea how to defend himself, he's never known how to do anything, much less use a weapon, or fight, I feel such hatred for her, my God, that I walk off and leave her talking to herself, and I go into the living room....

You did it, I think. I'm glad you did it. And I read the note once more.

I think about what my mother said and see that, in a certain way, she may be right. He is so clumsy about everything—about everything that everyone else does so naturally. What will he do in that new life, which must be just as unbearable and even more dangerous than this one? Yes, you must think about it all. You have to think that he may be killed, that he may already be dead and you'll never see him again. You must think about it all....

If he'd been with *us* he'd never have done this crazy thing! I hear someone shout at the front door. It is Adolfina, my aunt (accompanied by her little monsters Tico and Anisia), who has found out about it all and blames my mother for everything that has happened. She shoves her aside and comes up to me, cuffing me too and grabbing the note. And now she runs into the street shouting, so everybody knows, so he can never even come home again if things don't go well out there. And Tico and Anisia right behind, yelling even louder and laughing like crazy.

Holy Virgin, help me, because I don't want them to see me cry. And I don't cry. And I devote myself to waiting for you, Hector. For I know perfectly well that you will come back. I know it. You must. If not, what sense would any of this make? You are going to come back. And so I wait....

The rebels have cut the power lines. We are sitting in the living room, my mother and I, by the light of a candle that she has made herself out of a piece of soap. Mama is in the rocking chair. When she speaks, it's to complain. What a New Year's Eve, she says. I've never seen such a sad New Year's Eve in my whole life. She goes to the front door and opens it. She stands a moment by the door and then suddenly slams it. We may as well go to bed, she says.

I undress in the dark and lie down. The gunfire can be heard more clearly now. The sound of a plane, too, crossing over the town. Then the bombardment. Sometimes the smell of wet dirt comes in the window. I don't know where it comes from, since it hasn't rained for months. So, lying there, I try to figure out where that smell comes from, until dawn begins to break....

In this town, the only sound early in the morning is the crowing of roosters. First one, far off; then another, this time closer, answers him. And so the roof-raising chorus little by little takes shape. And at last, daylight. But at this moment a different sound is heard. Like shouting, the roar of thousands of voices that seem to sing, shout *Vivas,* cheer. In nothing but the slip which I have thrown on, I go into the living room. Hundreds of people are coming out on to their porches, gathering at corners. From over there a kind of parade appears, the demonstrators carrying a flag, the rebels' flag—if you're caught carrying this, it can cost you your life.

The murderer is gone! someone shouts.

It all becomes clear to me. I run to Mama's room. She is already awake; she gets out of bed and opens the front door.

Be careful! she shouts at a group of men on the porch, you're going to mess up my flower beds!

I run cheering into the street too. I run towards a commotion centred on several rebels. But Hector is not one of them. I run in and out of all the groups. I run right through the town. I don't go back home till the afternoon. Mama is nervously watching the garden. She looks fearfully out of the front door, closes it and goes back to the kitchen.

What a commotion, she says, we'll see what happens.... Your cousin, she finally says, it's strange he hasn't come back.

He'll come, I say, everyone can't come back the same day.

That's true, she says, Lord only knows where he is.

For a moment I don't say anything. Don't say he might be dead, I tell her now, raising my voice, perhaps unnecessarily.

God forgive you for thinking such things, she says now.

You're the one thinking them, I say.

You're rude, she answers. And I keep still. But I know very well that that was what she was thinking. She's always thinking the worst. Maybe by now she's so used to unhappiness that a little hope terrifies her, or confuses her: she wouldn't know what to do with it. But it may be that I'm mistaken; it may be that it's cruel of me to think that of her. Holy Virgin, I am so stunned by all this that I don't even know what I'm saying. Oh, and forgive me for I didn't even remember to thank you.

The next day. There are more rebels coming down from the mountains than yesterday. I ask them about him. But they know nothing. There are so many, they say, that the whole army won't be here for a week at least. I go back. My mother, calmer, is making dinner.

Today there's less food than ever, she says. With this mess of people I couldn't get anything.

I don't answer. I go to the dining-room and turn on the radio. Some woman is reciting a patriotic poem. I don't know whether this poem is good or bad—no doubt it's dreadful—but I listen and am filled with happiness. So night comes. The two of us are sitting once more in the living room.

What they have to do, says my mother, is get the food out and straighten things up once and for all.

They'll get everything straightened out soon, I say, and go on rocking, pumping with the tips of my toes, faster and faster.

You're crazy, Mama says, behave yourself. I go on rocking until, now later in the evening, she stands up. He isn't coming today, she says.

That's what you think. I'm going to stay up a while longer, I say. I hear her spraying all the bedrooms.

I undress slowly, listening for every sound. Someone is coming down the street, getting closer; he passes by the front of the house, and goes on. There is nothing to be heard now; just, in the darkness, the racket of the victrolas in Loma Colorada barrio, and the organ lording it over all the other noises. The bars in 'La Frontera' have opened again. That's where, so my mother tells me, the whorehouses are. Sometimes you can hear loud yelling (*It's a fight*) mixed with the screams and laughter of the women. The music from a victrola can be heard more clearly now that the organ has stopped. It's some vulgar song, in fashion for two or three months and then no one will remember it. Sometimes, I'm such a silly fool, I've cried listening to those songs; sometimes, silly fool, I've caught myself singing those songs....

I think I heard a tap on the window. Maybe he has come back. Or it might be a cricket. I think—I'm sure now—the tapping is repeated. I listen. Holy Virgin, the taps are soft, as though not to make too much noise, as though not to call attention to themselves, as though barely to be heard. Only I hear them, no one else. Who could tap like that? Who could be tapping that way, so softly, as though not to be heard? I jump into my clothes and run to the living room. I open the door. And he is there, on the porch, in his faded uniform, a rickety rifle, and a beard that's not a beard, laughing. Laughing, but not loud.

Mama, I say then. Hector's here.

And I laugh. I laugh like he does and I am entranced, looking at him.

Son! says Mama with a long shriek, and runs to the door where he is standing, still undecided whether to come in, waiting for me to tell him at last to come in. Son! my mother repeats once more, hugging him. And I am embarrassed to hear her say that word; it sounds so ridiculous coming from her. She hugs him again, she kisses him. She starts to cry. At last she leads him to the dining room, talking constantly. Oh, how worried she was, how happy she is now. Me, behind. Looking at him. Looking at his uniform, his skin tanned dark brown.

While Mama begins to prepare him something to eat I sit down next to him on a stool. The two of us are silent. And I am glad he doesn't tell me anything. We remain like that while my mother serves the improvised lunch (or breakfast), always talking, asking questions, chattering nonsense.

He answers everything, practically without saying a word. Yes, he says. No, he says.

Now you'll be able to get a good job, which is something we all could really do with, says my mother, when we're finishing the meal.

And I realize that all her unctuousness, every word, has had a purpose, a precise, utilitarian end, that it was more than simple hypocrisy. How can she be so self-seeking? How can she be so selfish? But suddenly I'm sorry I thought such a thing. She's not young anymore. After all, she has the right to think of her own security. But she goes on talking to him, giving him advice, hounding him. He mustn't let this chance go by, hurry and get a good position.

And he says uh-huh, uh-huh.

I get up and go into the living room. But the neighbours come in, embrace him too, ask him a million questions. He has to show them his rifle, give them lessons in assembling and dismantling it. He does everything slowly, hoarsely, clumsily.

Be careful with that gun, 'Son', says my mother.

And once more her words sound to me utterly false. I watch Hector manipulating some lever on the gun—I don't know what it's called. The shells fall on the floor and scatter all over the living room. He bends over to pick them up. I see his hands, and realize they're sweaty. And I think, He's the same, the same, Holy Virgin, the same man who left. He hasn't changed. And suddenly I begin to feel a sadness such as I've almost never known and then, without knowing why, I am happy.

I stand up in the middle of the living room and speak. You must be tired, you should rest. And I look at the neighbours.

Yes, he says, but I think I'll have a bath first.

I'll start it for you right now, says my mother. And she rushes out.

He says goodbye to the neighbours and goes into the bathroom. Holy Virgin, before he goes in he looks at me and smiles—although not much—and it is a smile of complicity, as though he were saying I don't give a damn about any of this....

I put on my best dress, my best shoes, apply powder and lipstick. When I come out of my bedroom he's standing at the front door, his hair combed and his uniform on, waiting for me.

Where are you going? says my mother.

For a walk, I answer, already taking his arm.

But Hector, she says—ignoring me—aren't you even going to wait for your coffee?

No, I answer for him, we'll get some somewhere....

An endless parade passes through the streets. There are loudspeakers on the corner that pour out one patriotic anthem after another. Everyone looks at us and smiles—looks at him, so young in his uniform. Some people say hello although they don't even know him. We finally come to the highway through the mob of cars, bicycles and milling people. Although we don't talk it's as though we were chatting about everything. Pushing, knocking against people and saying excuse me, we come to the centre of town. In one corner of Calixto García Park a large crowd has gathered. Everyone is angry. Some women are jumping up and down and shaking their fists, others are throwing rocks. Hector and I walk over to the disturbance. Several rebels are training their rifles on the crowd, protecting a sweaty man it wants to lynch. Some people manage to dodge around the guard and give him a kick.

Shoot him, he's a murderer! yells an old woman.

To the wall! To the wall! everyone shouts now.

Finally the rebels, protecting him with their weapons, take him away. They cross the park. The procession grows larger and larger as it moves along. We join in too, as I keep holding tight to Hector's arm. Both of us in silence. The crowd follows the rebels to the walled jail where, as I now learn, they have already executed several war criminals.... We enter along with everyone else. We cross the courtyard and at the far end see the high wall that fences in the compound and now serves as the firing-squad's backdrop. Everyone clusters around. Some people have climbed up into the trees, others cling to the bars of the windows. Although soon it will be dark it is still terribly hot. I look at Hector and see that he is perspiring too. I try to speak to him, to catch his attention, to tell him that if he wants to, we can leave. But he's not looking at me now. He looks straight ahead, to where the soldiers are now lining up just a few yards from the man.

129

Suddenly, there is silence. A silence in which not even our breathing can be heard. Out of this silence comes the unwavering voice of the criminal who himself directs the firing squad: *Ready!* he orders with an angry, firm voice, still the boss.

The new soldiers obey, raising their rifles. I watch them. They are so young. They wear their uniforms so well. New uniforms, apparently not the ones they wore in the battles. The rifles held to their shoulders.

Aim! The silence is now unbearable. The mob seems to have vanished. No one seems to surround us, and we seem to be alone, Hector and I: there's no sound or space—anything.

FIRE! The word is shouted as though very far away. The bullets shatter the man's head. Blood splashes across the wall. The body, perhaps from the force of the fusillade, stiffens upright, stands on tiptoes. Its arms shake. Its breast, riddled with bullets too, is covered with blood, soaking the shirt. At last it teeters slowly forward and falls....

Viva la Revolución! cries a voice from the crowd. And suddenly everyone (including us) begins to shout. *Viva la Revolución! Viva la Revolución!* People wave hats, handkerchiefs, little flags. Once more the shouting, this time worse than ever.... Mingling in with the mob, we come out into the street. I have to cling tightly to Hector so I don't get lost in all the pushing and jostling.

Let's go, he says. The shouting moves further off. We cross the highway, go through the deserted field near home. And now I realize he hasn't let go of my hand—since who knows when.

It is the middle of the night when we come in. My mother looks troubled, frightened, unsure, but at bottom threatening.

It's late, she says. Come and eat something. But Hector disobeys her for the first time. He lowers his head and goes to his room without looking at her.

We're too tired, I tell Mama. We saw them shoot a man.

Oh God, she says, crossing herself.

I go to the dining-room. As I cross the hallway I see Hector sprawled across the bed still wearing his uniform and his boots.

You two have to eat something, my mother says. I've even made you a dessert.

I don't answer. I go into my room and sit on the bed without turning on the light. I feel almost dizzy and at the same time I'm sorry for Mama and would even like to eat something, just to make her happy, but if I did I think I would be sick. I lie down in the dark. Gradually the man appears. He walks steadily. Ready, he says. Aim, he says. His bloody body teeters and falls beside my bed. I pull the sheets up over my head. Once more the man topples beside me. His skull smashes against the chest, his blood spatters the bed. Holy Virgin, Holy Virgin.... But the words to the prayer will not come, don't flow, will not appear; I don't remember a single prayer. I see only that bloody body which topples once more. I cry out. Did I really cry out? I may have cried out... But no, if I had, my mother would already be here. I'm so terrified I can't even shout. I'm also certain that I didn't cry out then, either. The surprise was so great that I couldn't have. Thank goodness. If I had cried out people might have thought I was a counter-revolutionary. But I'm sure I didn't shout. Not then or now.

And Hector must be thinking the same thing too. Holy Virgin, he's alone in his room, seeing the same thing, not crying out. I listen carefully. I hear only Mama snoring. A strange uneasiness comes over me, different from any fear I ever had before. My mother's snoring is stronger. I stand up. I open the door. I go out into the darkness of the hallway. I walk slowly, touching the walls with my fingertips, tiptoeing, Holy Virgin, so no one will hear me.... I come to his room. The light is on. He is sitting on the bed. Still dressed in his uniform.

Hector, I say.

He turns and looks at me, not surprised, not elated. He simply looks at me.

I go in and put my arms around him. I feel his sweating hands on my back. Still embracing him I say only Hector, Hector. And we cry. But very softly, so no one will hear us. Then we are still. Just holding each other, just together. All night....

How to make
a year
last 13 months!

Buy a subscription to **The Times Literary Supplement**
for a friend or relative as a gift and take advantage of our
special offer of a 13-month subscription (56 issues) for
the price of 12. Simply complete the coupon below and
send it with your cheque or postal order made payable to
Times Newspapers Limited.
*If more than one subscription is required, please enter
details on a separate sheet of paper. Offer applies to U.K.
only. Details of overseas subscriptions are available on
request from the address below.*

TLS
The Times Literary Supplement

Please send a year's subscription to The Times Literary Supplement to:

NAME_____

ADDRESS_____

_____

_____

_____

I enclose my cheque for £30.00 (Cheques made payable to Times
Newspapers Ltd.)

SIGNATURE_____ DATE_____

Address this coupon with your cheque to:
FRANCES GODDARD, The Times Literary Supplement, Priory
House, St John's Lane, London, EC1M 4BX.

GRA

ORVILLE SCHELL
CHINA'S OTHER
REVOLUTION

For anyone familiar with the great cities of Asia, which teem with activity, it was eerie to walk the streets of urban China while Mao still lived. In Chairman Mao's China, all private enterprises, even individual street vendors, had been branded 'tails of capitalism'. And so diligently had the government gone about chopping off these tails that the streets looked as if a neutron-bomb-like device had been detonated, destroying small businesses while leaving everything else intact. There were no kerb-side restaurants with their smells of food wafting in the air, no pedlars hawking their wares, no throngs of shoppers browsing and haggling with merchants on the pavements. The streets of Mao's China were crowded, but with silent, purposeful people, buying the bare necessities of life from dreary state-owned shops or going to and from work.

When I first went to China, in 1975, Mao Zedong and the so-called Gang of Four, led by Mao's wife, Jiang Qing, were still firmly in power. The shadow of the Chinese Communist Party fell across all aspects of life, freezing the Chinese people in a combination of fear and socialist rectitude. Politics was 'in command'. To put one's own interests above those of the Party and the task of 'building socialism' was a dangerous form of heresy. And to be branded a heretic in a land where there were few places to hide and fewer ways to escape was a grim prospect indeed. Should one momentarily forget the Party's dedication to creating a 'new socialist man', who would, in Mao's words 'serve the people' with all his 'heart and soul', slogans were everywhere—on billboards, walls, smoke-stacks, ships, dams, buildings, even mountainsides:

NEVER FORGET CLASS STRUGGLE

CARRY THE REVOLUTION THROUGH TO THE END

DOWN WITH ALL CAPITALIST ROADERS

Travelling in China at that time, I felt as if I had fallen down a well, like Alice into Wonderland, and entered a strange new universe in which all the imperatives of the outside world had been reversed. Whereas other countries eagerly sought to build economic relations with their neighbours, China was dedicated to isolation and self-reliance. Whereas most governments accepted class divisions, China's leaders waged an unceasing battle against them. And while most governments viewed politics as simply one aspect of life, China's leaders viewed it as life itself.

I returned to China several times after Mao's death, in 1976, and I watched as the country cautiously began a cultural transformation. Like a piece of paper in a fire, whose edges slowly burn before the flames finally move inward to incinerate the centre, old-style Chinese Communism was beginning to be consumed by change. Western influences were penetrating China's protective isolationism, creating unlikely contrasts. The Chinese people, once so mute, were beginning to express their curiosity about the outside world. Politics slowly receded in importance as China's leadership implemented a new political 'line', stressing a pragmatic approach to rebuilding the country's economy rather than class struggle.

A new political line is the Chinese Communist equivalent of the Christian notion of being born again. It offers the opportunity to jettison a bungled past and sally forth on a different political course into a better future. This is exactly how Mao Zedong came to power years ago, when the Chinese Revolution was rising from the ashes of traditional China. He and other Leftist intellectuals struggled to detach China from its Confucian past and to regroup the Chinese people behind a new ideology and identity, derived from the teachings of Marx and Lenin.

Now the Chinese Communist Party has declared Mao's political line defunct. Under the leadership of Deng Xiaoping, who consolidated his power in a series of political manoeuvres in the late 1970s, China's doors have been thrown open to the outside world. Militant egalitarianism and class politics have been abandoned in favour of increasing production. 'Black cat, white cat—it's a good cat if it catches mice,' Deng has told his people.

The first stirrings of change became evident in 1979 and 1980. Democracy Wall, on which Peking's activists posted petitions demanding greater freedom, came and went. So-called free markets, where peasants were allowed to sell produce from their recently reinstated private plots, began to appear all over China. The notion of working for one's own benefit rather than for the abstraction of socialism began to be discussed. Incomes started to rise. After 1981, these forces gathered full momentum, and when I first arrived in Peking in July 1983, after an absence of less than two years, I found the streets transformed. I felt as if I were walking back in on a film that had mysteriously speeded up in my absence, so that by the time I regained my seat a whole new plot development had begun; it was hard to imagine how, short of being at war, a country could begin to change so fast.

The Chinese Communist Party has always been fond of using the term *da gao,* which means 'to do something in a big way'—as in 'to build socialism in a big way' or 'to start a mass movement in a big way.' Although the present leaders of China, unlike their predecessors, now view political mass movements as disruptive and unproductive, they have lost none of the old penchant for doing things in a big way. Their current project is the decentralization and decollectivization of the Chinese economy—a radical departure from the past, which they have embraced with an almost desperate optimism and exhilaration.

As I set out my first morning in Peking to walk through the outdoor market that had sprung up on Dongsixi Street, in the quarter known as the East City, the first signs of change I encountered were several 'tails of capitalism'. An old woman squatting on the pavement was selling an ecumenical collection of gilt plaster statues of Buddha and the Virgin Mary. Next to her stood a young man with a tray slung around his neck; he was selling snapshots of singers and movie stars, many of whom lived in Taiwan or Hong Kong. A little further down the street, I saw a man with a tall bamboo pole strapped to his back. Dangling from the pole on a string was a life-size cardboard cutout of a sewing machine, which had a needle affixed to it. Drawing closer, I saw that the man held a small aluminium device shaped like a fighter-bomber, with which he threaded the needle over and over with masterly ease. 'Just amazing, I tell you!' he was saying in a throaty, rapid-fire rap like that of a street card sharp. 'There's nothing like it on the market! It saves time! Cannot be purchased at a shop! Would you like one or two?' At this point in his pitch, he paused and, holding the aluminium gismo up in the air, gazed in turn at several women in the onlooking throng. Sales were brisk. Next in line on the pavement was an old man who sat patiently and silently on a tiny wooden stool before a motley offering of medicinal bones, roots, and herbs spread out on a back issue of the *Worker's Daily.* Nearby, a severe-looking middle-aged woman sold a Chinese version of typists' white-out. As a knot of curious people gathered around her, she bent over a pad of paper and inscribed a

Chinese character with a traditional writing brush and ink. Then, taking some liquid from a large brown bottle, she swabbed the paper, making the black character vanish in an instant.

On a short street that runs towards the People's Market, the pavements were chock-a-block with small booths, all displaying retailers' licences on cloth banners—a formality most of the more itinerant pedlars ignored. These booths were constructed of boards laid across trestles or were simply set up on the backs of the bicycle carts in which the goods were hauled to and from the makeshift market each day. An elaborate patchwork of plastic tarpaulins was stretched overhead to keep out the scorching sun and the occasional shower. Most of these merchants sold clothing, with a heavy emphasis on T-shirts—an item of apparel which young Chinese are particularly fond of these days. T-shirts made in Hong Kong or abroad confer the most status on a wearer. One youth I spotted in Beihai Park—formerly a preserve of the Imperial family—wore a T-shirt inscribed with the message 'UNCLE SAM'S MISGUIDED CHILDREN, BEIJING, CHINA.' A Chinese construction worker who was working on the remodelling of the International Club wore a T-shirt marked 'DEPARTMENT OF COMMERCE, NARCOTICS SQUAD'. Perhaps the most popular T-shirt—so popular in fact, that I could not find one anywhere in Peking to buy for myself—showed a picture of a bodybuilder's naked torso. Beneath one flexed arm were written the words 'VIGOROUS AND GRACEFUL.'

In fact, as recently as June 1982, *China Youth News* had run an article declaring that young Chinese who wore T-shirts imprinted with such English-language messages as 'KISS ME' or 'USA', were guilty of 'ignorance, exhibitionism and spiritual pollution'. The Communist Youth League paper denounced Chinese shops which printed and sold such T-shirts, saying that they were 'catering to some people's blind worship of foreign things and a base taste for profit.' These efforts evidently did not amount to much.

As I neared the corner, two dissolute-looking youths wearing dark glasses arrived with a bicycle cart and began setting up shop beside the kerb. They were selling what looked like men's shirts in bright-coloured plaids. Since men in China do not ordinarily wear bright colours such as red—these are reserved for women and children—I walked over to the cart for a closer inspection. Unlike the other vendors, these two young men displayed no licence. When I examined the label on one of their shirts, I saw the name Sears, and when I asked them who their supplier was they just looked at each other with sly smiles and laughed.

At the end of T-shirt alley, I spotted a pedicab, its driver dozing on the passenger seat while he awaited a fare. I was surprised to see a pedicab; these small, rickshaw-like conveyances, which are powered by a man on a bicycle rather than on foot, had long been banned in China. The image of one human being straining on a bicycle to haul another human being around was one that came too close to suggesting the old exploitative society the Communists had set out to transform with their revolution. But sensitivity to such socialist niceties is evidently on the wane, for, as I watched, a potato-shaped woman, carrying several net bags bulging with food and packages, rudely tapped the driver on the chest with her fan and woke him up. After haggling over the price, she heaved her bulk into the pedicab and barked an order, and a moment later they were off, the calf muscles of the driver flexing as he struggled to get his vehicle moving. It was the first time I had seen such a sight since the early seventies.

After a long absence, a private sector is rapidly reappearing in China's economy, and a new class of privately employed Chinese is beginning to appear along with it. In October of 1981, Party and government leaders gave their official blessing to the proliferation of private businesses. In the first six months of 1983, retail sales by state-owned commercial enterprises were two and a half per cent higher than they had been in the same period in 1981, whereas sales by private businesses that had bothered to get government licences were 110 per cent higher. There are now privately run repair shops for television sets and radios, bicycles and motorcycles. Private barbers and shoemakers work in almost every neighbourhood, and myriad pedlars and repairmen, with their distinctive cries, have once again begun to roam the city's back alleys. Private tailors are the fashion among those who can afford them. Cooks, maids and nannies—once considered bourgeois affectations—are becoming commonplace in the households of middle-income families as well as in those of wealthy professionals.

In fact, in February 1984, the *Economic Daily*, a Shanghai-published newspaper covering finance, printed an article by Yang Zhengyan, the Deputy Secretary General of the Beijing Municipal Government, extolling the establishment of the newly founded

Housework Service Company, the capital's first privately run agency dedicated to finding jobs for domestics. In his article, 'The Question of Housekeepers and the Socialization of Housework', Yang noted: 'Although the employment of household help was criticized as gentrified, bourgeois, and exploitative during the Cultural Revolution, in reality such employment cannot be abolished.'

Why not?

'The current tendency is for people to want to have less housework, and more time for work, study, and recreation,' Yang explained, concluding that for those who could afford them, maids in China were now 'an inevitable phenomena of today's urban social life.'

In March 1984 the *Beijing Daily* reported that the Housework Service Company already had 2,500 customers and was getting 'loud applause' from city residents, who had already reportedly employed more than 30,000 live-in maids, many of them imported from poor rural areas.

Entrepreneurs are starting to open up small private inns, which Chinese travellers often prefer, because these establishments are cheaper than the state-run hotels and sometimes offer meals at no extra charge. A friend told me that, in an effort to get customers, some private inns now even include a young woman in the price of a night's lodging.

One particularly lucrative form of private enterprise is the restaurant business. Part of the reason a private restaurant can be so successful is that state-owned Chinese restaurants are among the most depressing places in the world. Although the food is not necessarily bad and prices are reasonable (particularly by Western standards), the restaurants themselves are almost invariably noisy, dirty, ill-lit, crowded, ugly, and badly managed. At mealtimes, one has to queue to get in the door, and, once inside, one must usually eat at a table heaped with the debris of earlier dinners. Employees are often lackadaisical, even surly and discourteous, and are more concerned with getting the customers out of the door so the establishment can close promptly at seven than with providing good service.

Interested in seeing what dining in China is like at one of the new private restaurants, I went out one night with two friends to the Jinjin Restaurant, at the corner of Dianmennei and Dianmenxi Streets, behind the Imperial City. The Jinjin was surprisingly spacious—unlike most private restaurants, which are crammed into tiny rooms. In Peking, where overcrowding is legendary and living or working space is at a premium, a location like the Jinjin's, facing on to a main street, can usually be obtained only if the proprietor has *guanxi,* or 'special relations', with an influential official or with someone who works in the municipal office responsible for assigning commercial space.

The Jinjin Restaurant was run by a family: the daughter cooked, the mother waited on tables, and the father sat with his abacus behind the front counter, handling the accounts. By Chinese standards, the restaurant was handsomely appointed. Fluorescent fixtures cast a brilliant light. Fans churned the hot summer air, making it possible to eat without sweating. The walls were adorned with examples of Chinese calligraphy. There were six tables, each covered with a plastic sheet and uncluttered by the usual assortment of fish heads, gristle, and bones. The food, which was at least twice as expensive as that in the state-owned restaurants, was delicious. It was served courteously by the harried mother, who scurried back and forth between the kitchen and the tables. A Chinese-made refrigerator near the front counter valiantly battled with the heat to produce partly cooled bottles of Peking beer. As we dined, I realized that this was one of the few times on all my trips to China when I was actually enjoying a meal that was not served in a fancy tourist restaurant or in one of the special back rooms that many of the better state-owned restaurants maintain for 'foreign guests' and other dignitaries.

B ut the Jinjin is, in its own way, a preserve of privilege. It is one of a small but growing number of refuges from the madding crowd which the new Chinese system allows its own people to enjoy—if they can afford to. In fact, in recent months the government has become so impressed by the success of private restaurant management that it has begun leasing state-owned 'eateries' to private individuals to run like any private enterprise in the capitalist world. After years of militantly thwarting any individuals who found a way to surge ahead of the pack economically, the Chinese leadership has now accepted the fact that not all people are or will be equal. It has decided that as long as the productive forces of the nation are generally moving forward, growing discrepancies between

141

rich and poor, and even the development of an incipient bourgeoisie, are an acceptable price to pay. Mao Zedong, of course, advocated an ideal of classless, equal development, in which no individual or segment of society was to advance at the expense of another. The salaries of educated people were not to rise faster than those of common workers. City people were not to enjoy more improvements in their standard of living than peasants in the countryside. In short, it was considered politically incorrect for any individual or family to become wealthy while others remained poor. Mao thought of himself as the great leveller.

In December of 1978, two years after Mao's death, the Third Plenum of the Eleventh Party Central Committee convened in Peking. The session declared that turbulent mass struggles were no longer the order of the day, and that if China was to develop successfully it must turn from class struggle to 'modernization', and completely restructure its economy. After a decade of the Cultural Revolution, with 'politics in command', the Chinese people were told to 'seek truth from facts' rather than from political ideology. They were told that their ability to produce, rather than their 'socialist purity', would be the new measure of success. The Central Committee called for the abandonment of the old Stalinist model of production, which rigidly maintained all planning and decision-making authority in the hands of the central ministries. Over the next few years, much of this authority began to be dispersed downwards, so that state-owned businesses became more independent economic units and their managers became responsible in large measure for planning, use of capital, distribution of profits—in short, for their success or failure. Workers had for years received a flat salary of between thirty and fifty-five yüan a month (three yüan are approximately equivalent to one pound sterling) no matter how efficiently they produced; now many of them found their pay geared to their output, with bonuses promised if business was good. This system has come to be known as the 'responsibility system'.

From the Third Plenum onwards, a new concept of industrial management and a new work ethic began to spread outwards from Peking. Workers who had been terrified of evincing even the slightest bourgeois taint were told that it was all right to serve themselves as well as 'the people'. 'GET RICH BY WORKING,' ran one slogan. 'TO GET RICH IS GLORIOUS' proclaimed another. Deng Xiaoping, in his

Selected Works, published in July 1983, wrote that it was now ideologically correct 'to make some people rich first, so as to lead all the people to wealth.'

These were arresting slogans for a Communist Party that had formerly threatened anyone who exhibited any privatistic tendencies or interest in personal gain with the ignominy of being labelled a 'capitalist roader', a 'Rightist', or—the last degree of political damnation—a 'counter-revolutionary'. In the past, people may have entertained fantasies of wealth, but few dared express them. Like fame, bourgeois contamination made one stand out: as an old Chinese aphorism put it, 'People are just as afraid of becoming well known as a pig is of becoming fat.' Party theoreticians now undertook not only to justify economic inequality but actually to speak of a need to 'overcome egalitarianism', as if egalitarianism were an insidious force completely at odds with the Chinese Revolution. One particularly striking bit of evidence that China's era of egalitarianism has ended was the announcement in 1983 by the People's Liberation Army that badges of rank, which had been abolished in 1965 by former Defence Minister Lin Biao, would be restored in August 1984.

The Party has launched a propaganda campaign to reassure those who still suspect that the new economic reforms are a passing fancy. In June 1983, a self-employed photographer, a private chicken farmer who had earned 20,000 yüan in one year, and another privately employed man, described as a 'bartender', became members of the prestigious National People's Congress, the rubber-stamp legislative organ of the Chinese government. The selection of such people under Mao and the Gang of Four would have been roughly equivalent to the seating of an avowed Marxist revolutionary in the United States Senate. In August, the government organized a conference in Peking which brought together more than 300 delegates from all across China who had been successful in setting up individual or collective private enterprises. They were addressed by none other than Party General Secretary Hu Yaobang. Sounding like the president of a local chamber of commerce, he asked these latter-day model workers, 'What would our markets and lives be like if there were no collective and individual economies to serve the daily needs of the people?... Every job which benefits the country and the people is to be respected.' Hu went on to criticize people who still held

143

the 'outdated' view that workers in state-owned enterprises were more 'ideologically respectable' than those in private business.

Soon after, newspaper articles approving of wealth gained through 'hard work' began appearing everywhere. Some bore headlines which could almost have been lifted directly from the newspapers of Taiwan or Hong Kong. 'HAVE NO FEAR OF BECOMING PROSPEROUS,' proclaimed one. 'MORE INDIVIDUAL ENTERPRISES NOW, BUT NOT ENOUGH,' advised another.

From the looks of things, by the time I arrived in China this propaganda offensive had already proved highly successful. More and more people seemed to be making more and more money with greater and greater vigour. In the English-language paper, *China Daily,* one rich peasant from Hebei Province analysed his situation this way: 'In 1982, I became prosperous on the sly. In 1983, I had to be brave to remain prosperous. In 1984, I can be prosperous without any worry.'

Although China under the Communists has never been as free of crime as many visiting Westerners supposed, a pronounced upsurge of criminal activity over the past few years has caused concern even among the highest echelons of the Chinese leadership. In January of 1982, the Party launched a nationwide anti-crime campaign. Chinese newspapers, which once were filled with slogans and long theoretical tracts, became so peppered with lurid accounts of crime and corruption that at times they read like tabloids; the object of such news stories was not to titillate or to sell papers but to warn offenders that criminal activity would be severely dealt with. *Red Flag* deplored the existence of 'elements hostile to the socialist system', who 'rob the state of property, kill and maim the nation's workers at their posts, hijack, rape women, traffic in women and children, tyrannize others, [and] trample upon the masses.' Well into the campaign, China's Minister of Public Security, Liu Fuzhi, announced that in 1982 750,000 street crimes had been reported—an average of 7.5 for every 10,000 people. (Whatever one might make of the figures or their accuracy, the announcement itself was unusual, since the Chinese government rarely divulges information that might embarrass the Communist Party.) The incidence of street crime had been rising, officials admitted, since 1956, when the rate was officially reported to be as low as 2.3 per 10,000.

A year after the anti-crime campaign began, the first publicized executions occurred. Wang Zhong, the fifty-six-year-old Party secretary of Guangdong's Haifeng County, was executed on 17 January 1983, by a pistol shot in the back of the head, for defrauding the state of about 70,000 yüan and for taking bribes from people who wanted to escape to Hong Kong. (The *People's Daily* called Wang's execution 'most gratifying news'.) The following day, a second Guangdong man—Li Jingfang, aged fifty-five—was executed for embezzling more than 600,000 yüan from a local bank.

When I arrived in China that summer, the anti-crime publicity campaign was just getting into high gear. According to one report, an increase in the number of executions was ordered by Deng Xiaoping himself, who had recently encountered a pack of gangsters on a highway near the coastal town of Beidaihe while travelling in a motorcade with President Li Xiannian; one of the President's aides had been slashed with a knife. Almost every other day, it seemed, there was a story in the newspapers about gangs. They were active even in the remote reaches of Inner Mongolia, where a gang known as the Bridgehead Squad, whose members had eagles tattooed on their left arms, was arrested in August. In the city of Tangshan, in Hebei Province, six different gangs, consisting of more than a hundred criminals, were rounded up, arrested, and accused of murder, assault, ransacking people's houses, robbery, and 'insulting women in public places'. Many of the gang members were ex-inmates of labour camps, in which, before the promulgation of a new criminal code, in 1979, 'anti-social elements' could be incarcerated without a trial. Another gang sentenced while I was in Peking had had its headquarters in the city of Anyang, in Henan Province, but had expanded its operations throughout three nearby provinces, kidnapping young women and selling them, for up to 900 yüan each, to peasants who could not find wives. Before the gang was broken up and arrested, in November of 1982, it had reportedly kidnapped and sold more than 150 women. The leader was sentenced to death, and thirty gang members received prison terms ranging from ten to twenty years.

By summer 1983, the government began publicly sentencing large numbers of criminals to death at 'prosecution rallies'. On 23 August, the Public Security Bureau held a rally at a Peking sports stadium, at which twenty-nine men and one woman were paraded in front of a jeering crowd before being taken away to be executed for their criminal activities. In the weeks that followed, the names of numerous other criminals were marked with red crosses on posters displayed in front of the public buildings all across China, a sign that the criminals, too, had been sentenced to death. One of those who received the death sentence last summer was the grandson of the renowned Marshal Zhu De, a general who had fought alongside Mao since the 1920s. Zhu Guohua, a Tianjin railroad worker, was accused of leading a ring of thieves who had reportedly gang-raped thirty women and of using the name of his famous grandfather to avoid arrest. He was put to death in September, along with eighty-one other sons and grandsons of Army officers, in what proved to be one of the largest mass executions of the anti-crime campaign.

When I arrived in Taicheng, the seat of rural Taishan County, Guangdong Province, in January 1984, billboards and walls in public places had been plastered with anti-crime posters for several months. Printed on large sheets of white paper with black print, the posters showed mug shots of criminals alongside brief descriptions of who they were and what offences they had committed. Those criminals ultimately executed had bold red Xs slashed across their faces.

One morning I was walking early in the streets of Taicheng when I suddenly saw columns of marching students, laughing and talking. By the time at least 1,000 had passed, I became curious about where they were going and what they were doing out of school *en masse* on a weekday morning. Following one long line, I found that they were marching through the gates of a large athletic field by the Tungji River, which flows by the edge of town. At one end of the field was a bandstand decked out with anti-crime banners. One of Taicheng's pre-execution rallies was scheduled to begin in half an hour.

Rushing back to the centre of town, I learned that a parade of criminals being taken to the rally was about to commence. Almost immediately I saw a phalanx of white-jacketed Security Bureau policemen on motorcycles heading down the main street shouting at pedestrians to clear the way. The street emptied quickly; an eerie silence hushed the crowd.

Moments after the police sweep, a procession of open-backed army trucks appeared in the distance and inched slowly towards us as people on the pavement craned their necks to get a better view. In the back of the first truck stood a single, grim-faced young man, hands bound behind his back, head lowered. Around his neck hung a white placard listing his offence and name, which was slashed with the familiar crimson X. The young criminal had an expression that mixed resignation with terror.

Three more trucks passed, carrying three more criminals condemned to death. All wore placards around their necks emblazoned with crimson Xs. Three more trucks followed, each filled with ten or more criminals convicted of non-capital offences. Bringing up the rear were two more trucks filled with young militiamen, rifles slung over their shoulders, their faces frozen in expressions of righteous defiance. The last vehicle conveyed soldiers of the People's Liberation Army, the two in front bracing machine guns on the cab of the truck as if expecting trouble at any moment. Only after the whole cavalcade had passed well beyond us did the crowd begin to murmur.

Hurrying back to the rally ground, I could already hear the sound of martial music drifting out across Taicheng. As I approached the gates of the field, the music suddenly stopped and a strident voice began blasting out over a loudspeaker. The students, thousands of them, were all sitting quietly on the ground with basketball nets, soccer goals, and other sports-field paraphernalia around them. The prisoners remained in their trucks, which had been parked next to the bandstand where they could be easily seen.

'How many have they shot already?' I whispered to a youth, who already looked very uneasy at my presence. At first he did not answer. Then, glancing around with wary eyes, he replied, 'Ten that I know of. But there have been more in the countryside.' That said, he darted away. Moments later a very agitated Security Bureau policeman approached me and said in halting but menacing English, 'Go out! Go out!' and pointed towards the gate.

That evening I met a twenty-two-year-old soldier who had just been demobilized in another part of China. As we walked the dark streets of Taicheng, he told me how, after the rally, two of the condemned men were taken back to their villages to be executed among their own people. The other two condemned men had been led down to the river bank, blindfolded, forced to kneel, and then shot in the back of the neck while 1,000 onlookers—this young soldier among them—lingered to watch.

When I asked why the authorities allowed people to watch, he laughed and said, 'They want us to. They want to scare people and make a big point.' He was silent for a moment, and then added, somewhat hesitantly, 'There is an old custom here in China, and they've revived it again. After a criminal's been shot, his family is sent a bill for the bullet. It's a reminder that a criminal not only brings punishment on himself but shame on the whole family in which he was raised.'

As early as mid-October 1983, diplomats in Peking were estimating that between 1,000 and 2,000 people had been executed throughout China since the campaign began. They reported that Chinese internal documents called for a quota of 5,000 executions and 50,000 arrests by the end of the year. However, by January 1984 many Western correspondents were coming to believe that the figure was actually much higher. Tiziano Terzani, Peking Bureau Chief for the German news weekly *Der Spiegel,* who was later expelled from China for his outspoken articles, calculated that the figure was closer to 15,000.

These Draconian measures appear to have been at least temporarily effective: the government announced at the beginning of January 1984 that the crime rate in the closing months of 1983 was down by forty per cent compared with the same period in 1982. Nonetheless, throughout 1984 reports of gang activity continued to circulate, such as those of the 'Five Fingers' and 'Two Wolves', seven gang leaders in Beian, Heilongjiang Province. When they and their gangs, composed largely of the sons of high-ranking cadres, were arrested after a knife fight with a policeman at a Beian restaurant, they stood accused of no less than 300 crimes of rape and violence.

The Party blamed the upsurge of crime on the 'chaotic' years of the Cultural Revolution, when young people went undisciplined, and on 'bourgeois influences' that had slipped into China as a result of its new open-door policy. What Party officials seem to have overlooked was that the 'bourgeois influences' were part of the reformed economic system, which they themselves instituted and continued to extol. Unemployment had left millions of youths loose on the streets of Chinese cities. In the countryside, people were no longer tied to their registered address, or *hukou,* by the need for government coupons for grain, oil, and cotton products. With new wealth and peasant-run free markets everywhere, such coupons were no longer indispensable. People could buy what they needed wherever they wanted, and were thus freed from the tightly-organized system that once held them firmly in place. Criminals could move about with ease. And the new private sector of the economy had opened a netherworld for criminals in China—a Sherwood Forest within the king's domain, into which outlaws, like Robin Hood's Merry Men, could retreat and live. Here, in the middle of organized Chinese society, criminals were able to survive and carry on the pursuit of individual wealth, which the Chinese leadership itself now glorified.

All the new problems which have arisen are, however, dwarfed by one: the rising population. Between the years 1974 and 1982, the population of China increased by 310 million people. Currently, twenty-five babies are born there each minute of the day. If this trend continues, there will be no way for China to raise its standard of living. Every increase in food production will simply be consumed by new mouths. These unsettling truths have goaded the Chinese government into instituting a policy of 'one couple, one child', in the hope of preventing the country's population, numbered at 1.008 billion in 1982, from exceeding 1.2 billion people by the year 2000. Families who limit themselves to one child are granted bonus payments, higher pensions, and preferential treatment in housing and schooling. Families who have more than one child risk pay cuts, reduction in medical care, and assessments with special taxes. Women are required to report their monthly periods to health officials, so that conception can be detected early. Pregnant women who have not sought permission to bear a child, or who already have a child, are strongly urged—and very often forced—to have abortions, sometimes as late as the second trimester.

In cities, where crowding is particularly acute, and where government propaganda campaigns and control are most effective, the 'one couple, one child' campaign has been quite successful. But nearly 80 per cent of China's population lives in the countryside, where, in the words of the *People's Daily,* the birth-control policy 'will win or fail'. The results in the countryside have not been encouraging. The Chinese government cites two reasons: 'backward ideology' and 'economic interests'. 'Backward ideology' refers to the Confucian aspiration of peasants to have large families, with at least one son to carry on the family name. 'Economic interests' is a term that officials leave vague, because to be more explicit would be to acknowledge one of the most contradictory and deleterious aspects of the responsibility system: namely, the pressure it has put on peasant households to rear as large a family work-force as possible. When rural life was collectivized, the backward ideology of the peasants was easier to overcome. Party cadres still wielded absolute power; moreover, the need to have a large number of children as a source of labour was obviated by the fact that people were farming together on collective land, making the size of individual families irrelevant. But now, with most rural households on their own, large families have suddenly become an economic necessity; recently, many peasants have begun to take their children out of school, in order to increase the labour power in their fields.

Even if a peasant and his wife conscientiously decide to abide by the government's birth-control policy, they may lose their resolve if their first child is female. Although it costs as much to raise a girl as it does a boy, and although birth-control officials count one child as one child regardless of its sex, peasants are convinced that a female child will not be as much help in the fields as a male child and that when a daughter comes of age she will marry and go off to live in the household of her husband. A peasant who has no sons not only will be left shorthanded in his fields, but will have no one to take care of him and his wife in their old age, and no honour.

The one traditional solution to this problem before the Revolution was infanticide. Now, under pressure from both the birth-control programme and the realities of the responsibility system, peasants are once again killing their girl babies. In November 1982, the *China Youth News* stated:

> Some of these unfortunate children are left by the roadside or abandoned on street corners while others are even drowned. Such cruel, inhuman and brutal actions cannot be tolerated.... If this phenomenon is not stopped quickly, then in twenty years a serious social problem may arise; namely, that a large number of men will not be able to find wives.

The paper noted that in certain rural areas three out of every five surviving babies were male. Recent reports from travellers indicate that in some parts of China up to 80 per cent of the surviving infants are male.

In March 1983, the *People's Daily* quoted a spokesperson for The Federation of Women's Associations as saying, 'The drowning and killing of girl infants and the maltreatment of mothers of infant girls ... have become a grave social problem. These phenomena are found not only in deserted mountain villages but also in cities; not only in the families of ordinary workers and peasants but also in the families of Party members and cadres.' In February 1983, a group of women from Hexian County, Anhui Province, wrote a desperate letter to the *People's Daily* which was printed under the headline WE ASK FOR A SECOND LIBERATION. None of these fifteen rural women had succeeded in giving birth to a son, although one had as many as nine daughters. Expressing an acute sense of shame at their failure, they wrote:

> No one wants to be a mother of an excessive number of children, yet not one of the fifteen of us is ready to give up. Even if we must die, we would still strive to have a son so that we might be able to hold up our heads.... Here where we live, a mother without a son suffers so much discrimination and cruelty that we feel it is worth risking our very lives to escape it.

Documenting the ways in which they were discriminated against, these women called on the government

> to adopt a law stipulating that whoever publicizes views preferring men over women and whoever insults mothers who only have daughters, be punished by law, and that the law be posted in large characters on walls in rural areas so that it will be deeply imprinted into the hearts of the people, and so that the momentum it creates will be as great as that when we obtained our first liberation.

All across China I saw posters that propagandized against infanticide and against the abuse of women who gave birth to females: MALE AND FEMALE ARE EQUAL, THE BIRTH OF A DAUGHTER IS LIKE RECEIVING A BLOSSOM, THE LAW GUARANTEES RIGHTS TO WOMEN AND CHILDREN WHICH MUST NOT BE VIOLATED.

Desperate to produce sons, many peasant women have turned to religion, and are once again making pilgrimages to temples, sacrificing to the traditional gods and spirits which once were, and evidently still are, believed to govern births. Others have turned to old-fashioned superstitious practices, seeking the help of priests, sorcerers, wizards, witches and mystics in the hope of giving birth to a boy. That it is even possible for women like these to turn, with varying degrees of openness, to such an array of traditional semi-religious practitioners is in itself arresting and certainly one of the most startling indicators of the regression of mores in rural China. Of course, it could hardly be said that such religious and superstitious practices ever completely disappeared from the Chinese countryside even at the height of the Cultural Revolution's temple-smashing, but certainly they were attenuated. Most peasants would not have dared publicly to seek help or solace in such 'feudal' practices. Exactly what their resurgence means today is hard to say, but it is almost impossible to overlook evidence of their revival.

While leaving the campus of Xiamen (Amoy) University in the coastal province of Fujian on a winter day in 1984, I stopped at one of the privately owned shops near the front gate which sold sweets, cigarettes and fruit. As I was paying for a few oranges, I noticed that these small shops also stocked large quantities of incense and 'gold paper', or fake wood-block-printed money, which Buddhist worshippers have traditionally burned as an offering to the gods. Since it seemed improbable to me that there could be much of a market for religious accoutrements at one of China's most renowned universities, I asked the shopkeeper who bought these goods. Motioning behind her to the rugged mountain which divides Xiamen, and on which I had already noticed the sloping roofs of several buildings constructed in traditional Chinese temple style, she replied, 'We sell them to the worshippers at Nanputou Temple over there.'

Nanputou Temple is one of the most beautiful in China. Situated on the slope of boulder-strewn Wulao Mountain, it was dedicated to the goddess of mercy Guanyin, by a Qing Dynasty General in 1683 after his reconquest of Taiwan. Closed during the Cultural Revolution, it was restored and reopened like so many other churches and temples after the fall of the Gang of Four and the ascendancy of Deng Xiaoping to power.

What I found striking about Nanputou on this visit was not only its physical beauty but the fact that so many Chinese, both young and old, came there to worship. They burned incense and left offerings of money to the Four Great Heavenly Kings (Si Da Jingang). They bowed and said prayers before the image of Sakyamuni (Gautama Buddha) in a pavilion up a flight of stone steps from the gate. They lit incense and made offerings of fruit. Then, before leaving, many of the faithful also stopped and burned a few packets of 'gold paper' in the small, tile-roofed brazier that stood to the side of Guanyin.

'What do people come here to pray for?' I asked one woman whom I had seen placing a bouquet of burning sticks of incense in front of Guanyin.

'Oh, the usual,' she replied, not without a little embarrassment. After we had chatted for ten minutes or so, and she felt more comfortable, she said, 'The men pray for wealth and long life. The women pray for a good marriage and to give birth to sons.'

For the last two decades, the Chinese government had relentlessly tried to extirpate every last sign of religion from society, proclaiming that there was no place in the Chinese Revolution for such feudal and useless superstitions. But now that China seems to have doubled back on itself in so many ways, religious worship is once again permissible, and temples and churches all over China are reopening.

Like its recent espousal of the capitalist ethic, the Party's rehabilitation of religion creates a contradiction between the past and the present which sometimes seems so enormous it is hard to believe that both periods belong to the history of the same country. Yet even now, after temples like Nanputou have been restored at great expense to the state and allowed to reopen, beneath the veneer of the religious freedom which the Chinese government today claims to guarantee its people, an ambivalence is evident. Proclamations notwithstanding, Chinese leaders continue to denounce religion.

Just as the Chinese Communist Party wished to release the productive energies of free enterprise without becoming contaminated by the whole value system of capitalism, so it seemed to wish to be known by the world as a country that allowed religious freedom, while at the same time trying to contain what it considered the undesirable side effects of unfettered religious life. And so, almost everywhere I looked in China, I saw the Chinese government trying to rein in the very religious forces its new policies had purportedly just liberated.

Chinese Marxist theoreticians confidently maintain that as long as the state owns the major share of the means of production no one need have any fear of incipient capitalism. A Party official from Jiangxi Province named Wang Yuanlong reflected this thinking in an interview with a correspondent from the *Beijing Review*.

> The gap between the rich and poor at the moment is caused mainly by the difference in their ability to work. It is not a sign of class polarization caused by exploitation.... We'll never allow the emergence of two antagonistic classes in the countryside a second time. Our goal is prosperity for all. But like people riding bicycles, not everyone can ride abreast of one another. Our peasants, too, do not all become better off at once. Some are better off earlier than others, [but] we must not go back to egalitarianism, in which case no one would be in a position to prosper.

In March 1983, on the centenary of the death of Karl Marx, General Secretary Hu Yaobang gave a long speech, entitled 'The Radiance of the Great Truth of Marxism Lights our Way Forward', which sounded as if it had come out of a time warp. 'From its very birth, Marxism has demonstrated its mighty power, with which no ideological system can compare,' he proclaimed with a confidence that seemed sublime.

> We have learned from Marx, conscientiously studied and drawn wisdom and strength from his works, and shall continue to do so.... The past century has demonstrated again and again that the history of Marxism is one of triumph over successive onslaughts by various antagonistic ideological trends [and that] its revolutionary drive has remained invincible.

Hu's oratory notwithstanding, while I was in China I met no one who was drawing 'wisdom and strength' from Marxism, much less moving forward under the light of its 'radiance'. I met few who gave more than the most perfunctory genuflection to Marxist ideology. What I saw and felt instead was the 'radiance' of people making money. Behind the official façade of confidence what one sensed was a failing socialist nerve.

When Chairman Mao finally came to power, he insisted that theory was indivisible from practice—a dictum that China's current leaders appear to have reversed, as evidenced in their seemingly Confucian belief that moral behaviour can be cultivated apart from what is happening in the real world. Their efforts to instil socialist values in the Chinese people while at the same time encouraging them to lead lives that more and more resemble those of people in capitalist countries violate the Marxist notion that the superstructural world of values inevitably grows out of the substructural world of class and economic system. Like diplomats who stubbornly continue to represent their country abroad long after the government that appointed them has been deposed, the custodians of China's 'spiritual socialist civilization' continue to preach the ethics of a system that is vanishing in front of them.

EDWARD SAID
REFLECTIONS ON
EXILE

E xile is strangely compelling to think about but terrible to experience. It is the unhealable rift forced between a human being and a native place, between the self and its true home: its essential sadness can never be surmounted. And while it is true that literature and history contain heroic, romantic, glorious, even triumphant episodes in an exile's life, these are no more than efforts meant to overcome the crippling sorrow of estrangement. The achievements of exile are permanently undermined by the loss of something left behind for ever.

But if true exile is a condition of terminal loss, why has it been transformed so easily into a potent, even enriching, motif of modern culture? We have become accustomed to thinking of the modern period itself as spiritually orphaned and alienated, the age of anxiety and estrangement. Nietzsche taught us to feel uncomfortable with tradition, and Freud to regard domestic intimacy as the polite face painted on patricidal and incestuous rage. Modern Western culture is in large part the work of exiles, émigrés, refugees. In the United States, academic, intellectual and aesthetic thought is what it is today because of refugees from fascism, communism and other regimes given to the oppression and expulsion of dissidents. The critic George Steiner has even proposed the perceptive thesis that a whole genre of twentieth-century Western literature is 'extraterritorial', a literature by and about exiles, symbolizing the age of the refugee. Thus Steiner suggests

> It seems proper that those who create art in a civilization of quasi-barbarism, which has made so many homeless, should themselves be poets unhoused and wanderers across language. Eccentric, aloof, nostalgic, deliberately untimely....

In other ages, exiles had similar cross-cultural and transnational visions, suffered the same frustrations and miseries, performed the same elucidating and critical tasks—brilliantly affirmed, for instance, in E.H. Carr's classic study of the nineteenth-century Russian intellectuals clustered around Herzen, *The Romantic Exiles*. But the difference between earlier exiles and those of our own time is, it bears stressing, scale: our age—with its modern warfare, imperialism and the quasi-theological ambitions of totalitarian rulers—is indeed the age of the refugee, the displaced person, mass immigration.

Against this large, impersonal setting, exile cannot be made to serve notions of humanism. On the twentieth-century scale, exile is neither aesthetically nor humanistically comprehensible: at most the literature about exile objectifies an anguish and a predicament most people rarely experience at first hand; but to think of the exile informing this literature as beneficially humanistic is to banalize its mutilations, the losses it inflicts on those who suffer them, the muteness with which it responds to any attempt to understand it as 'good for us'. Is it not true that the views of exile in literature and, moreover, in religion obscure what is truly horrendous: that exile is irremediably secular and unbearably historical; that it is produced by human beings for other human beings; and that, like death but without death's ultimate mercy, it has torn millions of people from the nourishment of tradition, family and geography?

To see a poet in exile—as opposed to reading the poetry of exile —is to see exile's antinomies embodied and endured with a unique intensity. Several years ago I spent some time with Faiz Ahmad Faiz, the greatest of contemporary Urdu poets. He was exiled from his native Pakistan by Zia's military regime, and found a welcome of sorts in strife-torn Beirut. Naturally his closest friends were Palestinian, but I sensed that, although there was an affinity of spirit between them, nothing quite matched—language, poetic convention, or life-history. Only once, when Eqbal Ahmad, a Pakistani friend and a fellow-exile, came to Beirut, did Faiz seem to overcome his sense of constant estrangement. The three of us sat in a dingy Beirut restaurant late one night, while Faiz recited poems. After a time, he and Eqbal stopped translating his verses for my benefit, but as the night wore on it did not matter. What I watched required no translation: it was an enactment of a homecoming expressed through defiance and loss, as if to say, 'Zia, we are here.' Of course Zia was the one who was really at home and who would not hear their exultant voices.

Rashid Hussein was a Palestinian. He translated Bialik, one of the great modern Hebrew poets, into Arabic, and Hussein's eloquence established him in the post-1948 period as an orator and nationalist without peer. He first worked as a Hebrew language journalist in Tel Aviv, and succeeded in establishing a dialogue between Jewish and Arab writers, even as he espoused the cause of Nasserism and Arab nationalism. In time, he could no longer endure the pressure, and he left for New York. He married a Jewish woman, and began working in the PLO office at the United Nations, but regularly outraged his superiors with unconventional ideas and utopian rhetoric. In 1972 he left for the Arab world, but a few months later he was back in the United States: he had felt out of place in Syria and Lebanon, unhappy in Cairo. New York sheltered him anew, but so did endless bouts of drinking and idleness. His life was in ruins, but he remained the most hospitable of men. He died after a night of heavy drinking when, smoking in bed, his cigarette started a fire that spread to a small library of audio cassettes, consisting mostly of poets reading their verse. The fumes from the tapes asphyxiated him. His body was repatriated for burial in Musmus, the small village in Israel where his family still resided.

These and so many other exiled poets and writers lend dignity to a condition legislated to deny dignity—to deny an identity to people. From them, it is apparent that, to concentrate on exile as a contemporary political punishment, you must therefore map territories of experience beyond those mapped by the literature of exile itself. You must first set aside Joyce and Nabokov and think instead of the uncountable masses for whom UN agencies have been created. You must think of the refugee-peasants with no prospect of ever returning home, armed only with a ration card and an agency number. Paris may be a capital famous for cosmopolitan exiles, but it is also a city where unknown men and women have spent years of miserable loneliness: Vietnamese, Algerians, Cambodians, Lebanese, Senegalese, Peruvians. You must think also of Cairo, Beirut, Madagascar, Bangkok, Mexico City. As you move further from the Atlantic world, the awful forlorn waste increases: the hopelessly large numbers, the compounded misery of 'undocumented' people suddenly lost, without a tellable history. To reflect on exiled Muslims from India, or Haitians in America, or Bikinians in Oceania, or Palestinians throughout the Arab world means that you must leave the modest refuge provided by subjectivity and resort instead to the abstractions of mass politics. Negotiations, wars of national liberation, people bundled out of their homes and prodded, bussed or walked to enclaves in other regions: what do these experiences add up to? Are they not manifestly and almost by design irrecoverable?

161

We come to nationalism and its essential association with exile. Nationalism is an assertion of belonging in and to a place, a people, a heritage. It affirms the home created by a community of language, culture and customs; and, by so doing, it fends off exile, fights to prevent its ravages. Indeed, the interplay between nationalism and exile is like Hegel's dialectic of servant and master, opposites informing and constituting each other. All nationalisms in their early stages develop from a condition of estrangement. The struggles to win American independence, to unify Germany or Italy, to liberate Algeria were those of national groups separated—exiled—from what was construed to be their rightful way of life. Triumphant, achieved nationalism then justifies, retrospectively as well as prospectively, a history selectively strung together in a narrative form: thus all nationalisms have their founding fathers, their basic, quasi-religious texts, their rhetoric of belonging, their historical and geographical landmarks, their official enemies and heroes. This collective ethos forms what Pierre Bourdieu, the French sociologist, calls the *habitus,* the coherent amalgam of practices linking habit with inhabitance. In time, successful nationalisms consign truth exclusively to themselves and relegate falsehood and inferiority to outsiders (as in the rhetoric of capitalist versus communist, or the European versus the Asiatic).

And just beyond the frontier between 'us' and the 'outsiders' is the perilous territory of not-belonging: this is to where in a primitive time peoples were banished, and where in the modern era immense aggregates of humanity loiter as refugees and displaced persons.

Nationalisms are about groups, but in a very acute sense exile is a solitude experienced outside the group: the deprivations felt at not being with others in the communal habitation. How, then, does one surmount the loneliness of exile without falling into the encompassing and thumping language of national pride, collective sentiments, group passions? What is there worth saving and holding on to between the extremes of exile on the one hand, and the often bloody-minded affirmations of nationalism on the other? Do nationalism and exile have any intrinsic attributes? Are they simply two conflicting varieties of paranoia?

These are questions that cannot ever be fully answered because each assumes that exile and nationalism can be discussed neutrally, without reference to each other. They cannot be. Because both terms include everything from the most collective of collective sentiments to the most private of private emotions, there is hardly language adequate for both. But there is certainly nothing about nationalism's public and all-inclusive ambitions that touches the core of the exile's predicament.

Because exile, unlike nationalism, is fundamentally a discontinuous state of being. Exiles are cut off from their roots, their land, their past. They generally do not have armies or states, although they are often in search of them. Exiles feel, therefore, an urgent need to reconstitute their broken lives, usually by choosing to see themselves as part of a triumphant ideology or a restored people. The crucial thing is that a state of exile free from this triumphant ideology—designed to reassemble an exile's broken history into a new whole—is virtually unbearable, and virtually impossible in today's world. Look at the fate of the Jews, the Palestinians and the Armenians.

Noubar is a solitary Armenian, and a friend. His parents had to leave Eastern Turkey in 1915, after their families were massacred: his maternal grandfather was beheaded. Noubar's mother and father went to Aleppo, then to Cairo. In the middle-sixties, life in Egypt became difficult for non-Egyptians, and his parents, along with four children, were taken to Beirut by an international relief organization. In Beirut, they lived briefly in a pension and then were bundled into two rooms of a little house outside the city. In Lebanon, they had no money and they waited: eight months later, a relief agency got them a flight to Glasgow. And then to Gander. And then to New York. They rode by Greyhound bus from New York to Seattle: Seattle was the city designated by the agency for their American residence. When I asked, 'Seattle?', Noubar smiled resignedly, as if to say better Seattle than Armenia—which he never knew, or Turkey where so many were slaughtered, or Lebanon where he and his family would certainly have risked their lives. Exile is sometimes better than staying behind or not getting out: but only sometimes.

Because *nothing* is secure. Exile is a jealous state. What you achieve is precisely what you have no wish to share, and it is in the drawing of lines around you and your compatriots that the least attractive aspects of being in exile emerge: an exaggerated sense of group solidarity, and a passionate hostility to outsiders, even those who may in fact be in the same predicament as you. What could be more intransigent than the conflict between Zionist Jews and Arab Palestinians? Palestinians feel that they have been turned into exiles by the proverbial people of exile, the Jews. But the Palestinians also know that their own sense of national identity has been nourished in the exile milieu, where everyone not a blood-brother or sister is an enemy, where every sympathizer is an agent of some unfriendly power, and where the slightest deviation from the accepted group line is an act of the rankest treachery and disloyalty.

Perhaps this is the most extraordinary of exile's fates: to have been exiled by exiles: to relive the actual process of up-rooting at the hands of exiles. All Palestinians during the summer of 1982 asked themselves what inarticulate urge drove Israel, having displaced Palestinians in 1948, to expel them continuously from their refugee homes and camps in Lebanon. It is as if the reconstructed Jewish collective experience, as represented by Israel and modern Zionism, could not tolerate another story of dispossession and loss to exist alongside it—an intolerance constantly reinforced by the Israeli hostility to the nationalism of the Palestinians, who for forty-six years have been painfully reassembling a national identity in exile.

This need to reassemble an identity out of the refractions and discontinuities of exile is found in the earlier poems of Mahmud Darwish, whose considerable work amounts to an epic effort to transform the lyrics of loss into the indefinitely postponed drama of return. Thus he depicts his sense of homelessness in the form of a list of unfinished and incomplete things:

> But I am the exile.
> Seal me with your eyes.
> Take me wherever you are—
> Take me whatever you are.
> Restore to me the colour of face
> And the warmth of body
> The light of heart and eye,
> The salt of bread and rhythm,
> The taste of earth...the Motherland.

Shield me with your eyes.
Take me as a relic from the mansion of sorrow.
Take me as a verse from my tragedy;
Take me as a toy, a brick from the house
So that our children will remember to return.
The pathos of exile is in the loss of contact with the solidity and the satisfaction of earth: homecoming is out of the question.

Joseph Conrad's tale 'Amy Foster' is perhaps the most uncompromising representation of exile ever written. Conrad thought of himself as an exile from Poland, and nearly all his work (as well as his life) carries the unmistakable mark of the sensitive émigré's obsession with his own fate and with his hopeless attempts to make satisfying contact with new surroundings. 'Amy Foster' is in a sense confined to the problems of exile, perhaps so confined that it is not one of Conrad's best-known stories. This, for example, is the description of the agony of its central character, Yanko Goorall, an Eastern European peasant who, en route to America, is shipwrecked off the British coast:

It is indeed hard upon a man to find himself a lost stranger helpless, incomprehensible, and of a mysterious origin, in some obscure corner of the earth. Yet amongst all the adventurers shipwrecked in all the wild parts of the world, there is not one, it seems to me, that ever had to suffer a fate so simply tragic as the man I am speaking of, the most innocent of adventurers cast out by the sea....

Yanko has left home because the pressures were too great for him to go on living there. America lures him with its promise, though England is where he ends up. He endures in England, where he cannot speak the language and is feared and misunderstood. Only Amy Foster, a plodding, unattractive peasant girl, tries to communicate with him. They marry, have a child, but when Yanko falls ill, Amy, afraid and alienated, refuses to nurse him; snatching their child, she leaves. The desertion hastens Yanko's miserable death, which like the deaths of several Conradian heroes is depicted as the result of a combination of crushing isolation and the world's indifference. Yanko's fate is described as 'the supreme disaster of loneliness and despair'.

Yanko's predicament is affecting: a foreigner perpetually haunted and alone in an uncomprehending society. But Conrad's own exile causes him to exaggerate the differences between Yanko and Amy. Yanko is dashing, light and bright-eyed, whereas Amy is heavy, dull, bovine; when he dies, it is as if her earlier kindness to him was a snare to lure and then trap him fatally. Yanko's death is romantic: the world is coarse, unappreciative; no one understands him, not even Amy, the one person close to him. Conrad took this neurotic exile's fear and created an aesthetic principle out of it. No one can understand or communicate in Conrad's world, but paradoxically this radical limitation on the possibilities of language doesn't inhibit elaborate efforts to communicate. All of Conrad's stories are about lonely people who talk a great deal (for indeed who of the great modernists was more voluble and 'adjectival' than Conrad himself?) and whose attempts to *impress* others compound, rather than reduce, the original sense of isolation. Each Conradian exile fears, and is condemned endlessly to imagine, the spectacle of a solitary death illuminated, so to speak, by unresponsive, uncommunicating eyes.

Exiles look at non-exiles with resentment. *They* belong in their surroundings, you feel, whereas an exile is always out of place. What is it like to be born in a place, to stay and live there, to know that you are of it, more or less for ever?

Although it is true that anyone prevented from returning home is an exile, some distinctions can be made between exiles, refugees, expatriates and émigrés. Exile originated in the age-old practice of banishment. Once banished, the exile lives an anomalous and miserable life, with the stigma of being an outsider. Refugees, on the other hand, are a creation of the twentieth-century state. The word 'refugee' has become a political one, suggesting large herds of innocent and bewildered people requiring urgent international assistance, whereas 'exile' carries with it, I think, a touch of solitude and spirituality.

Expatriates voluntarily live in an alien country, usually for personal or social reasons. Hemingway and Fitzgerald were not forced to live in France. Expatriates may share in the solitude and estrangement of exile, but they do not suffer under its rigid proscriptions. Émigrés enjoy an ambiguous status. Technically, an émigré is anyone who emigrates to a new country. Choice in the matter is certainly a possibility. Colonial officials, missionaries, technical experts, mercenaries and military advisers on loan may in a sense live in exile, but they have not been banished. White settlers in Africa, parts of Asia and Australia may once have been exiles, but as pioneers and nation-builders the label 'exile' dropped away from them.

Much of the exile's life is taken up with compensating for disorienting loss by creating a new world to rule. It is not surprising that so many exiles seem to be novelists, chess players, political activists, and intellectuals. Each of these occupations requires a minimal investment in objects and places a great premium on mobility and skill. The exile's new world, logically enough, is unnatural and its unreality resembles fiction. Georg Lukács, in *Theory of the Novel*, argued with compelling force that the novel, a literary form created out of the unreality of ambition and fantasy, is *the* form of 'transcendental homelessness'. Classical epics, Lukács wrote, emanate from settled cultures in which values are clear, identities stable, life unchanging. The European novel is grounded in precisely the opposite experience, that of a changing society in which an itinerant and disinherited middle-class hero or heroine seeks to construct a new world that somewhat resembles an old one left behind for ever. In the epic there is no *other* world, only the finality of *this* one. Odysseus returns to Ithaca after years of wandering; Achilles will die because he cannot escape his fate. The novel, however, exists because other worlds *may* exist, alternatives for bourgeois speculators, wanderers, exiles.

No matter how well they may do, exiles are always eccentrics who *feel* their difference (even as they frequently exploit it) as a kind of orphanhood. Anyone who is really homeless regards the habit of seeing estrangement in everything modern as an affectation, a display of modish attitudes. Clutching difference like a weapon to be used with stiffened will, the exile jealously insists on his or her right to refuse to belong.

This usually translates into an intransigence that is not easily ignored. Wilfulness, exaggeration, overstatement: these are characteristic styles of being an exile, methods for compelling the world to accept your vision—which you make more unacceptable because you are in fact unwilling to have it accepted. It is yours, after all. Composure and serenity are the last things associated with the work of exiles. Artists in exile are decidedly unpleasant, and their stubbornness insinuates itself into even their exalted works. Dante's vision in *The Divine Comedy* is tremendously powerful in its universality and detail, but even the beatific peace achieved in the *Paradiso* bears traces of the vindictiveness and severity of judgement embodied in the *Inferno*. Who but an exile like Dante, banished from Florence, would use eternity as a place for settling old scores?

James Joyce *chose* to be in exile: to give force to his artistic vocation. In an uncannily effective way—as Richard Ellmann has shown in his biography—Joyce picked a quarrel with Ireland and kept it alive so as to sustain the strictest opposition to what was familiar. Ellmann says that 'whenever his relations with his native land were in danger of improving, [Joyce] was to find a new incident to solidify his intransigence and to reaffirm the rightness of his voluntary absence.' Joyce's fiction concerns what in a letter he once described as the state of being 'alone and friendless'. And although it is rare to pick banishment as a way of life, Joyce perfectly understood its trials.

But Joyce's success as an exile stresses the question lodged at its very heart: is exile so extreme and private that any instrumental use of it is ultimately a trivialization? How is it that the literature of exile has taken its place as a *topos* of human experience alongside the literature of adventure, education or discovery? Is this the *same* exile that quite literally kills Yanko Goorall and has bred the expensive, often dehumanizing relationship between twentieth-century exile and nationalism? Or is it some more benign variety?

Much of the contemporary interest in exile can be traced to the somewhat pallid notion that non-exiles can share in the benefits of exile as a redemptive motif. There is, admittedly, a certain plausibility and truth to this idea. Like medieval itinerant scholars or learned Greek slaves in the Roman Empire, exiles—the exceptional ones among them—do leaven their environments. And naturally 'we' concentrate on that enlightening aspect of 'their' presence among us, not on their misery or their demands. But looked at from the bleak political perspective of modern mass dislocations, individual exiles force us to recognize the tragic fate of homelessness in a necessarily heartless world.

A generation ago, Simone Weil posed the dilemma of exile as concisely as it has ever been expressed. 'To be rooted,' she said, 'is perhaps the most important and least recognized need of the human soul.' Yet Weil also saw that most remedies for uprootedness in this era of world wars, deportations and mass exterminations are almost as dangerous as what they purportedly remedy. Of these, the state—or, more accurately, statism—is one of the most insidious, since worship of the state tends to supplant all other human bonds.

Weil exposes us anew to that whole complex of pressures and constraints that lie at the centre of the exile's predicament, which, as I have suggested, is as close as we come in the modern era to tragedy. There is the sheer fact of isolation and displacement, which produces the kind of narcissistic masochism that resists all efforts at amelioration, acculturation and community. At this extreme the exile can make a fetish of exile, a practice that distances him or her from all connections and commitments. To live as if everything around you were temporary and perhaps trivial is to fall prey to petulant cynicism as well as to querulous lovelessness. More common is the pressure on the exile to join—parties, national movements, the state. The exile is offered a new set of affiliations and develops new loyalties. But there is also a loss—of critical perspective, of intellectual reserve, of moral courage.

It must also be recognized that the defensive nationalism of exiles often fosters self-awareness as much as it does the less attractive forms of self-assertion. Such reconstitutive projects as assembling a nation out of exile (and this is true in this century for Jews and Palestinians) involve constructing a national history, reviving an ancient language, founding national institutions like libraries and universities. And these, while they sometimes promote strident ethnocentrism, also give rise to investigations of self that inevitably go far beyond such simple and positive facts as 'ethnicity'. For example, there is the self-consciousness of an individual trying to understand why the histories of the Palestinians and the Jews have certain patterns to them, why in spite of oppression and the threat of extinction a particular ethos remains alive in exile.

Necessarily, then, I speak of exile not as a privilege, but as an *alternative* to the mass institutions that dominate modern life. Exile is not, after all, a matter of choice: you are born into it, or it happens to you. But, provided that the exile refuses to sit on the sidelines nursing a wound, there are things to be learned: he or she must cultivate a scrupulous (not indulgent or sulky) subjectivity.

Perhaps the most rigorous example of such subjectivity is to be found in the writing of Theodor Adorno, the German-Jewish philosopher and critic. Adorno's masterwork, *Minima Moralia,* is an autobiography written while in exile; it is subtitled *Reflexionen aus dem beschädigten Leben* (*Reflections from a Mutilated Life*). Ruthlessly opposed to what he called the 'administered' world, Adorno saw all life as pressed into ready-made forms, prefabricated 'homes'. He argued that everything that one says or thinks, as well as every object one possesses, is ultimately a mere commodity. Language is jargon, objects are for sale. To refuse this state of affairs is the exile's intellectual mission.

Adorno's reflections are informed by the belief that the only home truly available now, though fragile and vulnerable, is in writing. Elsewhere, 'the house is past. The bombings of European cities, as well as the labour and concentration camps, merely precede as executors, with what the immanent development of technology had long decided was to be the fate of houses. These are now good only to be thrown away like old food cans.' In short, Adorno says with a grave irony, 'it is part of morality not to be at home in one's home.'

To follow Adorno is to stand away from 'home' in order to look at it with the exile's detachment. For there is considerable merit in the practice of noting the discrepancies between various concepts and ideas and what they actually produce. We take home and language for granted; they become nature, and their underlying assumptions recede into dogma and orthodoxy.

The exile knows that in a secular and contingent world, homes are always provisional. Borders and barriers, which enclose us within the safety of familiar territory, can also become prisons, and are often defended beyond reason or necessity. Exiles cross borders, break barriers of thought and experience.

Hugo of St Victor, a twelfth-century monk from Saxony, wrote these hauntingly beautiful lines:

> It is, therefore, a source of great virtue for the practised mind to learn, bit by bit, first to change about invisible and transitory things, so that afterwards it may be able to leave them behind altogether. The man who finds his homeland sweet is still a tender beginner; he to whom every soil is as his native one is already strong; but he is perfect to whom the entire world is as a foreign land. The tender soul has fixed his love on one spot in the world; the strong man has extended his love to all places; the perfect man has extinguished his.

Erich Auerbach, the great twentieth-century literary scholar who spent the war years as an exile in Turkey, has cited this passage as a model for anyone wishing to transcend national or provincial limits. Only by embracing this attitude can a historian begin to grasp human experience and its written records in their diversity and particularity; otherwise he or she will remain committed more to the exclusions and reactions of prejudice than to the freedom that accompanies knowledge. But note that Hugo twice makes it clear that the 'strong' or 'perfect' man achieves independence and detachment by *working through* attachments, not by rejecting them. Exile is predicated on the existence of, love for, and bond with, one's native place; what is true of all exile is not that home and love of home are lost, but that loss is inherent in the very existence of both.

Regard experiences as if they were about to disappear. What is it that anchors them in reality? What would you save of them? What would you give up? Only someone who has achieved independence and detachment, someone whose homeland is 'sweet' but whose circumstances makes it impossible to recapture that sweetness, can answer those questions. (Such a person would also find it impossible to derive satisfaction from substitutes furnished by illusion or dogma.)

This may seem like a prescription for an unrelieved grimness of outlook and, with it, a permanently sullen disapproval of all enthusiasm or buoyancy of spirit. Not necessarily. While it perhaps seems peculiar to speak of the pleasures of exile, there are some positive things to be said for a few of its conditions. Seeing 'the entire world as a foreign land' makes possible originality of vision. Most people are principally aware of one culture, one setting, one home; exiles are aware of at least two, and this plurality of vision gives rise to an awareness of simultaneous dimensions, an awareness that—to borrow a phrase from music—is *contrapuntal.*

For an exile, habits of life, expression or activity in the new environment inevitably occur against the memory of these things in another environment. Thus both the new and the old environments are vivid, actual, occurring together contrapuntally. There is a unique pleasure in this sort of apprehension, especially if the exile is conscious of other contrapuntal juxtapositions that diminish orthodox judgement and elevate appreciative sympathy. There is also a particular sense of achievement in acting as if one were at home wherever one happens to be.

This remains risky, however: the habit of dissimulation is both wearying and nerve-racking. Exile is never the state of being satisfied, placid, or secure. Exile, in the words of Wallace Stevens, is 'a mind of winter' in which the pathos of summer and autumn as much as the potential of spring are nearby but unobtainable. Perhaps this is another way of saying that a life of exile moves according to a different calendar, and is less seasonal and settled than life at home. Exile is life led outside habitual order. It is nomadic, decentred, contrapuntal; but no sooner does one get accustomed to it than its unsettling force erupts anew.

ff

NEW FICTION

JAYNE ANNE PHILLIPS

Machine Dreams

faber and faber

MACHINE DREAMS
Jayne Anne Phillips
A first novel by the highly acclaimed author of *Black Tickets*, described by Ian McEwan as 'A brilliant writer, utterly original and with an astonishing range.'
'A remarkable novelistic début and an enduring literary achievement.' *The New York Times*.
October, Cased £8.95

THE WALL OF THE PLAGUE
André Brink
Through the image of the great Plague which swept Europe in the fourteenth century, André Brink, author of *A Chain of Voices*, explores a contemporary society whose well-being is poisoned by the divisions of apartheid.
September, Cased £9.95

INFANTE'S INFERNO
G. Cabrera Infante
A vivid, humorous, highly-charged novel about the sensual education of a young journalist in Havana by one of Latin America's most inventive writers.
September, Cased £9.95

HER LIVING IMAGE
Jane Rogers
In this subtle, complex novel, Jane Rogers explores some of the choices about ways of living and relating that face women and men today. Of Jane Rogers' first novel *Separate Tracks*, *New Society* said, 'It deserves to rank with John Fowles' *The Collector*'. October, Cased £9.95

AN EVENING OF BRAHMS
Richard Sennett
Richard Sennett made his highly acclaimed début as a novelist with *The Frog Who Dared to Croak*. *An Evening of Brahms* is a musician's novel, a story about music and the lives of people who make it. October, Cased £9.95

DORIS LESSING
JANE SOMERS'S
DIARIES

I had been thinking about writing a pseudonymous novel for years. Like, I am sure, most writers. How many do? It is in the nature of things that we don't know. But I intended from the start to come clean, only wanted to make a little experiment.

The Diary of a Good Neighbour got written for several reasons. One: I wanted to be reviewed on merit, as a new writer, without the benefit of a 'name': to get free from that cage of associations and labels that every established writer has to learn to live inside. It is easy to predict what reviewers will say. Mind you, the labels change. Mine have been—starting with *The Grass is Singing*: she is a writer about the colour bar (obsolete term for racism), about communism, feminism, mysticism; she writes space fiction, science fiction. Each label has served for a few years.

Two: I wanted to cheer up young writers—who often have such a hard time of it—by illustrating that certain attitudes and processes they have to submit to are mechanical, and have nothing to do with them personally or with their kind or degree of talent.

Another reason, frankly if faintly malicious. Some reviewers complained they hated my Canopus series: Why didn't I write realistically, the way I used to do—preferably *The Golden Notebook* over again. These reviewers were sent *The Diary of a Good Neighbour,* but not one recognized me. Some people think it is reasonable that an avowed devotee of a writer's work should only be able to recognize it when packaged and signed; others, not.

Again, when I began writing my Canopus series, I was surprised to find I had been set free to write in ways I had not used before. I wondered if there would be a similar liberation if I were to write in the first person as a different character. Of course, all writers become different characters all the time, as we write about them: all our characters are inside us somewhere. (This can be a terrifying thought.) But a whole book would be a different matter, mean activating one of the gallery of people who inhabit every one of us, strengthening him or her, setting him or her free to develop. And it did turn out that as Jane Somers I wrote in ways that Doris Lessing cannot. It was more than a question of using the odd turn of phrase or an adjective to suggest a woman journalist who is also a successful romantic novelist: Jane Somers knew nothing about a kind of dryness, like a conscience, that monitors Doris Lessing, whatever she writes and in whatever style. After all, there are many different styles or tones of voice in the Canopus series—not to mention *Briefing for a Descent into Hell* and *Memoirs of a Survivor*—and sometimes in the same book.

Some may think this is a detached way to write about Doris Lessing, as if I were not she. It is the name I am detached about. After all, it is the third name I've had: the first, Tayler, being my father's; the second, Wisdom (now try that one on for size!), my first husband's; and the third my second husband's. Of course there was McVeagh, my mother's name, but am I Scottish or Irish? As for Doris, it was the doctor's suggestion, he who delivered me, my mother being convinced to the last possible moment that I was a boy. Born six hours earlier, I would have been Horatia, for Nelson's Day. What could that have done for me? I sometimes wonder what my real name is: surely I must have one?

Jane Somers also developed from my reflections about what my mother would be like if she lived now: that practical, efficient, energetic woman, who was by temperament conservative, a little sentimental, and only with difficulty (and a lot of practice) able to understand weakness and failure—though she was always kind. No, Jane Somers is not my mother, but thoughts of women like my mother fed Jane Somers.

I and my agent, Jonathan Clowes, decided that it would be fair to submit *The Diary of a Good Neighbour* to my main publishers first. In Britain these are Jonathan Cape and Granada. Cape (not its chairman, Tom Maschler) turned it down forthwith. Granada kept it some time, were undecided, but said it was too depressing to publish: in these fallen days, major and prestigious publishers can see nothing wrong in refusing a novel in which they see merit because it might not sell. Not thus, once, were serious literary publishers. I saw the readers' reports and was reminded how patronized and put-down beginning writers are.

Michael Joseph, who accepted my first novel all those years ago, has now twice published me as a new writer. On accepting *The Diary of a Good Neighbour,* the editor there said it reminded her of Doris Lessing, and she was taken into our confidence, and entered with relish into the spirit of the thing. The redoubtable Bob Gottlieb of

Knopf in New York said at once, 'Who do you think you are kidding?'—or words to that effect. Interesting that these two great publishing firms, crammed with people and the possibilities of a leak, were able to keep the secret as long as they wanted: it was dear friends who, swearing their amazing and tested reliability, could not stand the strain.

Three European publishers bought *The Diary of a Good Neighbour*: in France, Germany, and Holland. My French publisher rang up to say he had bought this book, had I perhaps helped Jane Somers who reminded him of me?

This surely brings us back to the question: What is it that these three editors—one in England, one in the United States, and one in France—recognized? After all, Jane Somers's style is different from Lessing's. Every novel or story, by any writer, has a characteristic note or tone of voice—a style, consistent and peculiar to itself. But behind this must sound another note, independent of style. What is this underlying tone or voice, and where does it originate in the author? It seems to me we are listening to, responding to, the essence of a writer here, a ground-note.

The Diary of a Good Neighbour was published in 1983. We—that is, agent, publishers and I—believed the reviewers would guess at once. But not one did. A few people, not all reviewers, liked the novel. It was mostly women in women's magazines who reviewed it, because Jane Somers was described on the dust jacket as a well-known woman journalist (it was enough, apparently, to say it for people to believe it). This neatly highlights the major problem of publishing: how to bring a book to the attention of readers. The trigger here was the phrase *woman journalists*: some potential reviewers, male, were put off by it. It is this situation—bringing a book to the attention of readers—that has given rise to all these new promotional schemes in Britain: the Ten Best Young Novelists, Thirteen Best Novels, the razzmatazz prizes, and so on. The problem can only exist, it seems to me, because so many books are being published. If there were only a few, there would be no difficulty. Ever more loudly shrill the voices, trying to get attention: this is the best novel since *Gone with the Wind, War and Peace* and *The Naked and the Dead*! Overkill earns diminishing returns and numbed readers return to former habits, such as relying on intuition and the recommendation of friends. Jane

Somers's first novel (first serious novel—of course she had written those romantic novels which were not reviewed at all but sold very well!) was noticed, and got a few nice, little reviews. In short, it was reviewed as new novels are. And that could easily have been that. Novels, even good ones, are being published all the time and have what publishers call 'a shelf-life' (like groceries) of a few months. Once they used the phrase as a joke, sending themselves up, but now they use it straight. 'The shelf-life of books is getting shorter,' you'll hear them say, 'it's down to a few weeks now.' As if it all had nothing to do with them. And it hasn't: the mechanisms for selling dominate their practices—the tail wags the dog. A first novel can be remaindered and go out of print and vanish as if it had never existed, if unlucky enough not to win a prize or in some way attract a spotlight, such as the admiration of a well-known writer who cries (see above), 'This is the greatest novel since *Tom Jones.*' Or, accommodating to the times, 'More exciting than *Dallas*!'

The American publisher was asked why more had not been done to promote *The Diary of a Good Neighbour*—which in the opinion of the inquirer, a literary critic, was a good novel—but the reply was that there was nothing to promote, no 'personality', no photograph, no story. In other words, to sell a book, to bring it attention, you need more than the book itself. This means that writers spend more time 'promoting' their work, because readers are now thoroughly conditioned to respond to the personality of the author. A publisher friend was heard recently to groan: 'Look what we've done! It's all our fault! We started it, not knowing where it would end! Twenty years ago we sold books; now we have to sell authors.' As for us, the authors, we are continually amazed that it is not the year or so of hard slog we put into a book and the simple fact that it is there—an expression of ourselves at our best and most intelligent—that persuade readers to buy the book: no, for that you need the television appearance. Many writers who resisted at the start have thought it all over, have understood that this, now, is how the machinery works, and have decided that if we have become part of a publisher's sales department, whether it is acknowledged or not, then we will do the job as well as we can. It is remarkable how certain publishers wince and suffer when writers insist on using the right words to describe what is happening. In very bad taste, the publishers think it is, to talk in this way. Nevertheless, you are pressured to do interviews, television and so on, but you are conscious that the more you agree, the more you are earning his or her contempt. (But, looking back, it seems to me that men publishers are more guilty of this hypocrisy than women.)

If Jane Somers had only written one serious novel, which sold, as first novels do—2,800 copies in the States, 1,600 in Britain—by now it would be remaindered and pulped, and she would be cherishing half-a-dozen fan letters. But she wrote a second. Surely this time people must see who the real author is? But, no.

Predictably, people who had liked the first book were disappointed by the second. And vice versa. Never mind about the problems of publishers: the main problem of some writers is that most reviewers and readers want you to go on writing the same book.

By now, the results of friends' indiscretions meant that some people in the trade knew who Jane Somers was and—I am touched by this—clearly decided it was my right to be anonymous if I wished. Some, too, seemed inclined retrospectively to find merit.

One of my aims has more than succeeded. It seems I am like Barbara Pym! The books are fastidious, well written, well crafted. Stylish. Unsparing, unsentimental and deeply felt. Funny, too. On the other hand they are sentimental, and mawkish. Mere soap opera. Trendy.

I am going to miss Jane Somers.

I was in the chemist's and this happened.

I saw an old witch. I was staring at this old creature and thought, a witch. Here she was, beside me. A tiny bent-over woman, with a nose nearly meeting her chin, in black heavy dusty clothes, and something not far off a bonnet. She saw me looking at her and thrust at me a prescription and said, 'What is this? You get it for me.' Fierce blue eyes, under grey craggy brows, but there was something wonderfully sweet in them.

I liked her, for some reason, from that moment. I took the paper and knew I was taking much more than that. 'I will,' I said. 'But why? Isn't he being nice to you?' Joking: and she at once responded, shaking her old head vigorously.

'No, oh *he*'s no good, I never know what *he*'s saying.'

He was the young chemist, and he stood, hands on the counter, alert, smiling: he knew her well, I could see.

'The prescription is for a sedative,' I said.

She said, 'I know *that*,' and jabbed her fingers down on to the paper where I had spread it against my handbag. 'But it's not aspirin, is it?'

I said, 'It's something called Valium.'

'That's what I thought. It's not a pain-killer, it's a stupefier,' she said.

He laughed. 'But it's not as bad as that,' he said.

I said, 'I've been taking it myself.'

She said, 'I said to the doctor, aspirin—that's what I asked for. But *they're* no good either, doctors.'

All this fierce and trembling, with a sort of gaiety. Standing there, the three of us, we were laughing, and yet she was so very angry.

'Do you want me to sell you some aspirin, Mrs Fowler?'

'Yes, yes. I'm not going to take this stuff that stupefies you.'

He handed her the aspirin, and took her money, which she counted out slowly, coin by coin, from the depths of a great rusty bag. Then he took the money for my things— nail varnish, blusher, eye-liner, eye-shadow, lipstick, lip-gloss, powder, mascara. The lot: I had run low on everything. She stood by watching, with a look I know now is so characteristic, a fierce pondering look that really wants to understand. Trying to grasp it all.

I adjusted my pace to hers and went out of the shop with her. On the pavement she did not look at me, but there was an appeal there. I walked beside her. It was hard to walk so slowly. Usually I fly along, but did not know it till then. She took one step, then paused, examined the pavement, then another step. I thought how I rushed along the pavements every day and had never seen Mrs Fowler, but she lived near me, and suddenly I looked up and down the streets and saw—old women. Old men too, but mostly old women. They walked slowly along. They stood in pairs or groups, talking. Or sat on the bench at the corner under the plane tree. I had not seen them. That was because I was afraid of being like them. I was afraid, walking along there beside her. It was the smell of her, a sweet, sour, dusty sort of smell. I saw the grime on her thin old neck, and on her hands.

The house had a broken parapet, broken and chipped steps. I went in with her, my heart quite sick, and my stomach sick too because of the smell. Which was, that day, of over-boiled fish. We walked along a dark passage to the 'kitchen'. I have never seen anything like it. It was an extension of the passage, with an old gas-cooker, greasy and black, an old white china sink, cracked and yellow with grease, a cold-water tap wrapped around with old rags and dripping steadily. A rather nice old wood table that had crockery standing on it, all 'washed' but grimy. The walls stained and damp. The whole place smelled, it smelled awful.... She did not look at me while she set down bread, biscuits and cat food. The clean lively colours of the grocery packages and the tins in that awful place. She was ashamed, but wasn't going to apologize. She said in an offhand but appealing way, 'You go into my room, and find yourself a seat.'

The room I went into had in it an old black iron stove that was showing a gleam of flames. Two unbelievably ancient ragged armchairs. Another nice old wood table with newspaper spread over it. A divan heaped with clothes and bundles. And a yellow cat on the floor. It was all so dirty and dingy and grim and awful.

Mrs Fowler brought in an old brown teapot, and two rather pretty old china cups and saucers. It was the hardest thing I ever did, to drink out of the dirty cup. We did not speak much because I did not want to ask direct questions, and she was trembling with pride and dignity. She kept stroking the cat—'My lovely, my pretty'—and she said without looking at me, 'When I was young my father owned a shop, and later we had a house in St John's Wood, and I know how things should be.'

And when I left she said, in her way of not looking at me, 'I suppose I won't be seeing you again?'

And I said, 'Yes, if you'll ask me.' Then she did look at me, and there was a small smile, and I said, 'I'll come on Saturday afternoon for tea, if you like.'

'Oh I would like, yes I would.' And there was a moment between us of intimacy: that is the word. And yet she was so full of pride and did not want to ask, and she turned away from me and began petting the cat: Oh, my little pet, my little pretty.

When I got home that evening I was in a panic. I had committed myself. I was full of revulsion. The sour, dirty smell was in my clothes and hair. I bathed and washed my hair and did myself up and rang a friend and said, 'Let's go out to dinner.' We had a good dinner and the whole time I sat looking around at the people in the restaurant, everyone well dressed and clean, and I thought, if she came into this restaurant ... well, she couldn't. Not even as a cleaner, or a washer-up.

On the Saturday I took her some roses and carnations, and a cake with real cream. I was pleased with myself, and this carried me over her reaction—she was pleased, but I had overdone it. There was no vase for the flowers. I put them in a white enamel jug. She put the cake on a big old cracked plate. She was being rather distant. We sat on either side of the iron stove, and the brown teapot was on it to warm, and the flames were too hot. She was wearing a silk blouse, black dots on white. Real silk. Everything is like this with her. A beautiful flowered Worcester teapot, but it is cracked. Her skirt is of good heavy wool, but it is stained and frayed. She did not want me to see in her 'bedroom', but I took a peep when she was in the 'kitchen'. The furniture was part very good: bookcases, a chest of drawers, then a shoddy dressing table and a wardrobe like a varnished packing case. The bed had on it an old-fashioned quilt, plump, of chintz. She did not sleep in the bed, I realized, but on the divan next door, where we sat. Everywhere in the room were piles of rubbish, what looked like rags, bundles of newspapers, everything you can think of: this was what she did not want me to see.

She talked and I listened. I did not leave till nearly seven. I came home, and switched on the fire, and thought it was time I did some cleaning. I sat by myself and thought of Mrs Fowler, by herself, the flames showing in the open front of her grate. I opened a tin of soup, and I watched television.

Next Saturday I took her a little pot of African violets and another cake.
Everything the same: the fire burning, the yellow cat, and her dirty white silk spotted blouse.

There was a reticence in her, and I thought it was because she had talked last Saturday for three hours, hardly stopping.

But it wasn't that. It came out almost when I was leaving.

'Are you a good neighbour?' she said.

'I hope perhaps I may become one,' I said, laughing.

'Why, have they put you on probation, then?'

I did not understand, and she saw I didn't. It turns out that the Council employ women, usually elderly, who go into old people's houses for a cup of tea, or to see if they are all right: they don't do much, but keep an eye on them. They are called Good Neighbours and they are paid so little they can't be doing it for the money.

On the third Saturday I took her some fruit, and saw it was the wrong thing. She said nothing, again, till later, when she remarked that her teeth made it impossible for her to eat fruit.

'Can't you eat grapes? Bananas?'

She said, with humour, that the pension did not run to grapes.

And she was off, on the subject of the pension, and what coal cost, and what food cost, and 'that council woman who doesn't know what she is talking about.' I listened, again. I have not pieced it all together yet. I see that it will be a long time before my ignorance, my lack of experience, and her reticence, and her rages—for now I see how they simmer there, making her eyes light up with what you'd think, at first, must be gaiety or even a sense of comedy—a long time before how she is, her nature, and how I am, my rawness, can make it possible for me to form a whole picture of her.

She went with me to the outside door when I left, and she was doing something I have seen on the stage or written in novels. She wore an old striped apron, because she had put it on to make the tea, and she stood pleating it with both hands, and letting it go smooth, then pleating it again.

'Shall I drop in during the week?' I asked.

'If you have time,' she said. And could not resist, 'And it will make a bit extra for you.' Yet she almost gasped as she said this: she did not want to say it, because she wanted to believe I was not an official, paid person, but just a human being who likes her.

But I went back to Mrs Fowler after work.

I had been thinking all day about my marvellous bathroom, my baths, my dependence on all that. I was thinking that what I spent on hot water in a month would change her life.

But when I went in, taking six milk stouts and some new glasses, and I cried out from the door, 'Hello, I'm here, let me in, look what I've got!' and I strode in down that awful passage while she stood to one side, her face was a spiteful little fist. She wanted to punish me, but I wasn't going to let her. I went striding and slamming about, and poured out stout and showed her the glasses, and by the time I sat down, she did too, and she was lively and smiling.

'Have you seen my new boots?' I asked her, thrusting them forward. She bent to peer at them, her mouth trembling with laughter, with mischief.

'Oh,' she half whispered, 'I do like the things you wear, I do think they are lovely.'

So we spent the evening, me showing her every stitch I had. I took off my sweater and stood still so she could walk round me, laughing. I had on my new camisole, *crêpe de Chine*. I pulled up my skirts so she could see the lace in it. I took off my boots so she could handle them.

She laughed and enjoyed herself.

She told me about clothes she had worn when she was young.

There was a dress that was a favourite, of grey poplin with pink flowers on it. She wore it to visit her auntie. It had been the dress of her father's fancy-woman, and it was too big for her, but she took it in.

'Before my poor mother died, nothing was too good for me, but then, I got the cast-offs. But this was so lovely, so lovely, and I did love myself in it.'

We talked about the dresses and knickers and petticoats and camisoles and slippers and boas and corsets of fifty, sixty, seventy years ago. Mrs Fowler is over ninety.

And she talked most about her father's woman, who owned her own pub. When Mrs Fowler's mother died.... 'She was poisoned, dear! *She* poisoned her—oh yes, I know what you are thinking, I can see your face, but *she* poisoned her, just as she nearly did for me. She came to live in our house. That was in St John's Wood. I was a skivvy for the whole house, I slaved day and night, and before *they* went to bed I'd take up some thin porridge with some whisky and cream stirred in. She would be on one side of the fire, in her fancy red-feathered bed jacket, and my father on the other side, in his silk dressing jacket. She'd say to me, Maudie, you feeling strong tonight? And she'd throw off all that feathered stuff and stand there in her corsets. They don't make corsets like that now. She was a big handsome woman, full of flesh, and my father was sitting there in his armchair smiling and pulling at his whiskers. I had to loosen those corset strings. What a job! But it was better than hauling and tugging her into her corsets when she was dressing to go out. And they never said to me, Maudie, would you fancy a spoonful of porridge yourself? No, they ate and drank like kings, they wanted for nothing. If she felt like a crab or a sole or a lobster, he'd send out for it. But it was never Maudie, would you like a bit? But she got fatter and fatter and then it was: Do you want my old blue silk, Maudie? I wanted it right enough! One of her dresses'd make a dress and a blouse for me, and sometimes a scarf. But I never liked wearing her things, not really. I felt as if they had been stolen from my poor mother.'

I did not get home till late.

I went back to Maudie last night. I said to her, 'Can I call you Maudie?' But she didn't like that. She hates familiarity, disrespect. So I slid away from it. When I left I said, 'Then at least call me Janna, please.' So now she will call me Janna, but it must be Mrs Fowler, showing respect.

I asked her to describe to me all those old clothes, for the magazine: I said we would pay for her expertise. But this was a mistake. She cried out, really shocked and hurt, 'Oh no, how can you... I love thinking about those old days.'

And so that slid away too. How many mistakes I make, trying to do the right thing.

Nearly all my first impulses are quite wrong, like being ashamed of my bathroom, and of the mag.

I spent an hour last night describing my bathroom to her in the tiniest detail, while she sat smiling, delighted, asking questions. She is not envious. No. But sometimes there is a dark angry look, and I know I'll hear more, obliquely, later.

She talked more about that house in St John's Wood. I can see it! The heavy dark furniture, the comfort, the good food and the drink.

Her father owned a little house where 'they' wanted to put the Paddington railway line. Or something to do with it. And he got a fortune for it. Her father had had a corner shop in Bell Street, and sold hardware and kept free coal and bread for the poor people, and in the cold weather there was a cauldron of soup for the poor. 'I used to love standing there, so proud of him, helping those poor people....'

And then came the good luck, and all at once, the big house and warmth and her father going out nearly every night, for he loved going where the toffs were, he went to supper and the theatre, and the music hall and there he met *her,* Maudie's mother broke her heart, and was poisoned.

Maudie says that she had a lovely childhood, she couldn't wish a better to anyone, not the Queen herself. She keeps talking of a swing in a garden under apple trees, and long uncut grass. 'I used to sit and swing myself, for hours at a time, and swing, and swing, and I sang all the songs I knew, and then poor Mother came out and called to me, and I ran in to her and she gave me fruit cake and milk and kissed me, and I ran back to the swing. Or she would dress me and my sister Polly up and we went out into the street. We had a penny and we bought a leaf of chocolate each. And I used to lick it up crumb by crumb, and I hoped I wouldn't run into anyone so I must share it. But my sister always ate hers all at once, and then nagged at me to get some of mine.'

'How old were you, on the swing, Mrs Fowler?'

'Oh, I must have been five, six....'

None of it adds up. There couldn't, surely, have been a deep grassy garden behind the hardware shop in Bell Street? And in St John's Wood she would have been too old for swings and playing by herself in the grasses while the birds sang? And when her father went off to his smart suppers and the theatre, when was that? I ask, but she doesn't like to have a progression made, her mind has bright pictures in it that she has painted for herself and has been dwelling on for all those decades.

In what house was it her father came in and said to her mother, 'You whey-faced slop, don't you ever do anything but snivel?' And hit her. But never did it again, because Maudie ran at him and beat him across the legs until he began to laugh and held her up in the air, and said to his wife, 'If you had some of her fire, you'd be something,' and went off to his fancy-woman. And then Maudie would be sent up by her mother with a jug to the pub, to stand in the middle of the public bar asking for draught Guinness. 'Yes, I had to stand there for everyone to see, so that *she* would be ashamed. But she wasn't ashamed, not she, she would have me over the bar counter and into her own little back room, which was so hot our faces were beef. That was before she poisoned my mother and began to hate me, out of remorse.'

All that I have written up to now was a recapitulation, summing-up. Now I am going to write day by day, if I can. Today was Saturday, I did my shopping, and went home to work for a couple of hours, and then dropped in to Mrs F. No answer when I knocked, and I went back up her old steps to the street and saw her creeping along, pushing her shopping basket. Saw her as I did the first day: an old crooked witch. Quite terrifying, nose and chin nearly meeting, heavy grey brows, straggly bits of white hair under the black splodge of hat. She was breathing heavily as she came up to me. She gave her impatient shake of the head when I said hello, and went down the steps without speaking to me. Opened the door, still without speaking, went in. I nearly walked away. But followed her, and without being asked took myself into the room where the fire was. She came in after a long time, perhaps half an hour, while I heard her potter about. Her old yellow cat came and sat near my feet. She brought in a tray with her brown teapot and biscuits, quite nice and smiling. And she pulled the dirty curtains over, and put on the light and put the coal on the fire. No coal left in the bucket. I took the bucket from her and went along the passage to the coal cellar. A dark that had no light in it. A smell of cat. I scraped coal into the bucket and took it back, and she held out her hand for the bucket without saying thank you.

Monday.
   Dropped in after work, with some chocolates. She seemed stand-offish. Cross because I did not go in yesterday? She said she had not gone out because it was cold, and she felt bad. After I got home I wondered if she wanted me to go and shop for her. But after all, she got along before I blew into her life—*crashed* into it.

Tuesday.
   I was asked today if I would go to Munich for the Clothes Fair. I was reluctant, though I enjoy these trips: realized it was because of Maudie Fowler. This struck me as crazy, and I said I'd go.

Went in to Maudie after work. The flames were busting out of the grate, and she was hot and angry. No, she didn't feel well, and no, I wasn't to trouble myself. She was so rude, but I went into the kitchen, which stank of sour food and cat food that had gone off, and saw she had very little there. I said I was going out to shop for her. I now recognize these moments when she is pleased that I will do this or that, but her pride is hurting. She lowers her sharp little chin, her lips tremble a little, and she stares in silence at the fire.

I did not ask what to get, but as I left she shouted after me about fish for the cat. I got a lot of things, put them on her kitchen table, boiled up some milk, took it to her.

'You ought to be in bed,' I said.

She said, 'And the next thing, you'll be fetching the doctor.'

'Well, is that so terrible?'

'He'll send me away,' she said.

'Where to?'

'Hospital, where else?'

I said to her, 'You talk as if hospital is a sort of prison.'

She said, 'I have my thoughts, and you keep yours.'

Meanwhile, I could see she was really ill. I had to fight with her, to help her to bed. I was looking around for a nightdress, but I understood at last she did not use one. She goes to bed in vest and drawers, with an old cardigan pinned at the throat by a nice garnet brooch.

She was suffering because I saw that her bed was not clean, and that her underclothes were soiled. The sweet stench was very strong: I know now it is urine.

I put her in, made her tea, but she said, 'No, no, I'll only be running.'

I looked around, found that a chair in the corner of the room was a commode and dragged it close to the bed.

'Who's going to empty it?' she demanded, furious.

I went out of the kitchen to see what the lavatory was like: a little cement box, with a very old unlidded seat, and a metal chain that had broken and had string extending it. It was clean. But very cold. No wonder she has a cough. It is very cold at the moment. February—and I only *feel* how cold it really is when I think of her, Maudie, for everywhere I am is so well heated and protected. If she is going out to that lavatory from the hot fire....

I said to her, 'I'll drop in on my way to work.'

I am sitting here, in bed, having bathed and washed every scrap of me, hair too, writing this and wondering how it is I am in this position with Maudie.

Wednesday.

Booked for Munich. Went in to Maudie after work. The doctor was there. Dr Thring. An old man, fidgety and impatient, standing by the door, away from the heat and smell of the place. He was confronting an angry, obstinate, tiny old woman, who stood in the middle of her floor as if she was in front of the firing squad, 'I won't go into hospital, I won't, you can't make me.'

'Then I won't come in to look after you, you can't make me do that.' He was shouting. When he saw me, he said, in a different voice, relieved, desperate, 'Tell her, if you're a friend, she should be in hospital.'

She was looking at me quite terrified.

'Mrs Fowler,' I said, 'why don't you want to go into hospital?'

She turned her back on us both, and picked up the poker, and jabbed the flames with it.

The doctor looked at me, scarlet with anger and the heat of the place, and then shrugged, 'You ought to be in a Home,' he said. 'I keep telling you so.'

'You can't force me.'

He exclaimed angrily and went into the passage, summoning me to follow. 'Tell her,' he said.

'I think she should be in hospital,' I said, 'but why should she be in a Home?'

He was quite at the end of his tether with exasperation and—I could see—tiredness. 'Look at it all,' he said. 'Look at it. Well, I'll ring up the Services.' And off he went.

When I got back, she said, 'I suppose you've been arranging with him.'

I told her exactly what I said, and while I was speaking she was coughing, mouth closed, chest heaving, eyes watering, and was thumping her chest with the heel of her fist. I could see that she didn't want to listen to what I said.

Thursday.

I was coming straight home from the airport, because I was suddenly tired. But made the taxi put me off at Maudie Fowler's. I stood there knocking and banging on the door. Freezing. Not a sound. I got into a panic—was she dead?—and noted, not without interest, that one of my reactions was relief. At last, an agitation of the curtains at the window of her 'front room', which she seems never to use. I waited. Nothing happened. I banged and banged, absolutely furious by them. I was ready to strangle her. Then the door opened inwards, sticking and scraping, and there she was, a tiny little bundle of black, with her white face sticking up out of it. And the *smell*. It is no good my telling myself I shouldn't care about such details. I care terribly. The smell... awful, a sour, sweet-sharp reek. But I could see she was only just able to stand there.

There was nothing 'charming' about me, I was so angry.

'Why do you keep me out in the cold?' I said, and went in, past her, making her move aside. She then went on ahead of me down the passage, a hand on a wall to steady her.

In the back room, a heap of dead cinders in the grate. There was an electric fire, though; one bar, and it was making noises which meant it was unsafe. The place was cold, dirty, smelly, and the cat came and wound itself around my legs miaowing. Maudie let herself slide into her chair and sat staring at the grate.

'Well, why didn't you let the nurse in?' I shouted at her.

'The nurse,' she said bitterly. 'What nurse?'

'I know she came.'

'Not till Monday. All the weekend I was here by myself, no one.'

I was about to scream at her, 'Why didn't you let her in when she came on Monday?' but saw there was no point.

I was full of energy again—anger.

'Maudie,' I said, 'you are the limit, the end, you make things worse for yourself. Well, I'll put the kettle on.'

I did. I fetched coal. I found the commode full of urine, but no worse, thank goodness. Thank goodness was what I thought then, but I see one gets used to anything. I then went out into the street with a carrier bag. A grey sleety rain. There I was, in all my smart things from Munich, scrabbling about in the skip for bits of wood. Faces at the windows, watching me.

Inside, I scraped out the grate, clouds of dust flying about, and laid the fire. With a fire-lighter. Wood and coal. Soon it was burning.

I made tea for both of us, having scalded the *filthy* cups. I must stop being so petty about it. Does it matter, dirty cups? Yes! Yes, yes, yes, *yes.*

She had not moved, but sat looking at the flames.

'The cat,' she said.

'I've given her some food.'

'Then let her out for a bit.'

'There's sleet and rain.'

'She won't mind.'

I opened the back door. A wave of cold rain came straight in at me, and the fat yellow cat, who had been pressing to get to the door, miaowed and ran back again, to the coal cellar.

'She's gone to the coal cellar,' I said.

'Then I suppose I'll have to put my hand in it,' she said.

This made me so angry! I was seething with emotion. As usual, I wanted to hit her or shake her and, as usual, to put my arms around her.

But my mind luckily was in control, and I did everything I should, without, thank God, being 'humorous' or charming or gracious.

'Have you been eating at all?'

No response.

I went out again to shop. Not a soul in the corner shop. The Indian sitting there at the cash desk looked grey and chilled, as well he might, poor soul.

I said I was buying food for Mrs Fowler, wanting to know if she had been in.

He said, 'Oh, the old lady, I hope she is not ill?'

'She is,' I said.

'Why doesn't she go into a Home?'

'She doesn't want to.'

'Hasn't she a family?'

'I think so, but they don't care.'

'It is a terrible thing,' he said to me, meaning me to understand that his people would not neglect an old woman like this.

'Yes, it is a terrible thing, and you are right,' I said.

When I got back, again I thought of death. She sat there, eyes closed, and so still, I thought not breathing.

But then, her blue eyes were open and she was looking at the fire.

'Drink your tea,' I said. 'And I'll grill you a bit of fish. Can you eat it?'

'Yes, I will.'

In the kitchen I tried to find anything that wasn't greasy, and gave up. I put the fish on the grill, and opened the door briefly to get in some clean air. Sleet notwithstanding.

I took her the fish, and she sat herself up and ate it all, slowly, and her hands trembled, but she finished it and I saw she had been hungry.

I said, 'I've been in Munich. To see all the clothes for the autumn. I've been seeing all the new styles.'

'I've never been out of England.'

'Well, I'll tell you all about it when you are a bit better.'

To this she did not respond. But at last, just when I thought I would go, she remarked, 'I've a need for some clean clothes.'

I did not know how to interpret this. I did see—I have become sensitive enough for that—at least that this was not at all a simple request.

She wanted me to buy her clothes?

I looked at her. She made herself look at me, and said, 'Next door, you'll find things.'

'What?'

She gave a trembling, discouraged sort of shrug.

'Vest. Knickers. Petticoat. Don't you wear underclothes, that you are asking?'

193

Again, the automatic anger, as if a button had been pushed. I went next door into the room I knew she didn't like me in.

The bed that has the good eiderdown, the wardrobe, the dressing table with little china trinkets, the good bookcases. But everywhere piles and heaps of—rubbish. I could not believe it. Newspapers dating back fifty years, crumbling away; awful scraps of material, stained and yellow, bits of lace, dirty handkerchiefs, shreds of ribbon—I've never seen anything like it. She had never thrown anything away, I think. In the drawers, disorder, and they were crammed with—but it would take pages to describe. Petticoats, camisoles, knickers, stays, vests, old dresses or bits of them, blouses... and nothing less than twenty years old, and some of them going back to World War One. The difference between clothes now and then: these were all 'real' materials, cottons, silks, woollens. Not a man-made fibre there. But everything torn, or stained, or dirty. I pulled out bundles of things, and every one I examined, first for interest, and then to see if there was anything wearable or clean. I found at last a wool vest, and long wool drawers, and a rather nice pink silk petticoat, and then a woollen dress, blue, and a cardigan. They were clean, or nearly. I worked away in there, shivering with cold, and thinking of how I had loved myself all these last days, how much I do love myself, for being in control, on top; and thought that the nearest I could get to poor Maudie's helplessness was remembering what it had been like to be a child, hoping that you won't wet your pants before you get to the lavatory.

I took the clothes into the other room, which was very hot now, the flames roaring up. I said to her, 'Do you want me to help you change?' The sideways, irritable movement of the head, which I knew now meant I was being stupid.

But I did not know why.

So I sat down opposite her, and said, 'I'll finish my tea before it's freezing.' I noted that I was drinking it without feeling sick: I have become used to drinking out of grimy cups, I noted that with interest. Once Maudie had been like me, perpetually washing herself, washing cups, plates, dusting, washing her hair.

She was talking, at random I thought, about when she had been in hospital. I half listened, wishing that doctors and nurses could hear how their hospitals are experienced by someone like Maudie. Prisons.

Reformatories. But then I realized she was telling me about how, because she had not been well enough to be put in the bath, two nurses had washed her in her bed, and I understood.

'I'll put on the kettles,' I said. 'And you must tell me what to do.'

I put on two kettles, found an enamel basin, which I examined with interest, for I have not seen any but plastic ones for a long time, and searched for soap and a flannel. They were in a hole in the wall above the sink: a brick taken out and the cavity painted.

I took the basin, kettles, soap, flannel, a jug of cold water, next door. Maudie was struggling out of her top layer of clothes. I helped her, and realized I had not co-ordinated this at all. I rushed about, found newspapers, cleared the table, spread thick papers all over it, arranged basin, kettles, jug, washing things. No towel. I rushed into the kitchen, found a damp dirty towel, rushed into the front room and scrabbled about, seeming to myself to be taking all day. But it was really only a few moments. I was bothered about Maudie standing there, half naked, and ill, and coughing. At last I found a cleanish towel. She was standing by the basin, her top half nude. There is nothing of her. A fragile rib cage under creased yellow skin, her shoulder bones like a skeleton's, and at the end of thin stick arms, strong working hands. Long thin breasts hanging down.

She was clumsily rubbing soap on to the flannel, which, needless to say, was slimy. I should have washed it out first. I ran next door again, tore a bit off an old clean towel and took it back. I knew she wanted to tick me off for tearing the towel; she would have done if she had not been saving her breath.

I slowly washed her top half, in plenty of soap and hot water, but the grime on her neck was thick, and to get that off would have meant rubbing at it, and it was too much. She was trembling with weakness. I was comparing this frail old body with my mother's: but I had only caught glimpses of her sick body. She had washed herself. Now I washed Maudie Fowler. Maudie might be only skin and bones but her body doesn't have that beaten-down look, as if the flesh is sinking into the bones. She was chilly, she was sick, she was weak—but I could feel the vitality beating there: life. How strong it is, life. I had never thought that before, never felt life in that way, as I did then; washing Maudie Fowler, a fierce angry old woman. Oh, how angry: it occurred to me that all her vitality is in her anger; I must not, must *not* resent it or want to hit back.

Then there was the problem of her lower half, and I was waiting for guidance.

I slipped the 'clean' vest on over her head, and wrapped the 'clean' cardigan round her, and then saw she was sliding down the thick bunches of skirt. And then it hit me, the stench. Oh, it is no good, I *can't* not care. Because she had been too weak or too tired to move, she had shat her pants, shat everything.

Knickers, filthy.... Well, I am not going on, not even to let off steam, it makes me feel sick. But I was looking at the vest and petticoats she had taken off, and they were brown and yellow with shit. Anyway. She stood there, her bottom half naked. I slid newspapers under her, so she was standing on thick wads of them. I washed and washed her, all her lower half. She had her big hands down on the table for support. When it came to her bottom she thrust it out, as a child might, and I washed all of it, creases too. Then I threw away all that water, refilled the basin, quickly put the kettles on again. I washed her private parts, and thought about that phrase for the first time: she was suffering most terribly because this stranger was invading her privateness. And I did her legs again, again, since the dirt had run down them. And I made her stand in the basin and washed her yellow gnarled old feet. The water was hot again over the flaring gas, and I helped her pull on the 'clean' bloomers. By then, having seen what was possible, they were clean to me, just a bit dusty. And then the nice pink petticoat.

'Your face,' I said. For we had not done that. 'How about your hair?' The white wisps and strands lay over the yellow dirty scalp.

'It will wait,' she said.

So I washed her face, carefully, on a clean bit torn off the old towel.

Then I asked her to sit down, found some scissors, cut the toenails, which was just like cutting through horn, got clean stockings on, her dress, her jersey. And as she was about to put on the outside clothes of black again, I said involuntarily, 'Oh, don't—' and was sorry, for she was hurt, she trembled even more, and sat silent, like a bad child. She was worn out.

I threw out the dirty water and scalded the basin, and filled a kettle to make fresh tea. I took a look out of the back: streams of sleet, with crumbs of greyish snow, the wind blowing hard—water was coming in under the kitchen door; and as for thinking of her going out into that to reach the lavatory, that freezing box—yet she *had* been going out, and presumably would again.

I kept saying to myself, She is over ninety and she has been living like this for years: she has survived it!

I took her more tea, and some biscuits, and left her by her big fire.

I put all the filthy outer clothes I had taken off in newspaper and folded them up and dumped them in the rubbish bin, without asking her.

And then I made a selection among the clothes from the drawers, and stripped the filthy sheets from her bed, and the pillowcases, and went out into the rain to the launderette, leaving them with the girl there to be done.

I made the place as neat as I could, put down food for the cat, who sat against Maudie's leg, being stroked. I cleared everything up. All this time Maudie sat staring into the flames, not looking at me when I looked at her, but watching me as I moved around, and when she thought I didn't know.

'Don't think I don't appreciate it,' she said as I laboured on, and on. I was sweeping the floor by then, with a hand brush and pan. I couldn't find anything else. The way she said this, I couldn't interpret it. It was flat I thought, even hopeless: she was feeling helpless in a new way. For, very clearly, no one had ever done this kind of thing for her before.

I went back to the launderette. The large competent Irish girl with whom I had exchanged the brisk comradeship of equals when leaving the stuff gave me the great bag of clean things and looked into my face and said, 'Filth. I've never seen anything like it. Filth.' She hated me.

I said, 'Thanks,' did not bother to explain, and left. But I was flaming with—embarrassment! Oh, how dependent I am on being admired, liked, appreciated.

I took the things back, through the sleet. I was cold and tired by then. I wanted to get home.... But I cleared out the drawers of a large chest, put the clean things in, and told Maudie where I had put them.

Then I said, 'I'll drop in tomorrow evening.'

I was curious to hear what she'd say.

'I'll see you then,' was what she said.

And now I am alone, and have bathed, but it was a brisk businesslike bath, I didn't soak for hours. I should have tidied everything, but I haven't. I am, simply, tired. I cannot believe that this time yesterday I was in the hotel, pampered guest, eating supper with Karl, cherished colleague. Flowers, venison, wine, cream—the lot.

It seems to me impossible that there should be *that* there; and then Maudie Fowler, *here.* Or is it *I* who am impossible? I certainly am disoriented.

I have to think all this out. What am I to do? Who can I discuss it with?

N ow we are nearly into summer.

What has happened since I sat down last to this unfortunate diary of mine? But I don't want to give it up.

At the Indian shop, I hung around until the owner, Mr Patel, said, 'Mrs Fowler was out on the street yesterday, screaming and shouting.'

'Oh yes, what did she say?'

'She was screaming. None of you were around trying to get me hot water and a bath when I had a baby, none of you cared when I didn't have food to give him. I've lived all my life without running hot water and a bath, and if you come back I'll get the police.'

Mr Patel says all this slowly, his grave concerned eyes on my face, and I didn't dare smile. He keeps his eyes on my face, reproachful and grave, and says, 'When I was in Kenya, before we had to leave, I thought everyone in this country was rich.'

'You know better now, then.'

But he wants to say something else, something different. I wait, pick up some biscuits, put them back, consider a tin of cat food.

At last he says, in a low voice, 'Once, with us, we would not let one of our old people come to such a life. But now—things are changing with us.'

I feel I personally should apologize. At last I say, 'Mr Patel, there can't be very many like Mrs Fowler left.'

'I have six, seven, every day in my shop. All like her, with no one to care for them. And I am only one shop.'

He sounds as if he is accusing me. He is accusing my clothes, my style. I am out of place in this little corner shop. And then, feeling as if he has wronged me, he takes a cake from the shelves, one that Maudie likes, and says, 'Give it to her.'

Our eyes meet again, and this time differently: we are appalled, we are frightened; it is all too much for us.

ANITA BROOKNER
A WEDDING

H ere is Sofka, in a wedding photograph; at least, I assume it is a wedding, although the bride and groom are absent. Sofka stands straight and stern, her shoulders braced, her head erect in the manner of two earlier generations. She wears a beautiful beaded dress and an egret feather in her hair. It must have been attached to a hat but the hat is hidden by her coiffure, which is in itself hat-shaped. Behind her stand her two daughters, beautiful also, but looking curiously tubercular; perhaps those wide-eyed pleading smiles add to this impression. The daughters are in white, with ribbons in their long hair, which I know to have been red. Sofka's eldest son, her pride and joy, smiles easily, already a lazy conqueror. In his white tie and tails he has the air of an orchestral conductor. He stands between the two girls, an escort rather than a brother, as he was to prove on so many occasions. The sickly and favoured younger son is nowhere in sight, unless he proves to be one of those touching and doomed-looking children seated cross-legged in the front row, the girls, with hair of unimaginable length, clutching posies of flowers, the boys in long trousers and jackets of a satiny-looking material, gazing soulfully at the photographer. Yes, Alfred must be the one on the right. All around them are lesser members of the cast, relations by marriage: a stout and equally beaded woman, several jovial men, a youngish woman with a cascading jabot of lace and an expression of dedicated purpose and, on the extreme left, edging her way into the centre, a pretty girl with a face like a bird. None of these people seems to have as much right to be in the picture as Sofka does. It is as if she has given birth to the entire brood, but having done so, thinks little of them. This I know to be the case. She gazes out of the photograph, beyond the solicitations of the photographer, her eyes remote and unsmiling, as if contemplating some unique destiny. Compared with her timeless expression, her daughters' pleading smiles already foretell their future. And those favoured sons, who clearly have their mother's blessing—there is something there too that courts disaster. Handsome Frederick, in his white tie and tails, with his orchestral conductor's panache: is there not perhaps something too easy about him, pliable, compliant, weak? Able to engage his mother's collusion in many an amorous escapade, but finally dishonourable, disappointing? Does Sofka already know this? And little Alfred, seated cross-legged between the girls who must be cousins and with one of whom he will shortly fall in love: do those eyes, heavy and solemn, shadowed with the strain of behaving well, bear in them the portent of a life spent obeying orders, working hard, being a credit, being a consolation, being a balm for his mother's hurt, a companion in her isolation? For her husband, their father, is absent, gone before, dead, mildly disgraced. Gambling, they say. In any event, he was an older man, scarcely compatible, out of reach to his young children, amused by his young wife but easily bored by her inflexible dignity. Out of it, in every sense.

And now I see that it is in fact a wedding photograph. The bride and groom were there all the time, in the centre, as they should be. A good-looking couple. But lifeless, figures from stock. Above the bridegroom's shoulder, standing on something, perhaps, Sofka gazes ahead, with her family's future before her. No one to touch her. As it proved.

I have no doubt that once the photograph was taken, and the wedding group dispersed, the festivities took their normal course. I have no doubt that great quantities of delicious food—things in aspic, things in baskets of spun sugar—were consumed, and that the music struck up and the bride and bridegroom danced, oblivious of their guests, and that the elders gathered in groups on their gilt chairs while the children, flushed with too many sweetmeats and the lure of the polished parquet floor, ventured forth until restrained by nurses or grandmothers. I have no doubt that as the evening wore on the cigar-scented reminiscences induced many an indulgent nod, a nostalgic smile never to be recovered in the harder commerce of daily life. I have no doubt that those anonymous and jovial men (husbands, of course) relaxed into the sweetness of this precarious harmony, as if they had at last found what married life had seemed to promise them, and their golden smiles, their passive decent good nature, the sudden look of worldliness their faces assumed as their lips closed voluptuously round the fine Romeo y Julietas and they lifted their heads a little to expel the blueish smoke, reminded their wives—censorious women, with higher standards—why they had married them. Sofka would be at the centre of this group, of any group. Handsome Frederick would be dancing, sweeping some girl off her feet, making suggestions which she would not dare take seriously, and perhaps neither would he, with his mother watching him. Later, perhaps, or so the girls would like to think. Little Alfred would manfully trundle his cousin round the floor, looking to his mother for approval, and in so doing lose both her approval and his own heart. The girls, Mireille and Babette (Mimi and Betty), would stay with their mother, waiting for her permission to dance. But the young men, faced with the prospect of negotiating for that permission, would not insist, and the girls would not dance much. Sofka gave out that the girls were delicate. And indeed they looked it.

I find it entirely appropriate and indeed characteristic that Sofka should have named her sons after kings and emperors and her daughters as if they were characters in a musical comedy. Thus were their roles designated for them. The boys were to conquer, and the girls to flirt. If this implies something unfinished, as if the process were omnivorous but static, that too would be characteristic. Sofka sees her children's futures as being implicit in their names, and she has given much thought to the matter; indeed, one wonders if she thinks about anything else. Her sons, handsome, with the legendary if short-lived handsomeness of those men who die young, are to establish themselves on the ruins of their father's fortune; they are to divide the world and conquer it between them. No matter that Frederick plays the violin so well, and that Alfred is so fond of reading; these accomplishments are for the drawing-room and the study and not for the world. In due course they will lay aside the violin and the books, brace their shoulders, face up to their responsibilities (to Sofka and the girls) and revitalize those factories which have been idle too long. Imperceptibly, they will become tycoons, captains of industry, as their father had been before them. That their father's little weakness—the one he confessed to, that is—might be hereditary Sofka would regard as ridiculous. She repels the thought before it is even formulated. In any event, the boys are so little their father's children; they are, by definition, hers alone. Has she not brought them up single-handed? And are they not a credit to her dedicated mothering? Frederick might break hearts, and he will have her permission to do so. There is nothing the virtuous Sofka admires so much as a man with a bad reputation. Alfred will be encouraged to follow his brother's example; he is too serious by nature and by inclination. See how he clasps his little cousin round her unindented waist and turns his face back to his mother to solicit her smile. And the little cousin already annoyed that his attention should be diverted from her. Better that Alfred should shrug his shoulders and pass on, saving himself, saving them all, from hurt. And he will be even more handsome than his brother when he grows older; he has a soulful poet's face, the ancient eyes of a child prodigy. Alfred is her hope and her investment; he is her second chance. For if Frederick breaks too many hearts to devote much time to the business, that is to say if his career as a *boulevardier* were to interfere with his attendance at the factory, then sad little Alfred, whom Sofka knows to be as serious, as inflexible of purpose as she herself, can be relied upon to assume all the burdens that might otherwise have been shared. With Alfred's help, Sofka knows, she will once again come into her kingdom.

Will the boys marry? Well, of course, they will, in so far as everybody marries. But that day might be indefinitely postponed. Sofka does not believe in early marriages; she sees nothing touching in youthful pleasure. She herself had been chosen by a man of substance, well past the age of infatuation. (Or so she believed.) She herself had sought dignity and she thinks that everyone should follow her example. The boys will marry eventually but their brides must be carefully chosen; they will have to be of a suitable pattern to conform to the family destiny. For the family by that stage would once again be rich, very rich. So that extravagant pleasure-loving girls would be out of the question. Sensible women, young enough to produce one or at the most two children, but otherwise fairly mature, and not necessarily very good-looking. Looks are not everything, says beautiful Sofka to her children. And the daughters-in-law will be of a similar background to herself and above all of a similar temperament; thus can Sofka hand on her sons to replicas of herself when she at last, and regretfully, concedes that it is time for them to marry. But that time is in the very distant future, ever more distant as time goes on. In this matter of her sons' marriages, Sofka is inclined to enact both justice and revenge. For if her mothering is to triumph, why should any other woman get the credit? And enjoy the advantage?

And for Mireille and Babette (Mimi and Betty), that time of settling down, as they so wistfully think of it, is so far off as to be almost unimaginable. In the manner of sheltered girls in that unliberated age they long to be married; they long for marriage in order that they might be virtuous young matrons, attentive to their duties and to their husbands' welfare, able to supervise servants and, eventually, the children's nurse. Able to present the breadwinner with evidence of good housewifery, his shirts impeccably laundered and scented with lavender and vetiver, his newspaper and journals intact and uncreased, his house and garden tended, his accounts faultless. Where did they unearth these dreams of innocence? They are beautiful, with a slightly hectic look of which they are probably unaware, and they have been given the names of characters in a musical comedy. And are expected to behave in the same way. For Sofka, that unbending matriarch, young women have a duty to flirt, to engage in heartless and pointless stratagems, to laugh, pretend, tease, have moods, enslave and discard. The purpose of these manoeuvres is to occupy their time, the time that women of a later generation are to give to their careers. By breaking hearts (but never seriously) the girls can give themselves plenty to talk about; they need never be bored, or a burden to their mother. And by keeping a good-natured group of young men in tow ('our crowd') they need never know the grip of a hopeless or unrequited passion and be spared the shame of being left unclaimed. Sofka is quite sincere in determining that her daughters should never be seen to be waiting. Perhaps she has had this experience herself? Her daughters must be too busy and too light-hearted to tie themselves down; they must laugh and parry even when the proposals are sincere. For there will, of course, be proposals, from one or other member of the crowd, but the prevailing temper will not encourage the girls to take them seriously. The girls will not want to take them seriously; they will be having too happy a time. Never mind the shirts scented with lavender and vetiver and the uncreased newspapers; there is a new show at the Savoy, and dancing in somebody's house on the river near Henley. And there will always be somebody to bring them home and see that they are taken care of; in any event, they can always rely on their brothers to set a good example in this respect. Marriage? The girls married? Sofka can hardly imagine it, although she has the details of their weddings quite firmly fixed in her mind. There is nothing imaginary about the weddings, only about the whole question of their married lives.

Because there is something about the girls that causes Sofka pain, a soft inward quaking pain. Is it those innocent large eyes, mild and questioning above the coy rouged smiles, that pronounces them unfit for the life their mother has decreed for them, and which she in all her integrity sees as their safeguard? Is there something doomed about those girls, although they are in perfect health, and devoted to their mother? What happens to young women, brought up to obedience, and bred to docility and virtue? What happens to such unprotected lives? How will they deal with the world, or the world with them? Sofka sees that her vigilance will be needed to spare the girls the hurt and the shame that even the unsuspecting can endure, even when they are harmless as well as beautiful. When she thinks of the soulful heartless women that she knows, women of her own age, who view the world through narrowed eyes, Sofka feels a hand clutch at her heart. Mimi and Betty, devoted sisters, devoted daughters, brushing each other's long hair at night for all the world as if they were still children, refusing to have it cut, as if they were still little girls.... What happens to such daughters? Sofka looks at them sometimes and feels that there is something like a sentence of death on them. Then she determines that they must laugh and flirt and learn all the teasing catchwords, and learn too to disguise the haunting innocence in their large eyes. But all in due course. Let them get used to their social life first. Let them harden naturally. And let them stay with their mother until then. No need to worry too much about partners. The boys can be trusted to bring them home in due course. And once the girls are safe in the bosom of 'our crowd', then Sofka can relax at last.

It was decreed, or it seemed to be decreed, that all the women in that family should have tiny names, diminutives, as if to underline their tiny sparkling natures. The little cousin with whom Alfred is dancing is Nettie (Annette). Somewhere in the background there is a Steffie, and a Carrie. Perhaps the large woman in the photograph is Carrie, a sister-in-law, unaware that she is no longer a diminutive. The husbands refer to these women as 'the girls', having long ago fallen in with the prevailing ideology, always slightly surprised that the girls have grown up and grown older, having met them in the distant past when they all knew each other and formed part of 'our crowd'. Since then they have been subsumed into the matriarchal pattern to which they resigned themselves without ever knowing what it was. Good-humoured, good-natured, undemanding, unambitious men, chatting over the week's news among themselves until summoned to supply a detail, a compliment, a justification, bidden to rejoin the group. Getting a little stout now, former pleasant looks forgotten, former energy wearing thin. Judged collectively as not quite good enough for the girls, but tolerated, necessary. Golden, indulgent fathers, awakening in their daughters secret dreams of hard fierce brutal men. Fathers of infinite kindliness, easily moved to tears by their children's beauty. Nettie's father is just such a man, easy-going, always smiling. Some would say weak. And Nettie herself will be the sort of child to enslave such a man, with her imperious manners and her arbitrary wishes, apt to fly into a passion and scream, and have to be taken on to her father's lap and soothed back to happiness. Her mother says that Nettie is 'highly strung', but she understands her perfectly well. Nettie's mother is one of those women who view the world through narrowed eyes. Nettie's mother is possibly the only person in her immediate circle of whom Sofka is slightly afraid.

Sofka herself is a diminutive, of course, although one never thinks of her as in any way diminished, rather the opposite. She is Sophie (Sophie Dorn).

I n the photograph the men wear tails or dinner jackets and the women long dresses with little hats, for this is a wedding in the old style, with something of a feeling for the old country. These weddings are important affairs, with the roster of the family's achievements on show. Quiet and retiring as their social lives may be, spent largely in each other's houses, playing cards or discussing the children, with a sharp eye for both perfections and imperfections of housekeeping, the women will prepare for a wedding as if they themselves were getting married. Long sessions with the dressmaker will replace the idle but watchful afternoons in one another's houses, then the shoes, the tiny tapestry bag, and of course the hat, will demand all their attention. The children will be indulged with new and impossibly pretty dresses, although these may be a little too young for them. The children will become petulant with the long hours standing in front of a glass, while a dressmaker crawls round them pinning the hem. The children do not really like this indoor life, to which they seem to be condemned; it sharpens their nerves and makes them touchy, although they have the beautiful rose-coloured bloom of days spent in gardens. There are gardens, of course, but they are supervised by gardeners. These days of bustle and calculation will culminate in the actual preparations for the wedding itself. Husbands, cheerfully and with resignation getting into their tails or their dinner jackets, quell an instinctive sinking of the heart as they view their wives' very great solemnity at this moment of their adornment. Iconic and magnificent, the women stand in the centre of their drawing-rooms, and it is difficult to remember that they were ever girls. The children, longing to run and to play, kick moodily around in their enchanting clothes; already they look like men and women, bored with an adult boredom, discontented enough to run for their lives.

Sofka sits in her morning-room, waiting for the car to come round. This is the traditional cry, the view halloo of wedding mornings or afternoons: 'Has the car come round?' Sofka's back is ramrod straight, her beaded dress immaculately appropriate, the hat tiny but triumphal. Around her sit the girls (Mimi and Betty) in their pretty Pre-Raphaelite dresses, and little Alfred, who is already pale with the heat and the strain. Alfred is always good, but the effort costs him a great deal. Lounging in the doorway, with the nonchalant stance of the Apollo Belvedere, is Frederick who enjoys these long celebrations, offering him the pleasure of surveying a large field of nubile girls, for weddings put such thoughts into the forefront of every mind. While waiting for the banquet, Frederick is perfectly happy to offer his arm to his mother or his sisters, and indeed is most at home in doing so, for it seems to be his only function within this family. Even now he is pouring his mother a tiny glass of Madeira, placing a small table at her elbow, smiling at her, and very gently teasing her, for she finds these events initially rather daunting. She is a shy woman, virtuous and retiring, caring only for her children, but determined to fulfil her role as duenna, as figurehead, as matriarch. This means presentation, panache, high purpose, and in their wake dignity, and responsibility, awesome concepts, borne constantly in mind. Like a general on the evening of a great campaign, like an admiral setting a course for his fleet, Sofka looks to the family fortunes and plans her performance accordingly. She surveys her children, is proud of them, trembles for them. The tremor conveys itself to her hand, and a tiny drop of Madeira gleams on the polished wood of the table. 'Mama,' says little Alfred. 'The car has come round.'

At the wedding they will dance, husbands with wives, fathers with daughters. Under watchful gazes the young people will flirt, amazed that no one is stopping them. The music will become slower, sweeter, as the evening wears on. The children will be flushed, glassy-eyed with tiredness, their beauty extraordinary, as if it were painted. On the gilt chairs the elders will sit and talk. Sofka judges the event a success. Her girls have been congratulated on their charming appearance and manners, her boys on their filial devotion. This is how it should be. Sofka's cheeks have lost their ivory pallor and her mouth wears a proud smile. Tomorrow she will receive telephone calls, no doubt with more compliments; she will give one or two tea parties, for there will be much to discuss. The verdicts of those sharp-eyed women, those sisters in the spirit, will be sought, their advice heeded. Strange how much calculation there is even in the most virtuous! Upstairs, in the old nursery, the girls are playing the piano. Little Alfred stands behind his mother's chair until told to go and play. When he receives this permission he hardly knows what to do, for he is rather bad at playing. Frederick, who is very good at it, is nowhere to be seen. Sofka pours coffee, offers cakes. Looking out into her garden, she sees that a wheelbarrow has not been put away. She frowns slightly. How tiresome that so innocent a detail should spoil the perfect picture of her day.

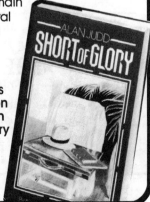

MARTIN AMIS
THE TIME SICKNESS

Twenty-twenty, and the *time* disease is epidemic. In my credit-group, anyway. And yours too, friend, unless I miss my guess. Nobody thinks about anything else any more. Nobody even pretends to think about anything else any more. (Oh yeah, except the sky, of course. The poor sky.)... It's a thing. It's a situation. We all think about *time,* catching *time,* coming down with *time.* I'm still okay, I think, for the time being.

I took out my handmirror. Everybody carries at least one handmirror now. On the zip trains you see whole carloads of people jackknifed over in taut scrutiny of their hairlines and eyesockets. The anxiety is as electric as the twanging cable above our heads. They say more people are laid low by *time*-anxiety than by *time* itself. But only *time* is fatal. It's a problem, we agree, a definite feature. How can you change the subject when there's only one subject? People don't want to talk about the sky. They don't want to talk about the sky, and I don't blame them.

I took out my handmirror and gave myself a ten-second scan. I felt so heartened that I moved carefully into the kitchen and cracked out a beer. I ate a *hero,* and a *ham salad.* I lit another cigarette. I activated the TV and keyed myself in to the Therapy Channel. I watched a seventy-year-old documentary about a road-widening scheme in a place called Orpington, over in England there. Yes, very boring, very boring indeed.... Boredom is meant to be highly prophylactic when it comes to *time.* We are all advised to experience as much boredom as we possibly can. To bore somebody is said to be even more sanative than being bored onself. That's why we tend to raise our voices in company and go on and on about anything that enters our heads. Me I go on about *time* the whole time: a reckless habit. Listen to me. I'm at it again.

The outercom sounded. I switched from Therapy to Intake. No visual. 'Who is it?' I asked the TV. The TV told me. I sighed, and put the call on a half-minute hold. Soothing music. Boring music.... Okay—you want to hear my theory? Now some say that *time* was caused by congestion, air plague, city life (and city life is the only kind of life there is these days). Others say that *time* was a result of the first nuclear conflicts (limited theatre, Persia versus Pakistan, Zaire versus Nigeria, and so on, no really big deal or anything) and more particularly of the saturation TV coverage that followed: all day the screen writhed with flesh, flesh dying or living in a queer state of age. Still others say that *time* was an evolutionary consequence of humankind's ventures into space (they shouldn't have gone out there, what with things so rocky back home). *Food,* pornography, the cancer cure.... Me, I think it was the twentieth century that did it. The twentieth century was all it took.

I went back to my call. It was Happy Farraday. That's right: the TV star. You've seen her on the Daydrama channel. *The* Happy Farraday. Oh, we go way back, Happy and me.

'Hi there, Happy,' I said, 'What's new?'

'—Lou?' her voice said warily. 'Lou, I don't feel so good.'

'That's not new. That's old.'

'I don't feel so good. I think it's really happening this time.'

'Oh, sure. Let's take a look at you,' I said. 'Come on, Happy, give me a visual on this.'

The screen remained blank, its dead cells seeming to squirm or hover. On impulse I switched from Intake to Daydrama. There was Happy, full face to camera, vividly doing her thing. I switched back. Still no visual. I said, 'I just checked you out on the other channel. You're in superb shape. What's your problem?'

'It's here,' said her voice. 'It's *time.*'

TV stars are especially prone to *time*-anxiety—to *time* too, it has to be said. Why? Well I think we're looking at an occupational hazard here. It's a thing. True, the work could hardly be more boring. Not many people know this, but all the characters in the Armchair, Daydrama and Proscenium channels now write their own lines. It's a new gimmick, intended to promote formlessness, to combat sequentiality, and so on: the market-research gurus have established that this goes down a lot better with the homebound. Besides all the writing talent is in game-conception or mass-therapy, doing soothe stuff for the non-employed and other sections of the populace that are winding down from being functional. There are fortunes to be made in the leisure and assuagement industries. The standout writers are like those teenage billionaires in the early days of the chip revolution. On the other hand, making money—like reading and writing, come to that— dangerously increases your *time*-anxiety levels. Obviously. The more money you have, the more time you have to worry about *time.* It's a thing. Happy Farraday is top credit, and she also bears the weight of TV fame (where millions know you or think they do), that collective sympathy, identification and concern which, I suspect, seriously depletes your *time*-resistance. I've started to keep a kind of file on this. I'm beginning to think of it as reciprocity syndrome, one of the new—

Where was I? Yeah. On the line with Happy here. My mind has a tendency to wander. Indulge me. It helps, *time*-wise.

'Okay. You want to tell me what symptoms you got?' She told me. 'Call a doctor,' I joked. 'Look, give me a break. This is—what? The second time this year? The third?'

'It's different this time.'

'It's the new role, Happy. That's all it is.' In her new series on Daydrama, Happy was playing the stock part of a glamorous forty-year-old with a bad case of *time*-anxiety. And it was getting to her—of course it was. 'You know where I place the blame? On your talent! As an actress you're just too damn good. Greg Buzhardt and I were—'

'Save it, Lou,' she said. 'Don't burn me out. It's real. It's *time*.'

'I know what you're going to do. I know what you're going to do. You're going to ask me to drive over.'

'I'll pay.'

'It's not the money, Happy, it's the time.'

'Take the dollar lane.'

'Wow,' I said. 'You're, you must be kind of serious this time.'

So I stood on the shoulder, waiting for Roy to bring up my Horse-fly from the stacks. Well, Happy is an old friend and one of my biggest clients, also an ex-wife of mine, and I had to do the right thing. For a while out there I wasn't sure what time it was supposed to be or whether I had a day or night context on my hands—but then I saw the faint tremors and pulsings of the sun, up in the east. The heavy green light sieved down through the ripped and tattered stratosphere, its fissures as many-eyed as silk or pantihose, with a liquid quality too, churning, changing. Green light: let's go... I had a bad scare myself the other week, a very bad scare. I was in bed with Danuta and we were going to have a crack at making love. Okay, a dumb move—but it was her birthday, and we'd been doing a lot of tranquillizers that night. I don't happen to believe that lovemaking is quite as risky as some people say. To hear some people talk, you'd think that sex was a suicide pact. To hold hands is to put your life on the line. 'Look at the *time*-fatality figures among the under classes,' I tell them. They screw like there's no tomorrow, and do they come down with *time*? No, it's us high-credit characters who are really at risk. Like me and Danuta. Like Happy. Like you.... Anyway, we were lying on the bed together, as I say, semi-nude, and talking about the possibility of maybe getting into the right frame of mind for a little of the old pre-foreplay—when all of a sudden I felt a rosy glow break out on me like sweat. There was this clogged inner heat, a heavy heat, with something limitless in it, right in the crux of my being. Well, I panicked. You always tell yourself you're going to be brave, dignified, stoical. I ran wailing into the bathroom. I yanked open the triple mirror; the automatic scanlight came on with a crackle. I opened my eyes and stared. There I stood, waiting. Yes, I was clear, I was safe. I broke down and wept with relief. After a while Danuta helped me back into bed. We didn't try to make love or anything. No *way*. I felt too damn good. I lay there dabbing my eyes, so happy, so grateful—my old self again.

'You screw much, Roy?' I asked as he handed me my car card.
'—Sir?'
'You screw much, Roy?'
'Some. I guess.'

Roy was an earnest young earner of the stooped, moustachioed variety. He seemed to have burdensome responsibilities; he even wore his cartridge-belt like some kind of hernia strap or spinal support. This was the B-credit look, the buffer-class look. Pretty soon, they project, society will be equally divided into three sections. Section B will devote itself entirely to defending section A from section C. I'm section A. I'm glad I have Roy and his boys on my side.

'Where you driving to today, sir?'
'Over the hills and far away, Roy. I'm going to see Happy Farraday. Any message?'

Roy looked troubled. 'Sir,' he said, 'you got to tell her about Duncan. The new guy at the condo. He has an alcohol thing. Happy Farraday doesn't know about it yet. Duncan, he sets fire to stuff, with his problem there.'

'His problem, Roy? That's harsh, Roy.'

217

'Well, okay. I don't want to do any kind of value thing here. Maybe it was, like when he was a kid or something. But Duncan has an alcohol situation there. That's the truth of it, Mr Goldfader. And Happy Farraday doesn't know about it yet. You got to warn her. You got to warn her, sir—right now, before it's too late.'

I gazed into Roy's handsome, imploring, deeply stupid face. The hot eyes, the tremulous cheeks, the moustache. Jesus Christ, what difference do these guys think a *moustache* is going to make to anything? For the hundredth time I said to him, 'Roy, it's all made up. It's just TV, Roy. She writes that stuff herself. It isn't real.'

'Now I don't know about none of that,' he said, his hand splayed in quiet propitiation. 'But I'd feel better in my mind if you'd warn her about Duncan's factor there.'

Roy paused. With some difficulty he bent to dab at an oilstain on his superwashable blue pants. He straightened up with a long wheeze. Being young, Roy was, of course, incredibly fat—for reasons of *time*. We both stood there and gazed at the sky, at the spillages, the running colours, the great chemical betrayals....

'It's bad today,' said Roy. 'Sir? Mr Goldfader? Is it true what they say, that Happy Farraday's coming down with *time*?'

Traffic was light and I was over at Happy's before I knew it. Traffic *is* a problem, as everybody keeps on saying. It's okay, though, if you use the more expensive lanes. We have a five-lane system here in our county: free, nickel, dime, quarter and dollar (that's nothing, five, ten, twenty-five or a hundred dollars a mile)—but of course the free lane is non-operational right now, a gridlock, a caravan, a linear breakers' yard of slumped and frazzled heaps, dead rolling-stock that never rolls. They're going to have a situation there with the nickel lane too, pretty soon. The thing about driving anywhere is, it's so unbelievably boring. Here's another plus: since the ban on rearview mirrors, there's not much scope for any *time*-anxiety. They had to take the mirrors away, yes sir. They got my support on that. The concentration-loss was a real feature, you know, driving along and checking out your crow's feet and gumline, all at the same time.... There used to be a party atmosphere out on the thruway, in the cheaper lanes where mobility is low or minimal. People would get out of their cars and horse around. Maybe it still goes on, for all I know. The dividing barriers are higher now, with the new Boredom Drive, and you can't really tell what gives. I *did* see something interesting, though. I couldn't help it. During the long wait at the security intersect, where even the dollar lane gets loused up by all the towtrucks and ambulances—and by the great fleets of copbikes and squadcars—I saw three *runners,* three *time* punks, loping steadily across the disused freightlane, up on the East Viaduct. There they were, as plain as day: shorts, sweatshirts, *running*-shoes. The stacked cars all sounded their horns, a low furious bellow from the old beasts in their stalls. A few dozen cops appeared with bullhorns and tried to talk them down—but they just gestured and *ran* defiantly on. They're sick in the head these punks, though I guess there's a kind of logic in it somewhere. They do vitamins, you know. Yeah. They work out and screw around; they have their nihilistic marathons. I saw one up close down at the studios last week. A security guard found her *running* along the old outer track. They asked her some questions and then let her go. She was about thirty, I guess. She looked in terrible shape.

And so I drove on, without incident. But even through the treated glass of the windshield I could see and sense the atrocious lancings and poppings in the ruined sky. It gets to you. Stare at the blazing noon of a high-watt bulb for ten or fifteen minutes—then shut your eyes, real tight and sudden. That's what the sky looks like. You know, we pity it, or at least I do. I look at the sky and I just think... *ow.* Whew. Oh, the sky, the poor *sky.*

Happy Farraday had left a priority clearance for me at Realty HQ, so I didn't have to hang around that long. To tell you the truth, I was scandalized by how lax and perfunctory the security people were becoming. It's always like this, after a quiet few weeks. Then there's another shitstorm from section C, and all the writs start flying around again. In the cubicle I put my clothes back on and dried my hair. While they okayed my urinalysis and X-ray congruence tests, I watched TV in the commissary. I sat down, delicately, gingerly (you know how it is, after a strip search), and took three clippings out of my wallet. These are for the file. What do you think?

Item 1, from the news page of *Screen Week*:
In a series of repeated experiments at the Valley Chemistry
Workshop, Science Student Edwin Navasky has 'proven'
that hot water freezes faster than cold. Said Edwin, 'We did
the test four times.' Added Student Advisor Joy
Broadener: 'It's a feature. We're real baffled.'

Item 2, from the facts section of *Armchair Guide*:
Candidate Day McGwire took out a spot on Channel 29
Monday last. Her purpose: to deny persistent but
unfounded rumours that she suffered from heart trouble.
Sadly, she was unable to appear. The reason: her sudden
hospitalization with a cardiac problem.

Item 3, from the update column of *Television*:
Meteorological Pilot Lars Christer reported another
sighting of 'The Thing Up There' during a routine low-level
flight. The location: 10,000 feet above Lake Baltimore. His
description: 'It was kind of oval, with kind of a black circle
in the center.' The phenomenon is believed to be a cumulus
or spore formation. Christer's reaction: 'I don't know what
to make of it. It's a thing.'

'Goldfader,' roared the tannoy, scattering my thoughts. The
caddycart was ready at the gate. In the west now the heavens looked
especially hellish and distraught, with a throbbing, peeled-eyeball
effect on the low horizon—bloodshot, conjunctivitic. Pink eye. The
Thing Up There, I sometimes suspect, it might look like an eye,
flecked with painful tears, staring, incensed.... Using my cane I
walked cautiously around the back of Happy's bungalow. Her
twenty-year-old daughter Sunny was lying naked on a lounger,
soaking up the haze. She made no move to cover herself as I limped
poolside. Little Sunny here wants me to represent her someday, and I
guess she was showing me the goods. Well, it's like they say: if you've
got it, flaunt it.

'Hi, Lou,' she said sleepily. 'Take a drink. Go ahead. It's five
o'clock.'

I looked at Sunny critically as I edged past her to the bar. The kid
was a real centrefold, no question. Now don't misunderstand me

here. I say *centrefold,* but of course pornography hasn't really kept up with *time.* At first they tried filling the magazines and mature cable channels with new-look women, like Sunny, but it didn't work out. *Time* has effectively killed pornography, except as an underground blood sport, or a punk thing. *Time* has killed much else. Here's an interesting topic-sentence. Now that masturbation is the only form of sex that doesn't carry a government health warning, what do we think about when we're doing it there, what is *left* for us to think about? Me, I'm not saying. Christ, are *you?* What images slide, what specters flit... what happens to these thoughts as they hover and mass, up there in the blasted, the totalled, up there in the fucked sky?

'Come on, Sunny. Where's your robe.'

As I fixed myself a vodka-tonic and sucked warily on a *pretzel,* I noticed Sunny's bald patch gently gleaming in the mist. I sighed.

'You like my dome?' she asked, without turning. 'Relax, it's artificial.' She sat up straight now and looked at me coyly. She smiled. Yeah, she'd had her teeth gimmicked too—by some cowboy snaggle-artist down in the Valley, no doubt. I poled myself poolside again and took a good slow scan. The flab and pallor were real all right, but the stretch marks seemed cosmetic: too symmetrical, too pronounced.

'Now you listen to me, kid,' I began. 'Here are the realities. To scudbathe, to flop out all day by the pool with a bottle or two, to take on a little weight around the middle there—that's good for a girl. I mean you got to keep in shape. But this mutton routine, Sunny, it's for the punks. No oldjob ever got on my books and no oldjob ever will. Here are the reasons. Number one—' And I gave young Sunny a long talking to out there, a real piece of my mind. I had her in the boredom corner and I wasn't letting her out. I went on and on at her—on and on and on and on. Me, I almost checked out myself, as boredom edged toward despair (the way boredom will), staring into the voided pool, the reflected skyscape, and the busy static, in the sediment of sable rain.

'Yeah, well,' I said, winding up. 'Anyway. What's the thing? You look great.'

She laughed, coughed and spat. 'Forget it, Lou,' she said croakily. 'I only do it for fun.'

'I'm glad to hear that, Sunny. Now where's your mother.'

'Two days.'

'Uh?'

'In her room. In her room two days. She's serious this time.'

'Oh, sure.'

I rebrimmed my drink and went inside. The only point of light in the hallway came from the mirror's sleepless scanlamp. I looked myself over as I limped by. The heavy boredom and light stress of the seven-hour drive had done me good. I was fine, fine. 'Happy?' I said, and knocked.

'Is that you, Lou?' The voice was strong and clear—and it was quick, too. Direct, alert. 'I'll unlatch the door but don't come in right away.'

'Sure,' I said. I took a pull of booze and groped around for a chair. But then I heard the click and Happy's brisk 'Okay'.... Now I have to tell you that two things puzzled me here. First, the voice; second, the alacrity there. Usually when she's in this state you can hardly hear the woman, and it takes an hour or more for her to get to the door and back into bed again. Yeah, I thought, she must have been waiting with her fingers poised on the handle. There's nothing wrong with Happy. The lady is fine, fine.

So in I went. She had the long black nets up over the sack—streaming, glistening, a cot for the devil's progeny. I moved through the gloom to the bedside chair and sat myself down with a grunt. A familiar chair. A familiar vigil.

'Mind if I don't smoke?' I asked her. 'It's not the lungburn. I just get tuckered out lighting the damn things all the time. Understand what I mean?'

No answer.

'How are you feeling, Happy?'

No answer.

'Now listen, kid. You got to quit this nonsense. I know it's problematic with the new role and everything, but—do I have to tell you again what happened to Day Montague? Do I, Happy? Do I? You're forty years old. You look fantastic. Let me tell you what Greg Buzhardt said to me when he saw the outtakes last week. He said, "Style. Class. Presence. Sincerity. Look at the ratings. Look at the profiles. Happy Farraday is the woman of men's dreams." That's what he said. "Happy Farraday is the—"'

'*Lou.*'

The voice came from behind me. I swivelled, and felt the twinge of tendons in my neck. Happy stood in a channel of bathroom light and also in the softer channel or haze of her slip of silk. She stood there as vivid as health itself, as graphic as youth, with her own light sources, the eyes, the mouth, the hair, the dips and curves of the flaring throat. The silk fell to her feet, and the glass fell from my hand, and something else dropped or plunged inside my chest.

'Oh Christ,' I said. 'Happy, I'm sorry.'

I remember what the sky was like, when the sky was young—its shawls and fleeces, its bears and whales, its cusps and clefts. A sky of grey, a sky of blue, a sky of spice. But now the sky has gone, and we face different heavens. Some vital casing has left our lives. Up there, now, I think, a kind of turnaround occurs. *Time*-fear collects up there and comes back to us in the form of *time*. It's the sky, the sky, it's the fucking *sky*. If enough people believe that a thing is real or happening, then it seems that the thing must happen, must go for real. Against all odds and expectation, these are magical times we're living in: proletarian magic. Grey magic!

Now that it's over, now that I'm home and on the mend, with Danuta back for good and Happy gone for ever, I think I can talk it all out and tell you the real story. I'm sitting on the cramped verandah with a blanket on my lap. Before me through the restraining bars, the sunset sprawls in its polluted pomp, full of genies, cloaked ghosts, crimson demons of the middle sky. Red light: let's stop—let's end it. The Thing Up There, it may not be God, of course. It may be the Devil. Pretty soon, Danuta will call me in for my *broth*. Then a nap, and an hour of TV maybe. The Therapy Channel. I'm really into early nights.... This afternoon I went walking, out on the shoulder. I don't know why. I don't think I'll do it again. On my return Roy appeared and helped me into the lift. He then asked me shyly, 'Happy Farraday—she okay now, sir?'

'Okay?' I said. 'Okay? What do you mean, *okay*? You never read a news page, Roy?'

'When she had to leave for Australia there. I wondered if she's okay. It'll be better for her, I guess. She was in a situation, with Duncan. It was a thing there.'

'That's just TV, for Christ's sake. They wrote her out,' I said, and felt a sudden, leaden calm. 'She's not in Australia, Roy. She's in heaven.'

'—Sir?'

'She's *dead,* God damn it.'

'Now I don't know about none of that,' he said, with one fat palm raised. 'All it is is, I just hope she's okay, over in Australia there.'

Happy is in heaven, or I hope she is. I hope she's not in hell. Hell is the evening sky and I surely hope she's not up there. Ah, how to bear it? It's a thing. No, it really is.

I admit right now that I panicked back there, in the bungalow bedroom with the chute of light, the altered woman, and my own being so quickly stretched by fragility and fear. I shouted a lot. *Lie down! Call Trattman! Put on your robe!* That kind of thing. 'Come on, Lou. Be realistic,' she said. 'Look at me.' And I looked. Yeah. Her skin had that shiny telltale succulence, all over. Her hair—which a week ago, God damn it, lay as thin and colourless as my own—was humming with body and glow. And the mouth, Christ... lips all full and wet, and an animal tongue, like a heart, not Happy's, the tongue of another woman, bigger, greedier, younger. Younger. Classic *time.* Oh, classic.

She had me go over and lie down on the bed with her there, to give comfort, to give some sense of final safety. I was in a ticklish state of nerves, as you'd imagine. *Time* isn't infectious (we do know *that* about *time*) but sickness in any form won't draw a body nearer and I wanted all my distance. *Stay out,* it says. Then I saw—I saw it in her breasts, high but heavy, their little points tender, detailed, *time*-inflamed; and the smell, the smell of deep memory, tidal, submarine... I knew the kind of comfort she wanted. Yes and *time* often takes them this way, I thought, in my slow and stately terror. You've come this far: go further, I told myself. Go closer, nearer, closer. Do it for her, for her and for old times' sake. I stirred, ready to let her have all that head and hand could give, until I too felt the fever in my lines of heat, the swell and smell of youth and death. This is suicide, I thought, and I didn't care.... At one point, during the last hours, just before dawn, I got to my feet and crept to the window and looked up at the aching, the hurting sky; I felt myself grey and softly twanging for a moment, like a coathanger left to shimmer on the pole, with Happy there behind me, alone in her bed and her hot death. 'Honey,' I said out loud, and went to join her. I like it, I thought, and gave a sudden nod. What do I like? I like the love. This is suicide and I don't care.

I was in terrible shape, mind you, for the next couple of months, really beat to shit, out of it, really out of it. I would wake at seven and leap out of the sack. I suffered energy attacks. Right off my *food,* I craved thick meat and thick wine. I couldn't watch any therapy. After barely a half hour of some home-carpentry show or marathon darts contest I'd be pacing the room with frenzy in my bitten fingertips. I put Danuta at risk too, on several occasions. I even threw a pass in on little Sunny Farraday, who came to stay here for a time after the cremation. Danuta moved out. She's back now. She's a good kid, Danuta—she helped me through. But the whole thing is behind me now, and I think (knock on wood) that I'm more or less my old self again.

Pretty soon I'll rap on the window with my cane and have Danuta fetch me another blanket. Later, she'll help me inside for my *broth.* Then a nap, and an hour of TV maybe. The Therapy Channel. I'm happy here for the time being, and willingly face the vivid torment, the boiling acne of the dying sky. When this sky is dead, will they give us a new one? Today my answering service left a strange message: I have to call a number in Sydney, over in Australia there. I'll do it tomorrow. Or the next day. Yeah. I can't make the effort right now. To reach for my stick, to lift it, to rap the glass, to say *Danuta*—even that takes steep ascents of time. All things happen so slowly now. I have a new feature with my back. I broke a tooth last week on a piece of *toast.* Jesus, how I hate bending and stairs. The sky hangs above me in shredded webs, in bloody tatters. It's a big relief, and I'm grateful. I'm okay. I'm good, good. For the time being at any rate, I show no signs of coming down with *time.*

RUSSELL HOBAN
A CONVERSATION
WITH THE HEAD OF
ORPHEUS

Prologue

Hermes and the Goddess and the Tortoise

The tortoise is small and timid, it harms no one; it withdraws into its shell when it is frightened. Like the moon it hides itself in darkness and because of this it is sacred to the Mother Goddess who in various of her aspects appears as Demeter or Aphrodite or Medusa or Eurydice.

Knowing this, Hermes killed the tortoise and scooped out its shell to make the lyre.

'Because you killed the tortoise and made an emptiness in which to sound your music,' said the Goddess to Hermes, 'those whose god you are may have the emptiness from which comes art or the love that fills the emptiness, but not both.'

'Only let them have the art,' said Hermes, 'and they'll find love for themselves.'

'They are condemned to lose it,' said the Mother Goddess.

'That's where they'll find the emptiness for the art,' said Hermes.

I often stay up till three or four in the morning; I like those small hours. I have an Apple II computer that I use instead of a typewriter and I have a Drake R7 receiver that I listen to while I work. I like to sit at my desk in the middle of the night; I feel like a telegrapher at a jungle outpost as my thoughts appear letter by letter in the green dancing of the phosphors on the monitor screen and the voices come in from All India Radio or Radio Moscow or the Voice of Greece or Rias in Berlin or whoever's transmitting the music I crave at the time. I seldom listen to English broadcasts; I don't want to know what the words mean—I just want to hear those voices coming from far away in the night, coming round the curving ionosphere and the great globe-encircling miles, night miles, ocean miles, where the deep fish glide in the deep deep dark and the kraken waits in the uttermost deep with its dark mind wild with the terror of itself.

Far, far away in the night are live human beings whose breathing can be heard as they speak, and they're looking at their illuminated dials as I look at mine at this end of the darkness that curves with the night miles to the heave and swell of the ocean dawn. And always on the night air sweet women singing in all the tongues of humankind, singing to the accompaniment of strange instruments, strange rhythms in places unseen but existing at this very moment, perhaps with dry dust rising on the plains or with monsoon rains beating down or with snow on mountain peaks impassable. And while I hear those sweet voices singing words that I cannot understand I watch my thoughts appear letter by letter in the green dancing.

I was listening to All India Radio and looking at two photographs of an olive tree that were on the copy-stand by the Apple. I'd photographed the tree four years before on the island of Skiathos where it stood on a hillside behind a monastery; there it lived its life and had its place in certain arrangements of wood and stone and words, in flashes and glimmers in the wind, in singing of a quick and silvery sort. In the sanctuary, images of Christ were hushed in darkness and the feeble glimmer of candles. Outside in the courtyard the light danced on stones from which grew trees that showed the earthy darkness of their trunks against the dazzle of whitewashed walls.

Letter by letter I watched my thoughts appear on the screen while from the radio came the sound of *Rag Mina Piktori*, played on the sarod by Ali Akbar Khan and transmitted through the night air from New Delhi on a frequency of 11.620 MHz in the General Overseas Service of All India Radio.

I was looking, looking, at the two photographs of the olive tree. Such a graceful, ardent thing it was (said the green letters on the screen) all dancing on the dry hill with its silvery-green flung out to catch the light and shadows and such breeze as might be passing. Light lived in the olive trees, flashing and glimmering like a shoal of fish turning where the sun slants through the green sea; light sang and twittered like birds in the silvery-green leaves.

The two photographs were taken from slightly different angles: both showed the olive tree on the hillside beyond what might have been the cement-block housing and grey pipes of a well. One of the photographs showed a bit more than the other of the boughs of another tree—I don't know what kind—between the viewer and the olive tree; because of this that photograph seemed to have more space and air in it than the other; sometimes the one seemed truer, sometimes the other. I found myself holding each one in turn closer to my eyes and marvelling that the life of the tree should so persist on this rectangle of paper: the tree was so much what it was that it could not be diminished; given any means of making an appearance it would live in the mind, cleverly keeping aloft and balanced on its shadowy trunk and branches the quick and silvery motion of its leaves.

I was astonished at the degree of reality with which the tree was coming to me. I couldn't think why I hadn't taken the time to sit down and be with it, be with all that it was when I was in the place where it was. Now it was inviting me to be with it in these pictures. A lightness and a singing moved in the silvery flickering of its leaves. The tree was girlish and artless in its beauty as the bright being of it continually moved between the seen and the unseen.

Rag Mina Piktori had begun as ragas often do, twanging and twunging desultorily as if the musicians were tinkering with its engine. Or as if tentative voices were speaking singly from different places; I could hear that the voices were listening for something as they spoke. There was a loud hum of interference that went like iron through the space where *Mina Piktori* was trying to put itself together. The voices tailed off into flickering bursts of dots on the little drums, the tabla; then the dots and the voices began to flicker their frequencies over and under the iron of the interference. I recognized that varying but steady occultation as the flickering here-and-gone in which the universe itself lives like music that we hear one note at a time. The interference became a necessary iron of reference as the dots and voices and the dancing intervals offered a progressively clearer and deeper seeing of the tree. With a little jump the hearing of the tree and the seeing of it became one.

I was recording the music, and when *Mina Piktori* was over I turned off the radio and played the tape while I went on looking at the two photographs of the olive tree. The longer I looked the more there seemed to be to see; I felt myself always on the verge of an important recognition. Flickering, flickering, sang the leaves; brightness and darkness moved through the branches and the trunk, hidden life in the secret hollows, young like a dancing girl, old like the Great Mother, the dark earth. Double, double, double, sang the tree, and as

I saw it all dancing on the hillside I seemed at the same time to see within the hollow of the young-old wrinkled trunk and down into the earth where all around me, as if I were inside a cylindrical mirror, I saw a face: a face not mine, a face not clear but almost recognizable, with a speaking mouth saying words almost intelligible.

It was between five and six in the morning. The moon was low in the sky. It was a waxing moon, a gibbous one; it was a particular moon. I raised the window shade. The street lamps outside the window were the same as always. I opened the front door and went out into the foredawn, into the hissing of the silence and the humming of the underground trains standing empty with lighted windows on the far side of the common. Unseen birds twittered but there was no crow to shout and flaunt its blackness.

I heard my footsteps; I saw under the lamps my shadow first before me, then behind. 'Nothing to declare,' I said.

I crossed the common and headed down the New King's Road. The Belisha beacons clicked as they blinked in the coldness of the morning. Cars at intervals hissed past me, in each one a face as questionable as the faces printed on the tin windows of toy cars from Japan. The shops stood like sleeping horses.

The lamps on Putney Bridge were still lit, the bridge stood in simple astonishment over the water, a stone-like creature of overness, of parapets and ghostly pale cool tones of blue, of grey, of dim whiteness in the foredawn with its lamps still lit against a sky growing light. Far below lay the river which is whatever it is called, the Thames or the Gunga or the Evros. Slack water it was, turn of the tide, the low-tide river narrow between expanses of mud, the moored boats rocking on this moment of unknowness.

A sort of singing filled my head; it seemed an aspect of the particles of light and colour that made in my eyes the picture of this time just before dawn. I thought of the dew on the grass where the olive tree stood, and the sound of the flute and the sheep bells with which The Voice of Greece begins its short-wave transmissions. There seemed perhaps to be a question in the air; I wasn't sure what it was.

'Yes,' I said, 'I will.' I spoke aloud because I wanted my answer to be recorded on the early air.

231

I was walking on the Putney side of the river, walking on the low-tide beach, hearing the lapping of the water on the stones. I was seeing the moon-glints on the water, I was smelling the low-tide smell of the mud and the stones by the river.

The singing in my head became the slowly spreading circles of an intolerable clangour; it was as if the brute bell of the universe were caged in my mind and bursting my skull. *'Eurydice!'* whispered a voice from the mud, from the stones. *'Eurydice!'*

I had sometimes thought of the head of Orpheus; I had thought of it drifting down the River Hebrus singing, singing across the sea to Lesbos. I had thought of it swimming under the moon to Lesbos.

I had known that the head of Orpheus would not be shining and incorruptible. I had known that it would be eyeless and bloated, with much of the flesh eaten away by the creatures of the sea who feasted on it as they listened, entranced, to the singing of it. In that state it would continue its existence known and unknown, seen and unseen.

Now it was stranded on the low-tide mud of the Thames. From it in this foreign dawn emanated the black sunlight of its immortal death. I picked up the sodden eyeless head. It was covered with green slime and heavy with barnacles; where the flesh had been eaten away I could feel the ancient skull. In my hands it hummed and buzzed like a hive of bees. The humming and the buzzing grew stronger; I could feel the rage in it and I was afraid.

The rage was inside me, it was swelling, it was more than I could contain, I thought that I should burst with it. I opened my mouth as the air shook like a transparent curtain and the head swelled into something large and dreadful that blackened the morning.

The mud that I was standing on had dropped away from under me, the grey sky over me was gone. With slap and gurgle, with rolling swell, there came green sunlit ocean in which I sank to the upward-rushing chill of deep green, blue-green, deep blue, blackness. Up to the surface I rose again, the Aegean sunlight hot on my face, dazzling in my eyes.

The rotting and eyeless head filled my vision. It was enormous, a floating island over which seabirds wheeled crying under the heartless blue of the sky. I tried to climb on to it as it rolled but my fingers slipped on the green slime and I scraped my flesh bloody on the barnacles as I fell back into the water. The great cavern of the mouth opened and showed its white teeth, its red tongue. *'Eurydice!'* it bellowed as the seabirds rose up screaming, *'Eurydice!'*

I clung to the hair that floated round the head and undulated with the swell. Looking down into the water I saw rising a vast and ivory nakedness and a woman's face of terrifying beauty. Her red-gold hair streamed round her, her green eyes were open wide, her pale silent mouth was open.

Under the blind head of Orpheus floated Eurydice, her long body rocking, her legs and arms open to receive his absent body. The seabirds screamed, uncaring. In black grief I sank down, down, down to the crushing blackness at the bottom of the sea where the kraken shudders endlessly and sends its terror widening in circles through the deeps. Down among the monstrous writhing of its tentacles I sank to the ultimate deep where the great head sits with its eyes for ever looking into blackness.

Rising with the terror I regained the green and sunlit surface, the screaming of the birds that wheeled above the island head of Orpheus and the vast rocking body of Eurydice. All the wide sea, all the blue sky shrank back into the mind of Orpheus, and again I was standing on the grey mud by the grey Thames in the grey October dawn.

'What do you want with me?' I said to the head.

'I want, I want, I want,' it said. It must have spoken Greek but I have no Greek and I was able to understand it. Now as I write this I cannot recall the actual voice that spoke to me; it was purer, more elemental, more profound than human voices are. I remember that the way it spoke seemed more animal than human. Yes, it was as if speech had suddenly become possible for an animal, and the creature after a lifetime of silence could no longer hold back utterance of its thoughts.

'Why have you brought me here; what do you want?' I said.

'You want,' said the head. 'You are found. You are found wanting.'

'"Found wanting!"' I said. 'What do you mean? How am I found wanting?' I wanted that voice to keep sounding in my ears.

The head was silent for a time. In my hands I felt the humming and the buzzing of it.

'Where am I?' it said.

'In London,' I said.

There was another silence. Then the head said, 'The ocean of my endless voyaging, the empty sky of my loneliness drained away like water out of a basin with a hole in it, and up through the hole rushed a greyness and the river of another time, another place. I have no eyes but in my mind I can see this place so grey and foreign to me. Your thoughts are hard and pulling and your speech is meaningless to me. What have you to declare?'

'Why do you keep saying that?' I said. 'I have nothing to declare.'

'I haven't kept saying that,' said the head. 'I haven't said it at all. What do you want? What have you done?'

'I haven't done anything,' I said, 'I don't want anything.'

'What am I to you?' said the head. 'I must be something to you or you couldn't have brought me to this place, this time.'

'Your story,' I said. 'That's what I want. That's what I am to you—the one who is found wanting your story. That's what I have to declare.'

'Why do you want my story?' said the head.

'I don't know,' I said, 'I just want it.'

The head laughed.

'Why are you laughing?' I said.

'You think you're lying but you're telling the truth,' said the head.

'If you know so much then you needn't have asked me,' I said.

'I didn't know it until you answered,' said the head. 'I know many things but not all at the same time. Do you know everything you know all at once?'

'Sometimes I don't know everything I know at all,' I said.

'Then you must be forgiving of me, you must be compassionate with me,' said the head.

'For what?' I said. 'You haven't done anything to me that requires forgiveness and compassion.'

'Have I not?' said the head.

'Not that I know of,' I said.

'Perhaps there will come a time when I shall do something, or a time when you will know,' said the head. 'What then? Will you forgive?'

'I can't really say,' I said. 'I've never been in a position to do much forgiving. I'm usually the one who's looking for forgiveness.'

'Do you want to hear my story?' said the head.

'I've already said so more than once,' I said.

'My story,' said the head. 'You must pay for it, there is a price if I tell it.'

'What's the price?' I said.

'The price is that if I tell it you'll know it,' said the head. 'You won't be able to get it out of your mind, it doesn't stop, it just goes on happening with whoever falls into it, maybe you.' The head began to laugh again.

'What are you laughing at?' I said.

'The everlasting curiosity of Hermes my father the heap of stones,' said the head. 'Hermes the thief-god, the-music-maker, the one who scooped out the tortoise and made the lyre. Do you want to hear my story or don't you?'

'You said I might fall into it,' I said.

'Are you afraid?' said the head.

'Yes,' I said.

'That's what happens when you're engodded,' said the head. 'Are you afraid of being engodded?'

'Yes,' I said.

'That's as it should be,' said the head. 'Now hear my story or throw me back into the river, I don't care which.'

'All right,' I said, 'I'll hear it.'

'I shall tell it,' said the head, 'not because I want to but because I am unable not to. The first thing you must know is that it was not Apollo who gave me the lyre, it was Hermes the flickering, the here-and-gone, the thief-god. And I shall tell you what Hermes was to me.

'My mother's name was Calliope. She was beautiful and wild, she was not the woman of any one man. We lived in Thrace among the shepherds who herded their flocks in the valley of the Hebrus. I never knew my father; it used to be said of such as I that we were fathered by Hermes the Journeyer, the god of the wayside. When I asked my mother where my father Hermes was she would say that he was never to be found where he was looked for. "Is he with you when I'm not looking?" I asked her. "No," she said. "He is the one who's gone, the one who never comes again."

'When I asked the shepherds where he was they would point to a heap of stones by the roadside, any heap of stones anywhere.

"There's your father," they told me. "Is he buried here?" I asked. "Hermes?" they said, "Not him, he'll never die." So that was all I knew of him: that he was in heaps of stones: that he was never where looked for; that he was the one who was gone and would never come again; and that he would never die.

'I too herded sheep, and like the other shepherds I played the pipes. One afternoon I was lying in the shade of an olive grove on a hillside. Lying in that flickering shade and looking up at the sky that moved among the leaves and very softly making my little music I could feel myself beginning to move with what lived in the olive grove. There seemed to be a silvery speaking in the leaves, and I began to feel as if I was living the same life as they, as if I had no separate being.

'Then it was as if the whole picture in my eyes jumped a little, and everything was more itself than it had been just a moment ago. In the light and in the shadows I could see places where I could go in, places where I could move with the light and shadows. I opened my mouth, I cried out in astonishment.

'When my voice went out of me I could feel it becoming something and Hermes was standing in front of me. It was a strange feeling, it was as if I had breathed my soul out of me and Hermes had made himself out of it. He had a special way of being there, he was made of flickering and motion and a dancing; his appearance danced in the eye all silvery and quick and shadowy. His face had not just one look, it looked many different ways all at the same time.

'"Listen!" he said. He had the lyre in his hand and he was touching the strings of it with a plectrum. The music that came out of the lyre wasn't only sound, it was also light and shadows and it was full of strangeness: there was brightness in the shadows, darkness in the light. He was singing:

Who would have thought, who would have thought?
Music from a tortoise-shell!
Not the tortoise, never the tortoise, he
Was too full of himself to think of
The music of his notness
In the bowl of his goneness.
That's why Hermes makes music from a tortoise
But no tortoise has yet made music from himself.

'The dancing lights and shadows were leaping up from the lyre like silver water from a fountain and his voice was doing the same. There was laughter in his voice, he was laughing at what his singing was doing: he could have made any words become silver lights and shadows, it didn't matter what he sang.

'With both hands he thrust the lyre at me and said, "Orpheus!"

'I took the lyre in my hands and immediately I became stupid and the lyre also became stupid; the strings jangled as if a boar were rooting in them.

'"Teach me!" I said, holding out the lyre to Hermes. But Hermes was no longer there. There was only a little heap of stones on the ground there in the shade of the olive trees.

'I touched the stones with my hand. I could feel the motion in them, the dancing. I put my ear to the stones and I could hear in them the singing of Hermes-in-the-stone. I heard it with my ear but it was nothing that could be played on any instrument.

'I tried to recall what I had heard when Hermes was before me playing the lyre but only words came back and not the music that made them into silver lights and shadows. The words sounded stupid when I tried to sing them and stupid music came out of the lyre when I tried to play it.

'I didn't know what to do then, I didn't know how to be the Orpheus that Hermes had commanded me to be. As bright and silvery as Hermes and his music had been, that was how dull and leaden I felt holding in my hands the lyre he had invented for the music that I could not play.

'The words of the song kept singing themselves tunelessly in my head and I began to think of the tortoise who had been too full of himself to think of the music of his notness in the bowl of his goneness. Then I tried to let my head go empty like the tortoise-shell of the lyre so that the bowl of my goneness could fill up with the music of my notness.

'I had been very good with the pipes, very smooth, very fluent. My head was full of good little tricks and tunes, and aside from the music there were the usual words and pictures, flickers and flashes, colours, lights and darknesses that all heads are full of. I wanted to empty my head of everything so that the music of my notness could come in but after a time I had to accept that the mind cannot simply be emptied like a bucket of slops; one has to learn how to be empty in the middle of the fullness so that what wants to come in can come in.

'So this became my life: trying to make a place in my mind for whatever wanted to come in; I stopped trying to make the music of lights and shadows that Hermes had made—indeed I wondered at my presumption in ever attempting it; I simply made what little music I could and tried not to interfere with what came to me.

'After a time I noticed that I was taking things in differently; I was living in a state of continual astonishment. One grey morning I watched the dawn mist rising from the river and I was overwhelmed by the taste of it on my eyes and in my mind. As I looked into the greyness and the mist on the river I sensed in it a presence that looked back at me. The light changed like music and it was afternoon. The flight of a kingfisher opened in the air over the river a blue-green iridescent stillness in which a dragonfly, immense and transparent, repeated itself with every wing stroke. High in the sky I saw a slowly revolving circle of storks and I felt in me a slowly revolving circle that moved with them.

'The greyness and the morning mist were gone but still I had the taste of them on my eyes and I knew that the presence that dwelt in the morning was also now looking at me out of the afternoon. It had in the stillness of it such beauty and such violence that I was unable to know whether I was perceiving it in terror or in ecstasy, unable even to know whether there was a difference between the two. My mouth dropped open, I was not able to think this thought with a closed mouth.

'That was the moment when I first saw Eurydice, and the first I saw of her was her legs wrapped around Hermes as they coupled in the leafy shade while the dragonflies printed themselves gigantically upon the transparent sunlit stillness on the river. Hermes was wearing winged sandals and the wings were beating as he thrust into her.

'I saw the naked beauty of her and in that instant she became everything to me, this woman mine and not mine; I saw her under the god but I knew that she was meant for me; I knew that until that moment my life had been an emptiness waiting for her.

'It felt as if from my open mouth there surged a thick and powerful green serpent and I knew this to be god-as-song. I had no choice in the matter; I was not able to close my mouth until the whole length of god-as-song had passed through it. I heard the sound of the lyre that I was playing; it was not so much music as motion become sound: it was the motion of all things, it was the motion that is the substance of all things.

'I had been standing on the riverbank when the singing began; when the singing stopped and the lyre was silent I found myself standing on a rock in the middle of the river. On both sides of the river the trees came down to the water's edge and swayed their tops against the morning sky. Then I opened my mouth and I howled because I knew that my beginning and my end were together in that song, I knew that the song that had come to me out of the silence and the love that had come to me out of the stillness were already from that moment beginning to return to where they had come from. All this while Eurydice waited for me in the leafy shade still wet with the semen of my father the god of shadows, the thief-god with winged feet who is there first.'

Here the voice of the head of Orpheus paused; the mottled sunlight and the leafy shade, the dragonflies and the river vanished into greyness. A desolation and a silence filled my mind. The sky was paling quickly.

'I waded ashore,' said the head of Orpheus, 'holding the lyre over my head. The water was up to my neck in the middle of the river and I was careful not to get the strings wet.

'Hermes was nowhere to be seen, there was only the naked marvel of Eurydice, her ivory nudity in the cool and leafy shade by the river. She seemed to be asleep, lying on her back with her thighs still open from clasping Hermes. The savage splendour of her beauty, the ivory of her and the arrant red-gold of her hair flaunted themselves in my eyes as that which must be unlawfully taken. It was Hermes the thief-god who put this idea into my mind; he is the patron god of the artist because all art is thieving, all art is the unlawful taking of what is not given and cannot be owned.

'When I was between her thighs she opened her wondrous green eyes and asked my name. Asked my name! No protest, no surprise, no outrage: my name was all that she required.

'"Orpheus," I said.

'"Orpheus!" she said. "I am Eurydice."

'Always I hear those words in my mind,' said the head, 'and always I see her nakedness rising from the green depths below me. And I think of how she lay there with her thighs open for whoever would enter her after the god of shadows, the thief-god. Because she believed that, the god having entered her, the next one would be the given of the god. Her giving of herself was all at once and without limit and the loss of her is the same; it is there every moment all at once and without limit; that it was inevitable does not lessen it.'

'How was it inevitable?' I said.

'What Eurydice was to me,' said the head, 'what she was essentially and in actuality, was the loss of her; she was that even when she was apparently the finding of her, the having of her. And I was the same to her; I was to her the loss of me. We were the two parts of a complementarity of loss, and that being so the loss was already an actuality in our finding of each other. From the moment that I first tasted the honey of Eurydice I tasted also the honey of the loss of her. What am I if not the quintessential, the brute artist? Is not all art a celebration of loss? From the very first moment that beauty appears to us it is passing, passing, not to be held.'

'And yet,' I said, 'people do love each other and live out their lives together.'

'I know nothing of people,' said the head, 'and I know nothing of affection or faithfulness or kindness. My nature is an elemental one: I had the joy of it and I have the pain of it.'

'And Eurydice also,' I said.

'Eurydice also what?' said the head.

'Eurydice also had the joy and has the pain.'

'Certainly she had the joy. How it is with her now I don't know; in death there is no community, I am cut off from her.'

'But I saw Eurydice with you,' I said. 'When I saw the island head of you, when the seabirds wheeled crying under the heartless blue of the sky I saw her naked like ivory under the water with her red-gold hair and her green eyes.'

'One used to hear stories of underworld,' said the head, 'where the souls of the dead squeaked like bats in the darkness. But there isn't even that, there's only one world for the living and the dead, and living or dead one must do the best one can with it. Often enough in heavy seas and black of night—and eyeless as I am I can feel the blackness—I've longed for a quiet underworld and the company of the other dead; but there's only the sea and the aloneness, the black of night and the heat of the sun and the pitiless mouthing of fishes.'

'Didn't you hear what I said?' I said. 'You aren't alone, Eurydice was with you in the sea. When you called her name she came rising from the green depths under you. You yourself have said to me that you see her nakedness rising from the green depths below you.'

'I have no eyes,' said the head. 'There is nothing, no one, no answer when I call. What you saw was a toy for the eye, Hermes is a trickster; I am alone.'

'Why are you alone?' I said. 'Why is there no community in death?'

'I am alone because it is my destiny to be alone,' said the head, and the buzzing of it seemed to intensify. 'There is no community in death for me; perhaps there may be for others.'

'In the stories,' I said, 'Eurydice died of a snake bite and you went to Tartarus to bring her back. If there's no underworld then where do Hades and Persephone have their kingdom?'

'It's not what you would think of as a kingdom or even as a place,' said the head; 'rather is it an aspect of all places: it's the otherness of whatever is. It's the emptiness in the fullness; it's the gone in the here. There is music, there is night; music is of the night, darkness is the nakedness of the world; day is the empty room, the pathetic little objects left behind by the one who is gone: day is underworld to night. The eye of day is the world of shadows where Hades and Persephone slake their lust.'

'And Eurydice?' I said. 'What happened to her? What was the manner of her death, and did you go to the world of shadows to bring her back?'

'There's a serpent in the stories,' said the head. 'You have said that.'

'Yes,' I said, 'there's a serpent.'

'Always they keep some grain of truth,' said the head. 'Now I shall tell you what happened to Eurydice, what happened to both of us. She was the given of the god, and at first it seemed to me that the music had been given to me so that I should be able to respond sufficiently to what she was; I made music all the time, but often before the song was finished she would gently take the lyre from my

241

hands and pull me into an embrace. Little by little the music began to seem artificial, a giving of art instead of self. Loving her required more and more of my time; the lyre hung silent on the wall.

'Taking it up again one day I found it had gone stupid; the strings jangled discordantly when I touched them; my voice came like a toad out of my mouth, I could make no music. I cursed Hermes for giving me Eurydice, and as I cursed him the lyre dropped from my hands, I had no hands with which to hold it, I writhed on my belly on the ground, I had no arms, no legs. Hermes stood over me with his staff, I twined myself around it.

' "Can you sing?" said Hermes. "Can you play the lyre?"

'I could not even speak to answer him. I could only writhe upon his staff and flicker my forked tongue wordlessly.

' "Do you want to make music again?" said Hermes. "First you must scoop yourself out as I scooped out the tortoise when I made the lyre; you must make in yourself an emptiness."

'Eurydice was walking towards the river. It was morning, and the low sun showed the shadowy litheness of her through the thin garment that she wore. Hermes lowered the staff and as I slid through the grass I felt the venom rising in me like song.

'O! what a singing there was then of shadows and of light, of emptiness and fullness, of the yearning of life for death and death for life! What a song of love that is lost and the loss that is love! What a song of beauty that is passing, passing, never to be held! O Eurydice! Eurydice!'

I let the head fall from my hands into the mud where it rolled crazily, fouling itself and howling, *'Eurydice! Eurydice!'*

I picked it up by the hair and clapped my hand over its mouth. 'You rotten filth!' I said. 'You monster! All that rubbish about a complementarity of loss! You killed her!'

The head went quiet and I took my hand away from its mouth.

'Once more I was Orpheus,' it said. 'My music returned and it was more than it had ever been, the emptiness in me opened more world to it. I believe that it is the music of this time in my life that is remembered when I am spoken of. Then I was engodded more than before and I was utterly possessed by what the god had opened me to. My singing was as free of artifice as the flickering of the leaves of the olive tree; I did not make that singing: it happened to me, it came out of my mouth, I was the voice of it with my mouth, I was the hands of it with my lyre.

'Night was my best time, night is the Great Mother from whom the world was born. My first engodded song had come in the golden stillness and the leafy shade of afternoon but that was the whim of Hermes as he coupled with Eurydice while I stood watching. Once I was open to real song I was entered by it always in the night. I remember the firelight on my eyes, I remember the blackness of the trees beyond the firelight, how they nodded in the night. I remember the wild beasts crouching near me with shining eyes, and all around me faces reflecting like mirrors an unseen world. In the dawns I found myself in strange places encircled by trees and stones and sleeping figures wet with dew.

'It was the death of Eurydice that opened me to my new music, and my new music made Eurydice more real to me than she had ever been in her lifetime. My new music made real to me what I had done and what I had lost. The more I sang the worse I suffered and the worse I suffered the more I needed to sing. My pain was more than I could bear and there was in it a joy that intensified it as the rain intensifies colour. Almost I wanted to kill myself but the thought of leaving my music and entering the silence stayed my hand.

'"Look," said Hermes one morning. Once again in the light and shadow of the low sun I saw Eurydice walking towards the river.

'"Look!" said Hermes again. Black-bearded Hades appeared and pale fair Persephone. Both were naked, and Eurydice stripped and gave herself to them, rolling with them in the wet grass.

'"You can be with her!" said Hermes, and he showed me a place of entry between the light and the shadow. "If you look back you must come back!" he said.

'I entered between the light and the shadow into a dim pale world of silence. Eurydice lay naked and alone by the river; when I took her in my arms she looked up at me as lovingly as before. Her lips moved, and very small and quietly, with the veriest shadow of a voice, she said, "Orpheus! I am Eurydice." Such a small, small shadow of voice, and her flesh was flesh of shadows.

'"Eurydice!" I said. "My music shall make you live again!" But my voice too was only the shadow of a voice. I tried to sing but I had no power, I was no longer engodded, the emptiness in me was the emptiness of no art. Surely the lyre will sing for me, I thought. But I had left the lyre behind.

'"Love needs no art!" whispered Eurydice in her tiny shadow-voice as she clasped me to her.

'A wave of despair swept over me, I twisted away from her, I turned my face towards where the god waited with the lyre. As I turned there passed swiftly on the edge of my vision the figure of Tantalus alternately bending to the water that receded from him and stretching out his hand for the fruit that swayed up out of reach.

'"No!" I shouted. I was alone by the river, under the trees. The sunlight had gone out of the day, the air was full of greyness. The lyre was in my hand but there was a chill in my belly, I was afraid to try whether song would come.

'Always when song came I had the feeling of god-as-song rising in me like a green serpent; I could feel it coming now but I was afraid of what the song might be and I tightened my throat against it. I sat there huddled by the river while the day passed, night came and went, and there was again the dawn mist rising from the river. Again and again the song rose in me and I closed my throat. I knew that there was nothing more for me in life, I knew that dismemberment was coming soon. I wondered how it would happen. Again I thought of killing myself but I waited for what the god would bring. From the greyness and the mist there looked out at me that same presence that had looked at me in the dawn of the first day that god-as-song had come to me.

'There was a circle of women around me, farm women with hoes, mattocks, billhooks. They looked as if they had been drunk the night before. Their faces were haggard; they looked exhausted and enraged, as if all the wine they had ever drunk had failed to bring them one real song. Yes, I thought: death comes like this in the morning without music.

'"Here is Orpheus, the great singer," said one of them. "Will you sing for us, Orpheus?"

'"Orpheus the great lover," said another. "Will you love us, Orpheus?"

'"He likes boys," said another.

'"He liked Eurydice," said another. "I have more to offer than she had. Look, Orpheus!" She pulled her smock over her head and danced naked before me. She was beautiful but she didn't know it and so she was angry. "Look, Orpheus!" she said, "Am I not a better armful than Eurydice?"

'"I have nothing left in me," I said. "No love, no music."

'"We'll see about that," said the one who had spoken first. She thrust the lyre at me. "Sing, Orpheus!" she said.

'So I let the song come then. I opened my throat to it, my last song, my song of silence. And it choked me as I knew it would, I died upon that song of silence that I could not sing. I was already dead when the hoes and the mattocks and the billhooks did their work.

'When my head was severed from my body consciousness came back into it. My mind had become what it is now, an organ of the curiosity of Hermes.'

'"An organ of the curiosity of Hermes"!' I said. In my mind was the vast bowl of ocean sky in which soared on great wings the wandering albatross over the endlessly voyaging head of Orpheus while below it swam great turtles and singing whales following paths unseeable. 'Only now do you become fully real to me as what you are,' I said: 'you are the first of my line, the progenitor; you are the endlessly voyaging sorrow that is always in me. You are that astonishment from which I write.'

'My song moved everyone,' said the head of Orpheus, 'even the stones, even the trees. And what has it come to? Endless punishment, endless voyaging, endless rotting in the burning sun and in the black of night; howling winds and raging seas, the lightning that never kills and the pitiless mouthing of fishes that never consume me. Sorrow without end for the loss of Eurydice and remorse without end for what I have done.'

'Remorse,' I said. Yes, remorse was inseparable from the strangeness and beauty of what could only be the idea of a voice sounding in my mind as it told me the story of Orpheus.

THE HOGARTH PRESS
Great Names Are Enjoying A New Life

£4.50

£4.95

£4.95

£6.95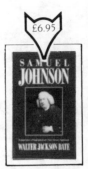

£3.95

£2.95

£2.95

£3.95

£4.95

£3.95

£3.95

£4.50

CHRISTOPHER HOPE

Christopher Hope published his first book of poems, *Cape Drives*, in 1974 for which he received the Cholmondeley Award. His first novel *A Separate Development*, banned for a period shortly after publication in South Africa in 1980, received the David Higham Prize for Fiction in 1981. A collection of short stories, *Private Parts and Other Tales* published in 1982 won the International P.E.N. Silver Pen Award for that year.

Kruger's Alp is a satirical fantasy of extraordinary invention and power built around the legends, the people and the political realities of South Africa.

KRUGER'S ALP

434 34660 8   272 pages   £8.95   HEINEMANN ▣

NOTES FROM ABROAD

Notes from East Germany
Timothy Garton Ash

The Carmen-Sylva Strasse, an evening in spring. Melancholy plaster faces stare down from the crumbling nineteenth-century façades. Down the narrow ravine of the street, the balconies bloom with clothes put out to dry. The neighbours are out too, gossiping, drinking beer from the bottle, shouting lazy insults across the ravine. Children play in the cobbled street. An old man, ragged, unshaven, picks his way among piles of rubbish on the pavement. Somewhere a gramophone pumps dance-tunes.

After eight o'clock, when the doors of the apartment houses are locked, the regular twilight chorus. Young men whistle up to the girls waiting for them on the half-lit balconies. From the corner pub, the sound of drunken banter, the occasional row. All the borough is here: the writer, athlete, soldier, bricklayer; an old gentleman in a frayed, grey three-piece suit and bow tie; a bearded lady, seventy at least, whom the waitress addresses as '*junge Frau*'.

Later, around eleven, there is one last rousing 'Hallelujah!', and a scarcely audible '*Scheisse!*' as a group of drunken youths stagger over the jagged paving stones on their way to bed. Later still the rumble of the last train, its lights momentarily visible as it flies past the end of the street. Then silence, complete, enveloping silence, until the brewers' drays at six in the morning.

I describe a night in the 1980s. But there is nothing here which you could not have seen in 1930. To enter this part of East Berlin is to walk through an etching by Grosz into a story by Isherwood. This *is* Berlin: the Berlin you failed to find in the West. But the appearance deceives.

To begin with, the names have changed. The Carmen-Sylva Strasse is now called the Erich-Weinert-Strasse, after a second-rate, communist poet. Then, in the morning you notice that the façades are covered with hundreds of wires, criss-crossing the plaster faces like the creases of old age: aerial wires to pick up Western broadcasts. The old man is not a tramp rummaging for food, but a pensioner looking for old bottles which he sells back to the state at a tiny shop just below my balcony, earning twenty or thirty *pfennigs* a time to augment his modest pension. In the pub, the workers are grousing about their 'premiums' and the amount that is deducted for what they call *Soli*: 'Solidarity Donations' for Vietnam or Angola.

In November 1932, in the last election before Hitler came to power, this tough working-class quarter voted overwhelmingly for the Communist Party. Under the Nazis, the borough was a centre of communist resistance. Even after a fortnight of storm-trooper terror following the Reichstag fire, more than 44,000 voted Communist in the local elections on 12 March 1933.

Today the borough is distinguished by its reluctance to vote communist. According to official figures for the local elections of 20 May 1979, there were 5,000 abstentions, while 679 votes were cast against the candidates of the 'National Front' (which includes candidates from a number of puppet parties as well as the ruling Socialist Unity Party). To appreciate these figures, it helps to know that, in the whole of East Germany, the vote for the 'National Front' was claimed to be 99.82 per cent, with an electoral turn-out of 98.28 per cent. In an East German polling station, a voter presents himself before a board of two or three officials, shows his ID card and collects a ballot-paper. To vote for the National Front, he folds his ballot-paper once and drops it, unmarked, into the box. To vote any other way, he has to walk across the room to mark his ballot-paper in a voting booth, beside which sits a *Vopo*. A *Vopo* is a 'People's Policeman'. The moment the voter steps towards the booth his name is noted. One independent-minded voter described the few paces to the polling-booth as 'the longest walk in my life'. The consequences may include demotion at work or, for a student, expulsion from the university.

'Never in German history,' the son of the first President of the Weimar Republic, Friedrich Ebert, declared at an election meeting in East Berlin, 'have the people's representatives been more democratically elected.'

I visited the lowest rank of the people's representatives—my borough councillors—in the bare, unheated backroom of their 'Club of the National Front' on a cold January evening. I asked if they had been elected.

'Yes, of course.'

'By a large majority?'

'Very large.'

'And are you from different parties?'

'No, by chance, we're from the same, party.' The Socialist Unity Party.

In talking about their duties, they never mention the people who elected them. But they say a great deal about the PLAN, a copy of which they present to me. 'The People's Economy Plan for the Borough of Prenzlauer Berg' is an example, in miniature, of the central planning by numbers that was introduced in the Soviet Union in the early 1930s: 'Book-holdings in the libraries are to be increased from 350,000 to 450,000 volumes. The number of borrowings is to be increased to 108.2 per cent.' Not 'People should be encouraged to borrow more books from the public libraries,' but 'The number of borrowings is to be increased to 108.2 per cent.' I pictured the borough librarian at the end of the year, having achieved only 105 per cent of last year's borrowings: 'Excuse me, madam, have you never read the works of Schiller? Only seventy volumes—let me sign them out in your name.'

The Plan concludes with the socialist competition 'BEAUTIFY OUR CAPITAL BERLIN: MACH MIT (JOIN IN). I witnessed 'MACH MIT' in practice when a poster went up in the hall of our apartment house announcing a 'MACH MIT' action to clear out the winter's rubbish on the following Saturday morning at eleven o'clock. I reported punctually for work. A quarter of an hour passed. Half an hour. Children peered curiously through the broken window-pane of the house door. Nobody, but nobody, *machte mit*. The winter's slush, old cigarette-ends, chewing-gum papers remained just where they were.

Here in Prenzlauer Berg I saw what one gifted observer has called 'the counter-revolution of reality'. East Germany clearly is a 'totalitarian' state in the sense that it *aspires* to occupy and direct its citizens' every waking moment. The very idea of 'free time' is suspect to all would-be totalitarian regimes. 'In socialism the contradiction between work and free time, typical of capitalism, is removed,' the official *Small Political Dictionary* explains. Moreover, 'free time must be purposefully and effectively deployed by all members of the socialist community.' Great energy is devoted to this mobilization of the population. School-children are 'won' for 'activity...in the productive sections.' Youths are 'persuaded' to participate in Defence Sport events. Millions turn out for the May Day parade. To this extent the regime does succeed in mobilizing the bodies of its citizens. But even East Germany is rarely able to mobilize their hearts and minds—as it undoubtedly did in the early years of reconstruction, after the misery of wartime destruction.

In my experience, East Germans make the most elaborate arrangements to withdraw from the collective political market-place into their own unpolitical niches. The split between the public and the private self, official and unofficial language, outward conformity and inward dissent—in short, the double life—is a phenomenon common to all Soviet bloc countries. The switch from one persona to the other is automatic, even for a fourteen-year-old. This double life naturally implies double standards: I applaud conduct by the state which I would never endorse in private life.

The typical, truly unpolitical East German is the one who turns out every year for the demonstration, hangs out his little flag on the National Day and votes in the elections. It is the people who stay away from the polls who are, paradoxically, the political Germans. Thus the remarkable abstention rate in my borough, Prenzlauer Berg, reflects a long tradition of protest and a certain unbroken working-class pride: 'Why should I take part in a farce?' as one building-worker put it. It also reflects at least a glimmer of the old-fashioned notion that a citizen's public conduct should bear some relation to his private conviction. In this looking-glass world, the non-votes are the votes that count.

Fifty years ago the Carmen-Sylva-Strasse voted in protest for the communists; today the Erich-Weinert-Strasse votes in protest against them. Fifty years ago the inhabitants had almost no money to buy anything; today there is almost nothing to buy. Fifty years ago they demonstrated on the first of May to express solidarity against the inhuman unemployment created by a capitalist economy. Today they attempt to withdraw from the compulsory May Day demonstrations of 'Soli' into the world of private enterprise represented by the allotment garden or the car. Fifty years ago they lived in dreadful insecurity; today in dreadful security.

The Weimar Question

Buchenwald looks on to Weimar. Goethe composed one of his greatest poems walking the hillside later chosen for the concentration camp. The smoke from its chimneys blew over the cultured life of wartime Weimar, over the classical theatre, the poetry readings and the chamber concerts. Weimar is, in Anna Seghers' words, 'the best and worst place in German history'. And the Weimar question—how was this barbarism possible in the heart of a 'civilized' country?—is *the* question of recent German history. Why did Germany's cultured bourgeoisie, the *Bildungsbürgertum,* fail to forestall or resist Nazism? How could extermination camp commandants play Bach in the intervals between supervising the gas chambers? Can we any longer believe that the humanities humanize?

In May 1945, speaking to an American audience about 'Germany and the Germans', Thomas Mann sought an answer in what he called the 'melancholy story' of German *Innerlichkeit*: from Luther to Goethe, German intellectuals had failed to incorporate the imperative of political and social responsibility into their central notion of what it is to be a civilized person. They raised an artificial barrier between the 'spiritual-artistic' world and the 'political-social' one. They supposed, wrongly, that the inner, spiritual freedom of culture could be divorced from outer, political freedom. In their 'musical-Germanic inwardness and unworldliness', they neglected the essential, outward and in the largest sense 'political' obligations of true *Humanität*—of being fully human. It was this fateful legacy, which—simplified and hardened beyond anything which they could have imagined—led to the acceptance of barbarism in one of the world's most 'advanced' and 'civilized' nations.

Mann's argument has paid the price of its influence, by debasement into cliché, although it has also been refined and extended by George Steiner, among others. It remains a classic statement.

When I went to live in East Germany, as an historian looking, among other things, at the cultural resistance to Nazism, I was interested to see if this German cultural tradition—the deliberate cultivation of inward spirituality, the cultured abstinence from political life—survives among today's East German intelligentsia. After all, they too face the challenge of a German dictatorship—though one which does not approach the extremes of Nazi inhumanity. (Buchenwald was used as an internment camp by the Soviets for several years after the war, but is now a carefully organized museum.) I found that the tradition persists.

Many of the educated Germans whom I got to know best live in a classical sort of 'inner emigration' from the totalitarian demands of the Party-state. They nourish themselves on the host of German music (the most mysterious, ambiguous, uncommitted of the arts—the art which Mann chose for his Dr Faustus), on European painting, poetry and fiction. They love and revere the enigmatic sculptures of Ernst Barlach—products of his own 'inner emigration' in the Third Reich. They drown out the sound of slogans with the music of Bach. Ignoring the state as far as possible, they nonetheless offer up the required tribute of outward conformity in the university or the workplace. When called upon, they will say and swear things in public which they privately abhor.

'Inner emigration' is the intellectual form of the double life. Of course the phenomenon is found in all the unfree societies of Europe today. But it does seem to me that it is more common, more intense, in the unfree part of Germany, than in Hungary, Poland or Czechoslovakia, and this may partly be explained by the special German heritage of *Innerlichkeit.* There is a body of contemporary East German literature which reflects and feeds this 'turning inward'.

Indeed the intensity of such writing has grown in the last decade, as many writers have finally despaired of changing their society by writing about it.

'We have all lost very much,' begins a moving poem by Eva Strittmatter:

> Don't fool yourself: also me and you.
> We were born open to the world.
> Now we keep the doors closed
> to him and her and them....

Interestingly, although her premises are anything but 'socialist', the melancholy individualist Eva Strittmatter has been not only published but praised by East Germany's official literary establishment. The explicit political *engagement* of 'socialist realism' is no longer required. Twenty-five years ago (at the Bitterfeld conference) the Party ordered its writers to describe the life of the workers: today it is quite relieved if they don't. The new literature of inwardness, being no threat to the state, is an acceptable alternative to a literature which engages *critically* with the external realities of East German life. The Party has had enough of that.

*I*n December 1971 the new Party leader, Erich Honecker, declared that 'there can, in my opinion, be no taboos in the field of art and literature. That concerns questions of content as well as style.' Younger East German writers took him at his word, and began to write honestly about their own experience: people in communist countries may commit crimes, be unhappy, beat their wives, like Western music—all these things were acknowledged—albeit obliquely, albeit in small editions, but still, officially acknowledged for the first time. Elder writers like Reiner Kunze and Stefan Heym were allowed to publish work that had lain in the drawer—or had been published only in the West. Younger writers like Volker Braun and Jurek Becker came into their own. There was an 'opening out' of new writing, as there was in Poland. What two young Polish critics called (in a book published in 1974) 'The un-depicted world' was at last being depicted.

We can say precisely when this literary spring ended. On 16

November 1976 the ballad-writer Wolf Biermann, while on tour in the West, was deprived of his East German citizenship. Twelve leading writers wrote an open letter of protest to the East German government. At least a hundred more subsequently added their signatures. The Honecker regime reacted viciously. All the signatories were punished in one way or another. Christa Wolf, perhaps the country's finest writer, was expelled from the Berlin committee of the writers' union—and from the Party. From this time forward, writers who had been encouraged, praised and published in the springtime of 'no taboos' were discouraged, denounced and barred from publishing. They experienced what in West Germany is known as *Berufsverbot*—but a *Berufsverbot* more absolute than any in West Germany, because of the state monopoly of the printed word.

Now, the paths of writers in East Germany and Poland diverged sharply. In Poland, the best, most critical and bravest writers reacted to official bans by challenging the state monopoly—and publishing themselves in *samizdat*. Over the next four years, they developed a whole counter-culture of independent publishing, with rival publishing houses and literary magazines like *Zapis* and *Puls*. In East Germany, writers emigrated. They emigrated inwardly—like Eva Strittmatter—or outwardly—to the West. Prominent among those who left for good were the poets Reiner Kunze and Sarah Kirsch, the playwright Thomas Brasch and the prose-writer Hans Joachim Schädlich. Kunze (who was particularly influenced by the Prague Spring, through his Czech wife) left most reluctantly, after official harassment made his life intolerable. One senior functionary told him he 'would not survive' what they had in store for him. At the end of the seventies, the Honecker regime relented somewhat, realizing the damage it was doing to its international reputation, and allowed authors like Jurek Becker, Klaus Schlesinger and the very popular Günter Kunert to live in the West while keeping their East German citizenship.

Like previous re-settlers, the East Germans now living in the West produced works in what I call the 'Owl of Minerva' school of literature. As the Owl of Minerva flies at dusk, so they, in flight from the system, made their reckoning with it. There is nothing from this generation which quite matches the range and profundity of Kantorowicz's *German Diary* or Milosz's *The Captive Mind* (two great 'Owl of Minerva' books from the 1950s). But the Owl of Minerva books from the 1970s are among the best writing in German during the last decade. Only one, Reiner Kunze's *The Lovely Years,* is accessible in English. Kunze exemplifies the best qualities of East German writing. His language is extraordinarily pure, in sharp (and conscious) opposition to the poisoned and inflated public language of the state. His short prose pieces are the written equivalent of a Grosz or Hockney drawing, with no single superfluous line. Word-etchings. His subjects have an evident importance—the systematic corruption of youth in East German schools, the 'un-personing' of writers in Czechoslovakia—and his moral stringency would satisfy the most astringent Leavisite.

Yet since he came to the West in 1977, Kunze's work has ceased to speak to his East German readers. And what is true of Kunze, is even more so of his fellow exiles or half-exiles. Why?

Of course there are practical difficulties. His books are no longer available in East German bookshops, and West German editions have to be smuggled in. Yet, compared with Polish, Czech or Hungarian writers in exile, the position of the (East) German writer in (half) exile is technically much better. He has all the resources of West German television and radio through which to reach his own people in the East. He has publishers and editors crying out to print his work, and thousands of West Germans ready to carry it to their friends and relatives over the border.

The explanation must lie deeper. Although this is treacherous, speculative ground, I do think that, artistically, they miss the challenge of a repressive system. Christa Wolf, who remains domiciled in East Germany, has been heard to remark privately that she doubts if she could work without the '*Reibung*'—the constant *friction* of a writer's life under communism. Paradoxically, censorship can make a writer's life easier as well as more difficult. The writer's energy is concentrated on one target, instead of being dissipated among the thousand subjects which cry out for attention in an open society. His talent is devoted to smuggling his message past the literary border guards, under the cloak of fable or in the false-bottomed suitcase of allegory. These very limitations, like the limitation of traditional forms—the sonnet or ballad—can have artistic advantages. And the mere fact of having smuggled his goods past the censor will be applauded by his readers.

Then, suddenly, he can write anything about anything. He experiences the *shock of artistic freedom.* Again, this experience is not confined to East German writers. You have only to look at the disorientation of some Polish writers in 1981. But Polish writers in exile are to a great extent insulated from that shock by a very strong—indeed overpowering—traditional understanding of their role as moral and political mentors of the nation. The great Polish Romantic poets lived in exile, yet were called the 'spiritual government' of Poland. Heine notwithstanding, there is no comparable tradition in German literature. Yes, there is the more recent precedent of German literature in emigration during the Third Reich: Thomas Mann's famous 'Where I am, is Germany.' But to raise that precedent is to see the essential differences.

*M*ann once remarked that the Nazi period was 'a morally good time'. I suppose he meant that the moral choices were then absolutely clear—black was black, white was white—and the moral duty of the writer easy to discern. The present is not (in Mann's ironic sense) 'a morally good time' in Germany. The choices are not clear, and the writer's political and moral task is far from plain. Brecht for his part wrote of the 'dark times' when

A talk about trees is almost a crime
Because it implies being silent about so many horrors....
But are the 'horrors' of the Honecker regime really such as to demand the concentrated artistic attention of the exiled writer? Many of my friends in East Germany would answer 'no'. Indeed, they would rather talk about trees.

The American exile of Mann and Brecht was at once complete and temporary. They were German writers plonked down on another continent, in a foreign culture, waiting to return home. They had no prospect or intention of becoming American writers. The exile of Kunze or Kiesch is at once permanent and incomplete. There is scant prospect of their ever being allowed 'home'. Yet they are still in Germany—German writers living among German readers. Czeslaw Milosz or Milan Kundera cannot become a 'West Polish' or 'West Czechoslovak' writer—the notion is meaningless—but East German writers can hope to become 'West German' writers.

Sadly, most of them now seem to be in a peculiar limbo—no longer speaking to their East German reading public, not yet speaking to West Germany. In the East they could publish nothing, but had everything to write about. In the West they can publish anything, but find nothing to write about. None of them speak any more to their own people, as Mann and Milosz continued to speak to their own peoples from Californian exile. If our criteria of 'rightness' is purely artistic, then it is authors like Christa Wolf and that grand old fox of East German literature, Stefan Heym, who have made the 'right' decision—to go on *living* in the East, while *publishing* (if need be) in the West. (But our criteria of rightness is not purely artistic.) This is not to endorse the simplistic argument that repression produces good literature. It is just to observe that, so far, this peculiar German *half-exile* seems to have crippled rather than inspired some of Germany's best writers.

Writers in Central and Eastern Europe are moral and political authorities in a way that no writer has been in England since Orwell and Bertrand Russell. But East German writers have been neutralized by emigration—in its inward and outward forms. Emigration, it has been said, is the German form of revolution.

LETTERS

Tisdall

To the Editor

Can I offer you a malevolent little fairy tale for some future edition? It features—and I can deck it out with Scott Fitzgerald or Budd Schulberg trappings if you wish—a brilliant young academic and writer grown twisted and desperate in the throes of bleak middle age. Twenty-five years ago he was a fellow of All Souls, and a young meteor for Harvard and Columbia. His first novel came garlanded in prizes. His energy was legend. He wrote plays and learned treatises in profusion. And then, strangely, the creativity drained away. The thunderclaps came slowly, and with diminishing returns. His first marriage crumbled. Over ten years—apart from a couple of trivial, penny-coining novels—he published only two books. And by the winter of 1983, he was reduced to scratching a living doing fill-in work at Bush House where, in three months, colleagues found 'little he wrote that was usable'. Age and disillusion and a burning political rage had laid a career waste. He was a small, podgy man with a crooked grin and a shiny suit, reduced to pursuing random passions and hawking them, fruitlessly, from paper to paper and magazine to magazine. There was some residual reputation: for a time friends helped him out: but the ashes of what might have been lay littered and cold.

Why, you may wonder, am I not first offering this stupendous article to the *Guardian*, the paper I edit? Because I wouldn't touch it with a barge pole. The facts of David Caute's career, as far as they go, are accurate enough. The quotes are accurate too, by Mr Caute's chop-sentence standards. So are the grin and the suit. But by any other test the thesis is pre-ordained hatchet-work and may, for all I know, be utter bunk.

I wouldn't print it. So why did you devote so much of your last issue [*Granta* 12] to the much-amended Caute rendition of the Tisdall case, which is precisely the same sort of factional, tawdry, driven exercise? To be clear: in my first letter to David Caute, last February, I wrote, 'I don't much mind being hung, drawn and quartered in this affair, if anybody wants.' That has always been, and remains, true. Mr Caute, or anyone else, may call me a fool or a coward or a deluded capitalist lackey. But it isn't necessary, in the process, so zealously to muddle and distort the facts of the matter. It simply isn't necessary.

There is no point, perhaps, in another 8,000 words, a Caute antidote. But can I outline just a few examples (out of dozens) of his technique, not because they're always the most important, but because they're the most simply disprovable?

— In his first drafts, widely circulated, Caute's central thesis was that I told Lord Rawlinson about the second document and that Lord Rawlinson told the Government. Caute never asked about this directly. He merely rushed into print. My last letter to him, of which you only printed the last couple of sentences, denied all this categorically. So in your version Caute merely puts it forward as 'another view' based (p. 180) on a conversation with Hugh Stephenson, who can't remember the five minutes he spent with me in a pub 'in those terms'. Repeat: none of this is true. And it can simply be shown as invention if you wish.

— The matter of *The Times* (p. 185). In his original draft, Caute accused me of telephone lobbying for support among other editors. Again, in that letter, I denied it. Again the charge is muted to a 'disconcerting overlap' and 'grateful' acknowledgement of a sympathetic *Times* leader in a letter to that paper. Just take that *Times* letter in full and look at it. The point—then nagging at a wound we knew to be open in Government circles—was to argue that we should have been prosecuted alongside Miss Tisdall, because to have done so would have put the Government's case against her in jeopardy. But Caute doesn't mention that because it doesn't fit his thesis.

— In the *Observer* episode (pp. 187–88) Caute portrays Chief Detective Superintendent Hardy scurrying round to that paper in search of the second document. But a few pages before he'd had us *telling* the Government that we'd had it. Had the Government failed to tell Mr Hardy? Or is Caute merely determined to put the worst gloss on every event, irrespective of the fact that they're mutually contradictory?

— On 7 February (p. 192) Caute says he asked Ken Dodd, my executive editor, about the second document and Ken didn't break down and tell him the whole story. What he doesn't say—but what Ken told him later in my presence—is that at that stage Ken hadn't a blind notion who this unknown chap in a raincoat was, asking odd questions. Does Caute unburden himself to every passing pedestrian?

— Miss Tisdall, says Caute, signed a confession covering both documents on 9 January, yet for ten weeks we 'maintained the fiction' that she had only leaked one. The wonders of hindsight continue. The charge against Miss Tisdall did not mention any number of documents; it was unspecific: and we—as her lawyers may confirm—had no notion of what she'd confessed to. All the time, too, there was the question of how severely the Government wished to proceed against her. None of what Caute 'knew' on 9 January was known to us until her full trial. It makes a difference.

— That 'visceral and threatening' reaction (p. 194). Not at all, if again you'd printed my whole letter. I don't believe that in a rough trade journalists should sue one another. But I'd love to be sued by David Caute.

Finally, Sir, a proposal. It was not, in the end, sensible to rehearse every jot and titter of the affair with Mr Caute. He wasn't actually interested in trying to understand what happened. But on the points above, or any other points, I am entirely happy to go through the written facts or verbal evidence with any member of your editorial board. Equally, I would be happy to see some outside body, like the Press Council, perform a similar role. I rely, perhaps naïvely still, on your own good faith. We may all, in our weak moments, be me; but I'd hate to think that we were all David Caute, too.

Peter Preston   Editor
The *Guardian*   London

Czech-mate

To the Editor

As a citizen of Prague—which I left only four years ago and to which I was promptly forbidden to return—and as a passionate citizen of Europe, I was deeply grateful for *Granta* 11: it represented not only the images of my city and the torments it has undergone but also its longing to re-discover its place in the heart of Europe.

Yet, after reading and re-reading Milan Kundera's essay 'A Kidnapped West or Culture Bows Out', I feel irritated. Has culture really 'bowed out' of Europe? Can culture do such a thing? I, too, lived through the 'happy marriage of culture and life' in Prague in 1968. I, too, have witnessed its 'inimitable beauty', and that beauty has 'cast a spell' on me, as it did on Kundera, for the rest of my life. But my concept of that culture is distinctly different from Kundera's—which strikes me as aristocratic and elitist.

The culture I witnessed was among the 'masses': it was in the workers and students who gathered spontaneously in Prague's square; in the non-violent but nevertheless powerful crowds that plastered the city with folk-art and poetry; in the population that, face to face with tanks and troops, succeeded in governing Czechoslovakia for a whole week after the Russian invasion. I believe in the people in the streets 'shouting in unison'. And I believe in their culture.

The whole character of society is changing. And so, too, is its culture. The change may undermine the aristocractic notion of culture: but is that such a bad thing? The spontaneous mass-cultures of, say, the peace movements 'dancing in circles' throughout Western Europe or of the 'rock-scene' among Eastern European youth may not be what some would regard as the 'supreme values' of humanity and may therefore go unpublished or unrecorded. But can we, on the other hand, really regard the great culture of Europe as always having been 'the expression of the supreme values' of humanity? Has there not always been a cultural giant somewhere who prepared or occasioned, intentionally or not, virtually every bloodthirsty revolution and holocaust in Europe and its colonies?

A new culture *is* emerging out of the old continent. It is not very presentable—uncouth even. It is markedly anti-aristocractic, often anti-intellectual. It is polarized between anger and abandon. It thrives on both despair and hope. It is intent on mass-survival and mass-dignity. And whether it is good or bad is beside the point: our culture cannot be defined by pre-established notions of what culture is meant to be. Even if culture does grow out of that of a previous era, it does so by denying what has come before. We can and should cherish our cultural inheritance, but we cannot actually inherit the culture itself. For what is culture if not the accumulating expression of a people, nations, whole continents, developing in the present time, and in space.

But I don't want to be misunderstood. There are limitations to Kundera's argument. But I rejoice in the fact that it is there. As I rejoice in the fact that I can now also find in Britain Kazimierz Brandys's *Warsaw Diary* and George Konrad's *Antipolitics*. And I suppose I can attribute it to one of the absurd, strangely justifiable turns of history that a Czech, a Pole and a Hungarian—men who shaped the post-war face of their 'socialist' countries, who experienced the hope and tragedies of, respectively, 1956, 1968, and 1980–81, who have had to cope with so much disillusionment— have emerged, more or less, as confirmed cultural aristocrats. But what they express is of greater consequence: all three of these great Central European writers introduce issues to the 'Far West' of Europe that have to be understood—and acted upon, if we are to lift the Iron Curtain and, in the words of George Konrad, 'go on to draw the two parts of a divided Europe together again.'

Zdena Tomin
London

To the Editor

There is no question that Milan Kundera is a brilliant writer of fiction, an accomplished story-teller, and an artist who has genuinely enlarged our understanding of what is possible in the novel. But, in his determination to show us that he is heir-apparent to the Nobel Prize for Literature, he also has to demonstrate that he is a 'thinker' as well. The result, however, is hardly commendable.

I suppose I can understand the reasons behind *Granta*'s publishing of 'A Kidnapped West or Culture Bows Out'. But I understand less why Kundera should write it or why he feels that we should be able to follow its (at best) tortuous logic. He laments, for instance, the dying of a culture that anyone in Western Europe would regard as merely anachronistic, pathetically 'Modernist', and unapologetically class-bound. (Although I suppose there is a perverse justification in the great émigré from socialism endorsing the great art of the bourgeoisie.) He laments the foreignness of an Asiatic Russia, ignoring the fact that Western Europe has long adored its music, long been inspired by its novels, and, more recently, admired its films: that Western Europe has, in short, long considered Russia part of the very Europe to which this Asiatic Russia is meant to be opposed. And, equally disturbing, he celebrates the Austro-Hungarian Empire, when there is little testimony from anyone who has suffered under its irrational regime that there was anything to celebrate about it until it was dissolved in 1918.

It may come as a shock that Kundera does not offer his article to *Granta* alone but hawks it to any and every magazine that will buy it. One such magazine was *Le Debat* in France. And one response to it is worth quoting. It is from François Bondy, who points out that 'The Habsburg monarchy was frivolous: it was an empire which never gave its Slav populations the slightest say in affairs and presented not security or protection but a "people's prison". It was, ultimately, a German movement—"in no way Asiatic." Lest we succumb to the intimidating rationalist tone in Kundera's prose,

267

Bondy offers one further observation: 'If Stalin's communism was so foreign to Europe, why did it have more supporters in Czechoslovakia than it ever did in Russia? Soviet pressure wasn't the main factor that enabled the Communist Party to establish its dictatorship over a still unoccupied country in 1948!'

Kundera is a polemicist—a welcome thing. But he is also a sentimentalist—something which deserves scrutiny of a more critical nature.

Ian Thompson
London

To the Editor

I have never seen a 'revue' as described by Milan Kundera. But, if it contains articles like Kundera's 'A Kidnapped West or Culture Bows Out' and 'Somewhere Behind', and Salman Rushdie's 'Outside The Whale', it surely is worth *Granta*'s emulating!

A. Ikkos
London

More Goddam Complaints

To the Editor

I must say that I was very disappointed to find that the latest issue of *Granta* devoted almost one hundred pages to an account of the Rolling Stones pop group. Should I wish to read about pop music I can pick up my son's copy of *Sounds*

which is always lying around. I had hoped that *Granta* would be more of a vehicle for original writing—there is a need for such a magazine.

Gloria Haines
High Wycombe
Buckinghamshire

Civilized Debate?

To the Editor

Mario Vargas Llosa's letter [*Granta* 12] on the Uchuraccay massacre contains his familiar mixture of evasions and accusations. In my letter [*Granta* 11], I did not suggest that the report prepared by the commission of which Vargas Llosa was a member was intended as a cover-up. I have no reason to doubt that he honestly believes what he writes. What I did say was that the commission of inquiry was appointed by the Peruvian Government at a moment when it was under very strong pressure to clear up what had happened at Uchuraccay and bring the culprits to book. It is by no means fanciful to suppose that the seasoned politicians in Lima saw the naming of the independent commission as a way of taking the heat off them. As the noted Peruvian historian, Pablo Macera, said at the time, if Congress had appointed its own commission of inquiry—as it was entitled to do—it would have included members of the political opposition. The appointment of a three-man commission by the President pre-empted such a possibility. Its conclusions, as it happens, were very acceptable to the Government.

It is worth pointing out, in this connection, that even such a staunchly pro-Government publication as *Caretas* magazine now advocates the appointment of a broadly-representative commission to investigate allegations of massacres made recently against the security forces. When, in mid-July, eye-witnesses reported that twenty people found dead in Ayacucho villages had been arrested earlier by uniformed members of the counter-insurgency forces, *Caretas* urged President Belaúnde to set up a commission of inquiry that would include representatives of the Catholic Church, the military command, the judiciary, the Attorney-General's office and the main political parties, as well as the President's own personal choices.

If such a broadly-based commission had been appointed after the Uchuraccay incident, it is possible that a great deal of public controversy might have been avoided. The judicial investigation into the Uchuraccay events is still floundering. There have been no fewer than four chief-prosecutors involved in the case in less than six months, and at the end of May the Ayacucho court refused an application from the prosecutor for more time to pursue his inquiries. A few weeks earlier, one of his predecessors, Dr Benjamín Madueño Yansey, had resigned 'as a protest against the situation in Ayacucho, where the judicial authorities receive no support at all from those whose duty it is to provide it.'

Was Vargas Llosa not, perhaps, a little naive to accept the President's invitation to join the commission?

As for the question of evidence about what happened at Uchuraccay, Vargas Llosa again comes up with nothing conclusive. Most of the contrary evidence he dismisses by the simple expedient of saying that it comes from the extreme Left, from the 'enemies of democracy' against whom Vargas Llosa has resolved to do battle. It is not the first time that he has sought to condemn me through guilt by association. What he does not say is that most of my comments are similar to the observations of such eminently respectable bodies as Amnesty International (which Vargas Llosa goes out of his way to praise) and the London-based security consultants, Control Risks.

The conclusions of the independent commission on the Uchuraccay events are based largely on what the *comuneros* and the military authorities said and made available to Vargas Llosa and his colleagues. But it is surely not beyond the realms of possibility that neither the *comuneros* nor the military authorities told the whole truth. Enough of the story does not add up to suggest that both had something to hide. Moreover, Vargas Llosa chooses to ignore such difficult points as the role of Fortunato Gavilan, the lieutenant-governor of Uchuraccay; the mystery surrounding the photographs taken by the dead journalists; the deaths of many of the witnesses and suspects of the massacre over the next few months; and the presence of large numbers of counter-insurgency police in the neighbourhood of the Yanaorcco telecommunications post, near

Uchuraccay, in the days immediately preceding the massacre.

Vargas Llosa's argument that there had been no time for the military to set up and train 'paramilitary bands' by the time the massacre took place is remarkably ingenuous. Since the counter-insurgency police units moved into Ayacucho in 1981, there had been plenty of time for all manner of contacts to be established, even if *sinchi* patrols did not often pass through Uchuraccay and there was no police post in Tambo. It was well known at the time that the armed forces were providing logistical and intelligence support to the police, though of course operational details were not publicized. One wonders, for example, why the *comuneros* made the manifestly untrue statement (even Vargas Llosa rejects it) that the journalists arrived waving a red flag if the *comuneros* had not been trained by someone to do so.

Undercover operations and psychological warfare may be a mystery to Vargas Llosa, but senior Peruvian officers have learned all about them, with the help of experts from the United States, Israel, Argentina and Europe. In the days immediately preceding and following the Uchuraccay massacre the Lima newspapers were full of reports derived from military communiques of villagers confronting heavily-armed guerrillas with sticks, stones and machetes, and either killing them or putting them to flight. These events apparently happened spontaneously all over the emergency area, but the accounts bear unmistakable signs of an orchestrated campaign. Could the Uchuraccay killings have been an incident in this campaign which went wrong? Vargas Llosa does not even consider such a possibility.

I did not, of course, insinuate that Vargas Llosa is a 'fanatic intolerant of the slightest criticism of Peru's system of government.' One is forced to wonder whether he actually read or understood my letter. I did say, quite clearly, that in his anxiety to defend Peru's fragile democracy, and to attack those whom he regards as its enemies, he is in danger of becoming a propagandist himself. Vargas Llosa says that I, along with other European journalists, caricature Latin America and perpetuate an image of barbarism. He is clearly unfamiliar with my work on Latin America over a period of fifteen years. In the specific case of Uchuraccay, the massacre was barbarous; Vargas Llosa says as much himself. Perhaps it is understandable that isolated Indians might behave barbarously—that is one of the problems of underdevelopment. But if it is suggested that the national power structure with which Vargas Llosa identifies is capable of barbarous conduct, he regards *that* as extremism of the worst kind. But to my mind no good purpose is served by closing one's eyes to what is going on, however unpleasant it might be.

(I do not, by the way, regard Peru as a barbarous place. I lived there for four years, and my eldest daughter was born there. She has been brought up to be very proud of her Peruvian citizenship.)

Perhaps I have also been naive. I took Vargas Llosa to be an open-minded person, capable of engaging in civilized debate and accepting that others might hold different opinions from his. Instead, he turns out to be intolerant of criticism, and capable of conducting a campaign of insults against me in the Latin American press, since the day I dared to disagree with him publicly. It would appear that Vargas Llosa has decided to appoint himself as the sole interpreter of Latin American reality to the rest of the world. Not everybody agrees that he is uniquely qualified for this task; the Uruguayan novelist, Mario Benedetti, for one, has challenged him, and so did the audience at a recent seminar on his work in Spain. Perhaps he put his finger on the problem afflicting him when he wrote, in a recent essay on his native Arequipa, that *arequipeños* are known to suffer from 'a kind of transitory madness which suddenly turns the mildest . . . into a belligerent and obnoxious person.'

Colin Harding
London

Mario Vargas Llosa's report on the events at Uchuraccay, 'The Story of a Massacre', is in Granta 9. Granta *wishes to apologize to Colin Harding and Mario Vargas Llosa for the fact that Colin Harding's previous letter [Granta 11] was, for reasons of space, substantially compressed and that the passage dealing with last January's protest march in Lima, Peru, was ambiguous, suggesting that it was a protest against the findings of the commission of inquiry of which Mario Vargas Llosa was a member. Colin Harding had originally written, correctly, that the protest was against the failure of the Peruvian judicial authorities to complete an entirely separate inquiry into the same incident.* Granta *accepts that Mario Vargas Llosa's accusation [Granta 12]—that Colin Harding is guilty of 'half-truths, lies and distortions'—was the consequence of our own subediting.* Granta *regrets the unjustified slurs on Colin Harding's professional reputation.*

Notes on Contributors

Milan Kundera's most recent novel, *The Unbearable Lightness of Being,* was published last spring. He has contributed to *Granta* 6 and *Granta* 11. **Josef Škvorecký** left Czechoslovakia in 1968, and now lives in Canada, where he and his wife run the Czech publishing house '68 Publishers. His new novel, *The Engineer of Human Souls,* is published in February. **James Fenton** was a freelance correspondent in Southeast Asia from 1973 to 1975. *The Memory of War and Children in Exile,* a collection of his poetry written since 1968, was published last year. **Someth May** now lives in Oxford, and is currently writing an autobiography based on his experiences in Cambodia. **John Berger**'s 'Boris' appeared in *Granta* 9. *And Our Faces, My Heart, Brief as Photos*, essays and observations on time, is published in the autumn. **Nella Bielski** was born in the Ukraine. Her books include *Oranges for the Son of Alexander Levy*, which was published in Britain in 1982. **Reinaldo Arenas** was born in 1943 and is the author of a number of novels and stories. He left Cuba in May 1980, and now lives in New York. **Orville Schell** is the author of *In the People's Republic* and *Watch Out for the Foreign Guests.* He was last in China in spring 1984, and currently lives in Bolinas, California. **Edward Said** is Parr Professor of English and Comparative Literature at Columbia University. *The World, the Text, and the Critic*, a collection of essays, was published last spring. He is currently writing about Palestine, in collaboration with the photographer, Jean Mohr. **Doris Lessing**'s *The Diaries of Jane Somers* will be published, this time under her own name, by Michael Joseph in the autumn. **Anita Brookner** is the author of four novels: *A Start in Life, Providence, Look at Me,* and *Hotel du Lac*, which was published in September. **Martin Amis** is the author of five novels, including *Money*, published in September. He has contributed to *Granta* 4 and *Granta* 7. **Russell Hoban** is a frequent contributor to *Granta*. 'A Conversation with the Head of Orpheus' is extracted from an early version of a work-in-progress, tentatively entitled *The Medusa Frequency*. **Timothy Garton Ash** is the author of *Solidarity*.

Photo Credits (in order of appearance): Keystone, Syndication International, Yves-Guy Berge/Sygma, Keystone, John Hillelson, James Andanson/Sygma, Popperfoto.